LORETO, BAJA CALIFORNIA

First Mission and Capital of Spanish California

ANN & DON O'NEIL

Para José Luis

Con amistad

Ann O'Neil
12/01

TIO PRESS

Dedicated to Marla Daily and Kirk Connally.
It never would have happened without them.

CREDITS
Front Cover Photograph: Our Lady of Loreto Mission Church, Leland Foerster
Frontispiece Map: Ana M. Gutíerrez
Back Cover Photograph: Brenda MacGowan

Project Management and Design: Vandecasteele Design & Printing

LORETO, BAJA CALIFORNIA
FIRST MISSION AND CAPITAL OF SPANISH CALIFORNIA
1st Edition

For information, address correspondence to:
Tio Press
4448 Morella Avenue
Studio City, California 91607 U.S.A.
E-mail: tiopress@aol.com

ISBN 0-9708541-0-2

Library of Congress Control Number: 2001091975

Manufactured in the United States of America

Contents

Maps, Photographs & Illustrations

Introduction

In the spring of 1973, we came to Loreto in Baja California, Mexico, from different parts of the world. Don had been working as an engineer in Japan and South America for the previous five years, and I had just moved to San Diego from Cleveland, Ohio. Don came to Loreto to fish, and I came on vacation with my father. We fell in love with Loreto, and with each other, and have been here ever since.

When we first arrived in Loreto, the transpeninsular highway was not completed, there was no telephone, and the local generator produced uncertain electricity. But the fish were plentiful, the people kind and friendly, and the sea and mountains and desert reminded us of the world as it must have looked in the beginning. From Loreto we have traveled and camped all over Mexico and Central America in many beautiful places, but when we came home we always agreed that Loreto is the loveliest place we have ever been.

Although we are *extranjeros*, we have felt very much at home since the beginning of our life here. We love the tranquillity and slow pace of living, the light and shadow on the mountains and islands, the many moods of the Sea of Cortez, the unpolluted air, and the wonderful people we have come to know. We have attended weddings and baptisms and fifteenth-birthday and funeral Masses in the first California mission. Children visit us to have soccer balls and bicycle tires inflated or for old magazines, for English lessons or just to talk. People from all over the world come sit on our porch and enrich our lives. We have shared with our neighbors the joy of new life and the sorrow of loss. We have watched generations of children grow up and have played a small part in that process.

Before our first trip to Loreto in May of 1973, we knew very little about this isolated arm of Mexico. The Baja California Peninsula extends 1,000 miles south from the U.S. Alta California border and is separated from the mainland of Mexico for most of its length by a narrow sea, the Gulf of California, which is also called the Sea of Cortez. We had been to the crowded border cities but knew nothing about the land that lay far south of them.

The paved two-lane highway, which now runs the length of the Baja California Peninsula, was not completed until December of 1973, and only the most intrepid travelers ventured down the dirt roads before then. We first flew to Loreto from Tijuana on a twin engine plane which stopped in Guerrero Negro, Mulegé, and Loreto on its way to La Paz, the capital of the Territory of Baja California Sur. Flying over the hundreds of miles of desert and mountains gave us an idea of the vastness and mystery of this sparsely inhabited land.

Although it is only 700 miles south of the United States border, when we landed in Loreto we found ourselves in a very different culture, in a different climate, in a different geological setting. The town is located on the eastern coast of the Sea of Cortez. It is warm and sunny, and the air is clear and clean. It was a delightful surprise to find ourselves in a lush green little town with tropical palm trees and brilliant bougainvillas, facing the clear blue waters of the gulf to the east and backed by the rugged mountains of the La Giganta range to the west.

We soon came to realize the Loreto area is not only very beautiful and a fisherman's Mecca but also has a most interesting history, which includes Indians and priests, pirates and pearl fishers, revolutionaries and ranchers, and some very remarkable people. We began to ask questions about the land and sea around us.

We learned that this land had once been a part of the mainland, but about twenty-five million years ago it began to slowly separate to the northwest along a crack which residents of upper California know all too well: the San Andreas Fault. As the gap widened, the Pacific Ocean filled the space between, and as the Ice Age came to an end ten thousand years ago and the glaciers melted, the sea level rose as much as 300 feet. Mountains and hills formerly attached to the peninsula became islands. We were surprised to learn that the Baja California Peninsula is longer than Italy.

We learned that the Baja California Peninsula is divided

into four natural subdivisions:

The Frontier, which includes the territory from the 30th parallel to the international boundary and runs in a straight line from the junction of the Gila and Colorado rivers to just south of San Diego and is similar in flora and fauna to the Mexican state of Soñora and the southern part of upper California.

The Central Upper Region, the narrow, rugged land from the 30th parallel to the 28th parallel, which is mountainous with little level land except for mesas paved with lava.

The Central Lower Region, the setting for Loreto, extending from the 28th parallel to the Cape region. It is mountainous to the east and there are many thousands of acres of desert flat land on the west, some of which is now being extensively farmed using non-replaceable ground water trapped beneath the surface millions of years ago.

The Cape Region, extending south of the capital city of La Paz is semi-tropical with more rainfall than the central area.

We learned that the Gulf of California gets water mainly from the tropical Pacific Ocean, that its length extends 669 miles from the mouth of the Colorado River to the tip at Cabo San Lucas and varies in width from about 60 to 125 miles. The peninsula was formerly much longer, but sediment deposits from the Colorado River created a delta and dammed off the upper end, forming the Imperial Valley of Alta California. The Gulf has had several names. One of the early names, common several hundred years after its discovery, was *Mar Bermejo* or Vermillion Sea in reference to the periodic occurrence of trillions of tiny vermilion-colored organisms, *Flagellate infusoria*, which join together to form large red carpets on the blue waters. Now, the gulf is usually called *el Mar de Cortés* or, in English, the Sea of Cortez, in honor of the conqueror of New Spain who initiated the first explorations of the peninsula.

We learned that the climate on the eastern side of the peninsula is warmer than the west, because the gulf is a shallow evaporation basin, the largest in the Pacific Ocean. This evaporation causes a high degree of salinity, which increases the surface temperature of the water and, consequently, of the air passing over it.

We learned that the Sierra de la Giganta mountain range to the west of Loreto is a massive fault block which tilts southwesterly toward the Pacific Ocean. Cerro de la Giganta, 10 miles north of Loreto, is the highest mountain in the chain at 5,832 feet, and the conical peak called El Pilón de las Parras, just behind Loreto, rises to 4,400 feet. The rugged ranges along the spine of Baja California are volcanic breakthroughs, which must have created a magnificent spectacle as they threw up rocks from deep in the earth along with volcanic ash and lava.

We learned that the three islands visible to the north, east, and south of Loreto are called, respectively, Isla Coronados, Isla del Carmen, and Isla Danzantes. Carmen Island, directly in front of Loreto, is the largest. The island is 58 miles square and about 18.5 miles long from north to south. It has fresh water and a large salt bed, which for many years provided the principal employment for the men of Loreto. Coronados is about 3 square miles and Danzantes about 2 square miles; both are uninhabited desert islands. The three islands protect the Bay of Loreto from the worst of the storms from the sea.

Many years ago we had gone to the library in San Diego looking for a book about Loreto and were startled to find there was none. Surely, we thought, there must be a book about the first European settlement in California, the site of the first of all the California missions, the capital of both lower and upper California for seventy-nine years, a place with so much interesting history.

We decided that some day, if nobody else did, we would write a book about the town. We would do the research together. I would write it, and Don would be in charge of logistics and backup. But first we would have to explore the peninsula, experience life in Loreto, and try to find out all we could about this pueblo we call home.

We told each other we would write the book when we got very old. And now we are.

Preparing this account of Loreto and its history has taken us many years. For the stories about the native inhabitants, the Jesuit years, the experiences of the Franciscan and Dominican Orders and the early civil government of Loreto, we spent many, many hours in the libraries of La Paz, the University of California, and the Sherman Library in Corona del Mar, California. We have also collected a comprehensive library of our own.

The detective work of searching for information about Loreto in books has been intriguing and interesting, but the research we have most enjoyed has been recording the oral histories of Loretanos. We talked to people who represented different facets of life in the history of the area. In the process, we have met some of the most fascinating, unusual, lovable people we have ever encountered. Their accounts of their lives and memories are a vital contribution to preserving the history of this town where Europeans began their settlement of the land they called California.

Chapter One

THE ORIGINAL INHABITANTS OF LORETO

Imagine waking up in the morning naked, lying on the ground in the middle of a desert wilderness. Imagine that in order to survive you have to walk for many miles over rocky terrain through thorny cactus and brush, looking for water and edible seeds and plants and, if you're lucky, a rodent or a bat or a lizard to keep you alive for another day. The original inhabitants of Loreto lived this way for thousands of years.

The lives of the people of the Baja California Peninsula appear to have remained relatively unchanged until the coming of the Europeans. Because of the arid desert land in which they lived, they had no agriculture and survived by hunting and gathering their food. Most of what we know about them comes from the early explorers of the 16th century and, primarily, from the Jesuits, who arrived at the end of the 17th century. During their seventy years in Baja California, the Jesuits wrote volumes of reports to their superiors in Mexico City and letters to their patrons and relatives abroad that left a thorough record of their observations about the customs, culture, and physical appearance of the people they had come to "save." *Before the Europeans Came*

There has been relatively little scientific study done in Baja California, especially compared to the ongoing studies of the pre-Columbian civilizations of mainland Mexico. Anthropologists and archeologists have done some investigation of the indigenous population, but there are no remains of pyramids, no stone columns engraved with writing, no statues to give a picture of the lives of the people who inhabited this land, as there are on the mainland of Mexico.

Archeologists have found bison, camel, and horse bones in the Comondú and La Purísima area near Loreto which are estimated to be about four thousand years old. These bones show evidence of having been burned and cut, indicating human presence.

Scientists speculate that man has inhabited the peninsula for at least twelve thousand years. Piles of clamshells and primitive arrowheads known as Clovis points have been carbon dated to about nine thousand years. The evidence indicates that people came to Baja California from the north, and stories the Indians told the Jesuits about their origins would confirm this. They said that the inhabitants of the peninsula had been defeated by other tribes in the north and forced to flee to the south. They believed that when good people died they would go north where food was plentiful, but bad people went south where the land was even more sterile.

Arrowheads, stone pipes, gravesites, rock art, and carved sticks for throwing have been found and analyzed. From these, anthropologists have surmised that the people that lived in the central area, including Loreto, had cultural levels superior to the inhabitants of the rest of the peninsula. They have labeled this the Comondú Culture. It is thought to have been from two to three thousand years old.

The impressive and mysterious rock art found between the Bahía de los Angeles and the Loreto area is thought to be part of the Comondú Culture. The huge and unique paintings of San Borjita, near Mulegé and the San Franciso range north of Loreto are the most spectacular. When the Jesuits questioned the natives about their makers, they were told that the huge mysterious figures had been painted by giants. These great mural paintings have been dated in the range of 2000 B.C. to 500 A.D. In the Loreto - San Javier - Comondú area there are a number of less spectacular rock paintings. They often appear to represent an account of game, fish or turtles caught, and there are occasional handprints.

Spain was eager to find a shortcut to their profitable trading centers in the Philippines. Europeans for hundreds of years thought that Baja California was an island, and as early as

1533, explorers were sent up the Sea of Cortez and along the Pacific Coast to find the northern end of the "island."

Many scholars believe that the name "California" came from a novel that was popular in Spain about the time of Cortés' conquest of Mexico in 1519, *The Adventures of Esplandián* by García Ordóñez de Montalvo. The description of an island called California in the novel stimulated the imaginations of the men of that era.

> Know ye that at the right hand of the Indies there is an island named California, very close to that part of the Terrestrial Paradise, which was inhabited by black women, without a single man among them, and they lived in the manner of Amazons. They were robust of body, with strong and passionate hearts and great virtues. The island itself is one of the wildest in the world on account of the bold and craggy rocks.

> Their weapons were all made of gold. The island everywhere abounds with gold and precious stones, and upon it no other metal was found. They lived in caves well excavated.

The book was probably read aloud during the long voyages of discovery from Spain. The rugged coasts of Baja California fit the description of the island in the book. Gazing at the land from the sea, the lonely sailors may have hoped to find robust and passionate women on shore.

Cortés' Attempts to Settle Baja California

Hernando Cortés had heard that the sea around the "island" of California was rich in pearls. He sent the first ship to explore Baja California in 1533. It was a disastrous journey. The pilot of the ship murdered the captain during the voyage, and when the mutinous crew landed in La Paz they proceeded to rape the women and shoot many of the men. In retaliation, the Indians* killed the pilot and twenty-two of his crew. The few survivors who made it back to the mainland reported they had seen beautiful pearls in the area, so Cortés sent a second

---

* The first European explorers of the peninsula repeated the mistake of Christopher Columbus who thought he had discovered India. He called the people he found "Indians." Since that has been the commonly used word for the indigenous people of the American continent for six hundred years, it will be used in these stories.

ship in 1535, this time with five hundred soldiers to subdue the primitive people. After all, he had conquered all of present mainland Mexico with four hundred men in 1521. But lack of food and water, disease, and the hostile Indians drove them out again. The Californians had learned their lesson with Europeans and discouraged attempts at settlement for the next two hundred years.

Other early navigators noted the Loreto area, but it was during the exploration of the Gulf of California by Francisco de Ortega in 1633 that the area was visited and described. He wrote:

> ...we circumnavigated this entire Isla del Carmen; it seemed to us to be more or less one hundred and twenty leagues in circumference. There the sun was shot, and I found that it is not twenty-nine degrees; and on the mainland side there is a small island next to the mainland. It forms a bay, which has very good anchorage, and at the end of it there are many reed-grass stands which have water. We gave the name Los Danzantes to this bay because the Indians which we find in the said bay came out to receive us dancing and playing flutes made from cane. They are people more bellicose than those of the port of La Paz. Here we took on water in a large pool that is there. This pool contains water throughout the year.

In 1685, Admiral Isidro Atondo y Antillón explored the Loreto area with Padre Eusebio Kino and wrote that he came to a large bay, which had been named San Dionisio by Captain Don Blas de Guzmán the previous year. He described it as having a large water hole and large reed grass stands and many tall and thick mesquite trees. He wrote:

> It is all low lying land and said bay is protected from the northwest and north winds because they come over the land, and the direction of the north wind is protected by Isla de Coronados which would be about four leagues, and from the east and southeast there is the protection of Isla del Carmen.

The Three Baja California Nations

At the time of the discovery of the peninsula in the 16th century there were three distinct groups of people with different languages and customs and blood relations. From Cabo San Lucas to north of La Paz, the land and some of the islands of the Gulf were the territory of the Pericú. From north of La Paz

16

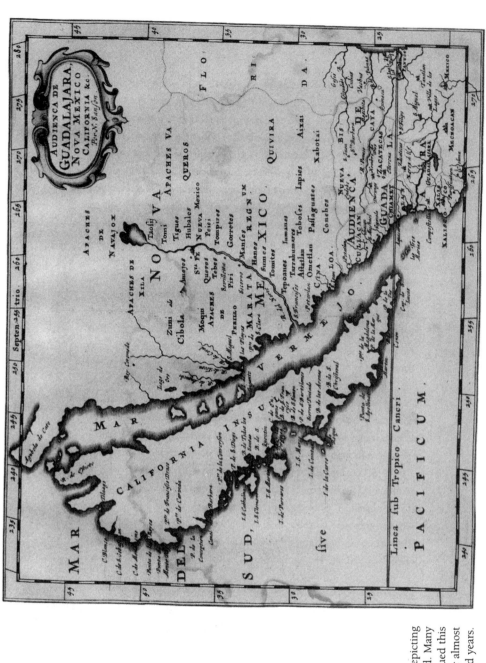

1600s map depicting
Baja California as an island. Many
cartographers continued this
error for almost
a hundred years.

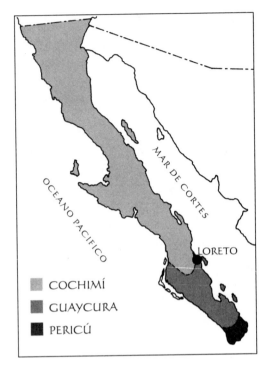

COCHIMÍ
GUAYCURA
PERICÚ

The three Indian
nations of the
peninsula.

to Loreto lived the Guaycura, and north of Loreto was the land
of the Cochimí. The Guaycura claimed territory on both coasts
to about 50 miles north of Loreto. The land of the Cochimí
extended all the rest of the way up the peninsula, except for a
pocket between the Guaycura coastal lands that ended at about
the present area of the San Javier mission. The Jesuit priests,
who came to the Loreto area in the late 17th century, happened
to land in a place that formed the boundary between two
nations, the Guaycura and the Cochimí.

The Pericú   The Pericú were described as being fiercer and more warlike than the Guaycura and the Cochimí, although that could
have been because they had been attacked by Cortés' men and
almost every other group of European explorers, who considered them sub-human and had no compunction about abusing
or killing them. Don Pedro Porter y Casanate, navigator and
explorer, visited the cape area in 1644 and said that "the men
are more robust, strong and well-featured than the natives of
New Spain, their hair is somewhat blond, they wear it very

long, and they go naked." In 1709, the English privateer Captain Woodes Rogers (who is remembered as the captain who had picked up Alexander Selkirk, "Robinson Crusoe," from his island in the South Pacific) visited the cape area and described the natives differently. "Their long hair is black and straight and hangs to their thighs. They are of much blacker complexion than any other people I had seen in the South Seas." The Jesuits, however, described them as being notably fairer than the rest of the *Californios*. In 1721, Father Ignacio María Napoli said, "I have not seen men taller than these, of well proportioned body, stout, and very white and bright red, and particularly the boys seem like Englishmen or Flemings for their whiteness and ruddiness." Napoli went on to surmise that some individuals were the offspring of Englishmen, since at that time English privateers waited around the tip of the peninsula to intercept the Manila galleon, and no doubt the men came ashore from time to time.

The Guaycura

The Guaycura were divided into three branches, related linguistically. The language of the Guaycura had a common root, but people from the southern end of their territory had great difficulty talking with the people from the north, as was the case with all three language groups on the peninsula. The Guaycura were described as being of medium build, well proportioned and sturdy, with a somewhat darker skin than the Pericú. Padre Kino described them as being of "a very lively and friendly disposition, of good stature, strength, and health, and very happy, laughing and jovial." He also found them to be fickle, crafty, easily offended, without regard for other people's property, shy, and easily frightened. These were the people of Loreto.

The Cochimí

The Cochimí, whose territory extended from the Loreto area to approximately 160 miles south of the present Mexico/United States border, also had many groups with a common linguistic root but with the same difficulty in communication among widely separated bands. The Jesuit fathers found these people to be the most docile, the easiest to convert, and the least troublesome. They were capable and easy to teach. Padre Benno Ducrue, a Viennese Jesuit who lived in Baja

19

California for fifteen years, from 1753 to 1768, said they were also lazy, sensual, untruthful, and violent in expressing their emotions. These were the people of San Javier.

Although the bands occasionally met with their neighbors for dances, contests and fighting, people did not travel far from the area where they were born. They were afraid of intruding on the territories of their neighbors and were too busy finding food each day to travel to areas where they were not familiar with the water sources and edible plants. Therefore, their dialects, even within their own nation, were different, as were their customs and religion.

All three nations were divided into bands of a few to about 100 people related through blood or marriage. The Jesuits called these bands *rancherías*. They possessed no land, but each ranchería did their hunting and gathering within a circumscribed area of as much as 30 miles. They had no permanent structures and moved from water hole to water hole in their territory.

Peninsular Clothing The Indian men of Baja California did not wear clothing. The men of the Guaycura band of the Loreto area, who called themselves Monquí, only wore a finely woven belt around their waists. Some wore a little net tied around their heads decorated with mother-of-pearl and little round beads. They also wore a necklace of carved mother-of-pearl figures alternated with beads. The Cochimí cut their hair short and wore a headdress of mother-of-pearl, which resembled a crown. The Pericú men also wore a sort of crown made of small snail shells. All the men of the peninsula pierced their earlobes by cutting a slit with a sharpened stone and inserting a thin smooth stick into the slit, gradually widening the hole by putting in thicker sticks until it was able to hold a hollow cane. They used the canes to carry deer sinews, arrowheads made of worked stones, or cactus spines.

The European missionaries were embarrassed by what they considered to be this indecent nudity, and they tried earnestly to persuade the men to cover themselves. The Indians, however, found the wearing of clothes ridiculous, as Padre Miguel del Barco said, "much as we are amused at the

Model of a Guaycura woman, made at the Universidad Autónoma de Baja California Sur, La Paz from a skeleton found on an archeological dig. Photo: Oroz, Loreto.

sight of dressed-up monkeys." When they were given clothing, it was often found discarded later by the side of the road. The Jesuit Padre Juan Ugarte, while establishing a mission at San Juan Baptista Ligüí, had two boys living with him so they could teach him the language and could later act as instructors in Christianity. He cut and sewed some blue woolen cloth and had the boys put on their new garments. When their relatives saw them, they howled with laughter and made such fun of them that the boys took their clothes off and hung them in a tree when they visited their families. They would retrieve them from the tree and put them on when they went back to the priest.

The women and girls wore a skirt and a sort of cape, the materials of which varied among the three nations. The priests gave them credit for modesty because they "protected their womanhood." The Pericú women made their skirts from palm leaves, which they smashed until the threads were exposed. These threads were tied together and hung in thick skeins. The skirts consisted of two parts. One part circled the back and the hips and hung to the calves; the other part of the skirt was

21

worn in front and reached only to the knees. A small cape of the same material reached from the shoulders to the waist.

The Cochimí women wore capes made of deerskin or other animal pelts and skirts made of the joints of very small reeds which were strung together on thin cords from the agave plant. These cords were then tied to other cords, which went around their waist.

The women of the Guaycura nation wore skirts fashioned from the small stems of reed grass tightly woven together, and they sometimes wore capelets of deerskin or woven reed grass. On their hair they wore a small net woven from fine grass thread or fiber. They made necklaces from mother-of-pearl figures, little berries, stems of reed grass, and small snails. These hung almost to their waists. They also pierced their ears but only for wearing decorative earrings made of the same materials as their necklaces.

Padre Juan María Salvatierra recorded a story about the women's noisy skirts on the day the Jesuits first landed on the beach at Loreto. He wrote:

> The women wear a skirt from the waist to below the knees. This dress is tightly woven from reeds and other grasses, a material which makes a rustling sound much like that of maize kernels when shaken. Inasmuch as the natives had never seen pigs before, they were very curious about them, especially on finding them so tame that they could come right up to them without being harmed. When the women also came up close to see the pigs, the animals, on hearing the rustling of the skirts which sounded like corn grains being rattled, ran after the women, grunting the whole time. The faster the women ran, the louder was the rustling of their skirts as though calling the pigs with greater insistence. The amusing incident lasted until real corn was brought to quiet the animals.

Both men and women wore some protection on their feet while traveling far or when it was very hot. Their sandals were made of deerskins held by cords around the foot, two coming from either side of the heel to the instep where they were tied in a large knot. Two other cords passed between the toes and were tied at the instep.

Living as they did in a desert environment where food and water were scarce, survival was a full-time occupation for the Indians of Baja California.

There was a distinct division of labor between the men and women. The men spent their days preparing to hunt and fish, making bows and arrows, planning war with their neighbors, and practicing dances. Since game was scarce, their contribution to the food supply was not great, and they frequently came back from their hunting trips empty handed and hungry.

The men of the Monquí group of Loreto fished and were able to supply food more easily than those who depended solely on hunting. Early explorers saw men from Loreto on sturdy rafts, very well made from cane, which would hold three or four fishermen. The whole family could also gather fish on the shore when the yellowtail boiled in feeding frenzies and sometimes leapt out of the water onto the beach, as they did until not many years ago when commercial fishing depleted the sea.

It was the women who daily scoured the land to bring home the food for the family. They gathered seeds, fruits, plants, and roots when they were in season and available.

Indian woman with basket. Illustration by Jesuit Padre Ignacio Tirsch, the only California missionary who left illustrations of life in Baja California in the 18th century. Padre Tirsch was a native of Bohemia, and his work is preserved in the Czech Republic National Art Museum in Prague. Tirsch illustration: Courtesy of Glen Dawson.

Lizards, snakes, rats, and certain spiders and worms were also on the family menu. Another delicacy was the lice they found and ate one by one when they deloused each others' heads. The women also supplied water for the family as well as firewood for roasting seeds and keeping warm. Except in the very hot months, the families always slept by a fire.

The Guaycura and Cochimí women prepared the food they had gathered. Seeds from annual plants were collected. The three-cornered seeds, about the size of small peas, from the San Miguelito plant, *Antigonon leptopus*, were especially useful. They first toasted all the seeds they had found by putting three or four handfuls on a wooden tray and covering them with hot charcoal. They moved the tray around continuously until the seeds were done and then removed everything from the tray with their hands and repeated the process. When all the seeds were toasted, they cleaned them by picking off the pieces of charcoal and other foreign objects. The Jesuits who tasted this food complained of the noise the bits of remaining charcoal made when they chewed. Some of the seed was eaten while it was still hot, but most of it was ground between two stones and reduced to a coarse flour which was eaten dry.

The women gathered small dry figs from native fig plants and fruit from two species of palm trees in the *Phoenicaceae* family, which the Europeans found to be bitter and to cause diarrhea. Cactus fruits that could be eaten included the fruit called *tuna* from the nopal plants, *Opuntia basilaris*, which are tasty and juicy when ripe. The seeds from the nopal were ground into flour, and the fleshy pads were bound to wounds and bruises and were also thought to cure warts. The small red bitter fruit of the Old Man (viejito) cactus, *Lophocereus schottii*, was eaten when other food was scarce.

The fruit of the biznaga (barrel cactus) *Ferocactus acanthodes*, was not very tasty and was also eaten only when no other food was available. The pulp of the stem was chewed in times of emergency for its food and water content. This cactus supplied spines used for awls, needles, tattooing, and fishhooks. The barrel cacti were made into cooking pots by cutting off the tops, scooping out the pulp, and placing hot stones in the cavity for heating food.

Native peninsular plants illustrated by Padre Ignacio Tirsch. Tirsch illustration: Courtesy of Glen Dawson.

The fruit of the cardón, *Pachycereus pringlei*, was a staple, which the women ground before eating or steeped in water as a tea. The cardón ribs were used for fishing spears and poles for picking cactus fruit and, when dried, made a very hot fire. Slabs of cardón flesh were applied to wounds and acted as a painkiller, disinfectant, and healing agent for ulcers.

Agave or mescal plants kept families alive for months when there was no other food. They roasted the heads in a pit lined with heated stones. The heads were put on top of the stones, covered with trimmed leaves and fibers and then another layer of dirt on which a fire was built. After three days of roasting, the mescal was removed from the pit and eaten or stored for the future. Charcoal from the burned agave was used for tattooing. Crushed or chewed agave leaves were an emergency source of water and food. The blossoms contain a great deal of sweet nectar which the people enjoyed drinking. The seeds were ground into flour. This useful plant also provided fibers to make fishing nets and carrying bags. The agave was never fermented into liquor, as it was on the mainland. The

Baja Californians never discovered any mind-altering substance, such as peyote or fermented fruit or cactus.

Women gathered the abundant seed pods from the palo blanco, palo verde, and mesquite trees and ground them into flour. The fruit of the candelabra cactus, or *cochal,* tastes somewhat like currants. The flowers of the ocotillo were eaten raw or soaked to make a tea.

But the most highly prized of all their food was the fruit of the pitaya cactus. When the fruit ripened in the fall months, even the men joined in the search for this eagerly awaited treat. A rib from the cardón cactus with a hook on the end was used to pick the fruit, and it was gathered in the purse-like nets which both men and women generally carried with them.

There are two kinds of pitaya fruit: sweet pitaya, *Lemaireocereus thurberi littoralis* and sour pitaya, *Machaerocerus gummosus.* Sweet pitaya fruit comes from the organ pipe cactus, which is a many-branched erect cactus. The flowers are cream colored with light purple tips and open at night. The fruit, about the size of a tennis ball, ripens in late summer and fall and tastes something like watermelon. The pitaya agria is a sprawling, spiny cactus, which forms dense thickets. The large flowers are white with long purple tubes. They are very fragrant and open only for one night. The bright red golf to tennis ball sized fruit matures in November, and, although it is not sweet, has a very pleasant taste.

The period of pitaya feasting was the only time of the year when there was enough to eat. The tribes were able to travel and gather together to participate in general orgies of eating, dancing, games, and the activity which guaranteed the perpetuation of the population. Father Salvatierra reported that "the three months of the pitahaya season are celebrated like the three carnival days before Ash Wednesday in some European countries, when to a great degree people go out of their senses. These Indians also go out of their senses, dedicating themselves completely to their feasting, dancing, invitations to parties of distant *rancherías,* and their peculiar type of merrymaking and buffoonery, and in which they often spend entire nights laughing and feasting. The clowns among them do a very good job of entertaining the rest."

If the fruit was not eaten fresh, it was dried in the sun and eaten later. To make certain that they utilized this wonderful fruit to the fullest, the tribes had a custom that the Jesuits called "the second harvest." The small black seeds of the pitaya, distributed throughout the fruit, were eaten along with the pulp. During this season when they ate nothing else, each family laid flat rocks or dry broadleaf plants in a designated spot where they defecated each day. When it dried, the women put it in their trays and broke up and discarded everything but the pitaya seed. When only seeds were left, they threw hot coals on them and toasted them as they did other seeds. Then the seed was ground and eaten as a powder.

This powder was once offered as a treat to Padre Francisco María Piccolo, and he ate it to show his appreciation for the gift, unaware of its origin. When his fellow Jesuits heard what he had eaten, they teased him about it for years.

Another custom the Europeans found disgusting was the natives' use of their own urine to clean their hands and faces. But in the desert where water was so scarce, it made better sense to reserve water for drinking, not washing.

Indian Women as Beasts of Burden

The life of a woman in this society was not an easy one. In addition to supplying and preparing most of the food for the family, she had to carry all the implements the family needed as they moved from place to place. Her burden included: a large wooden tray, a wooden bowl, a bone used as an awl for repairs, a small stick to start fires, a net in the form of a purse, two small boards for carrying hawk feathers for arrows, some flints, a shell for drinking water, a bow and arrow, and, in the Loreto area, large nets for fishing. All these were carried on her back in a large net made of agave fiber. Women were also responsible for making the nets and repairing the trays.

Indian Women as Mates and Mothers

In addition to their other loads, the women carried the children. Babies were carried in a net, open at the top, which was supported by strings crossing the mother's forehead. When the child grew a bit older, its mother carried it in her arms. Two or three-year-olds sat on their mothers' shoulders, the child clutching her hair.

A pregnant woman was always accompanied when she went out to gather food and often gave birth wherever she happened to be. She then returned to the campsite, carrying her baby, and only then lay down to take care of herself. The new baby was smeared with a paste made of ground charcoal and urine, which protected it somewhat from the weather in the absence of clothing. The woman returned almost immediately to her task of searching for water, seeds, and firewood.

Women sometimes found it necessary to kill their children when there was not enough food to sustain them. More frequently, they induced an abortion by having another woman apply violent pressure on their abdomen to kill the fetus. Many women did this regularly after the birth of their first child.

The Jesuit Jacob Baegert observed that often the women of the Guaycura with whom he worked chose their husbands. He discovered this when he tried to counsel married couples who were having difficulties. When he suggested to the man that, since he had chosen this woman, he should try to live in peace with her, the man would reply, with feeling, that he had not sought this wife, but rather that she had claimed him. Polygamy was fairly common among the Pericú of the south, but was unusual among the Guaycura and Cochimí.

Marriage customs differed among the various groups. In the Loreto area the man presented his chosen woman with a wooden tray called an *oló*. To show her consent, the woman accepted it and gave the man a small net. This contract was easily broken if one or the other partner became dissatisfied. Once the couple was married, the mother of the bride never looked at her son-in-law again, because it was thought she would go blind if she did. Adultery was considered a crime and a reason to take revenge except on two occasions: one was during festivals and dances, and the other was when the rancherías held competitions and the victor could choose any woman he wanted without fear of retaliation. In some groups it was also the custom for a widow to marry the brother or the closest relation of her deceased husband.

One chore that was not required of the women was housework, since most groups did not use any kind of shelter

A hunting party illustrated by Padre Ignacio Tirsch. Tirsch illustration: Courtesy of Glen Dawson.

except the shade of trees or, in bad weather, natural caves. When it was very windy and cold, rocks or brush were piled in a circle, and the family slept inside it. In Loreto some families made shelters of palm leaves. They did not like to sleep under a roof and resisted vigorously when the missionaries insisted they build small huts. Some of the old people could not become accustomed to living and sleeping inside, and died when they were forced to do so.

When the men went hunting, they never returned with much game. When they killed a deer, the meat was divided up among all the men who participated in the hunt, leaving only a small portion for the hunter's family. To trap deer, some of the men formed a line to drive and frighten the deer, which would run toward the other men who were waiting, with bows and arrows to shoot them. If they were successful in killing an animal, all the men in the hunting group gathered. While some stripped off the skin and opened up the body, others built a fire. They took out the intestines and then threw the meat on the fire so they could eat it immediately. They snatched the partly cooked meat from the fire with their fingers, ate until

Indian Men as Hunters

29

their hunger was satisfied, and then distributed the rest to be taken home to their families. The deer slayer was awarded the skin, but he did not eat the meat because it was believed that if he did he would never be able to kill another deer. It was also believed that a young man who did not yet have children would never have any if he ate rabbit.

The men roasted small game – rabbits, rats, bats, squirrels, and lizards – by throwing it on the hot coals of a fire. They turned it over once, shook off the charcoal or ashes that had stuck to the meat, and ate it barely cooked. Europeans found the sight of lizards cooking on the hot coals repulsive, because they bloated on the fire and looked horrible. They observed that the Indians would eat anything that wouldn't poison them except badgers, because they thought the badger's footprints looked human. The priests believed that this indicated that the natives had never been cannibals.

Hunting and *Fighting* *Equipment*   The men made only a simple arched bow for hunting and for fighting. They dried a piece of solid wood, *palo de arco,* on the fire to straighten and give it more strength. They cleaned it, leaving the middle about three fingers thick, and scraped it to taper it gradually toward the ends, which were less than the thickness of one finger. A string made from deer tendons or intestines was tied to one end, the bow was heated again and bent to the proper shape, and the taut cord was tied to the other tip. The smallest bows measured about 30 inches across and the largest about 45 inches.

The arrows were about a yard long. The first third of the arrow, toward the arrow's tip, was made of a thin piece of lightweight hard wood and the remaining two-thirds of reed grass about the thickness of a little finger. The wood portion was sharpened at one end and the other was slipped into the hollow section of the reed and the two sections glued together with tar. Then flattened tendons were wound around the junction many times to make it secure. The joint was evened out and strengthened so that when the wooden tip penetrated the body, the reed part could slip in as well. Three hawk feathers about 4 inches long were split lengthwise and fastened to the reed section, using tar and tendons, at an equal distance from one another, forming a triangle. These arrows were used for hunting small game and for target practice.

For war or for hunting big game or deer, flints were added to the tips of the arrows, using tendons to attach them. These inflicted greater injury and prevented them from falling out of the body. Long sticks with sharpened tips were also used in fighting.

The men also made reed flutes, which they played during their dances. Smoking pipes were carved from sandstone or other soft rock.

Flutes and Pipes and Baskets

The pipes were in the shape of an eight to twelve inch tube, divided in the middle by a pebble of irregular shape, which permitted the air and smoke to pass. The lower half was filled with wild tobacco and ignited with a live coal. These pipes were the property of the shamans, although during some of their festivities they were passed from hand to hand. These are the only artifacts found on the peninsula made of polished stone.

The small baskets the men made were used to carry water, as plates for eating, and as hats for the women. Baskets were made of closely woven reed fibers.

Strife among the various tribes was common, usually caused by offenses by some individuals against others or because some group had fished or collected fruits in an area another group was accustomed to using. The men announced their intention of going to war by noisily stocking up on arrows and flints and making sure their adversaries knew what they were up to, hoping to intimidate them so they wouldn't actually have to fight. If it came to a battle, they approached their enemy, whooping and shouting but in no military formation. When they were within bow-and-arrow range the clash began, and the only order seemed to be that when the men became exhausted or ran out of arrows they moved to the rear. During hand-to-hand combat they used the sharp wooden lances.

War

The Europeans observed that the people of the south were the most warlike, inflicting so many casualties on each other that the groups were becoming smaller. The priests also observed that the people of Loreto and others in the north felt hatred and the need for vengeance against one another, but not to the same degree as the southerners. They were more sociable and agreeable, more responsive to reason and less obstinate and stubborn. They seemed to feel that staying alive was the measure of victory in war, and they weren't ashamed of running away in order to do so.

Dancing

During times of peace, the men constantly practiced dancing. They danced to celebrate weddings, good luck in hunting and fishing, the birth of a child, victories over their enemies, for joy during the pitaya harvest, and for any other reason they could find. The bands invited one another to these festivities, which often lasted a week or more. They had many specific dances, all pertaining to some aspect of their lives, such as war, fishing, walking, burying, carrying loads, and so on. Children learned to dance when they were as young as three or four and participated in the celebrations.

California Languages

The Jesuits found that their task of learning the language of the people they had come to save was even more difficult in California than on the mainland of New Spain. The languages of the three Baja California nations had nothing in common with each other or any mainland language, and, moreover, the dialects within each differed widely since the bands were so isolated. In addition, they had no words for many European concepts. Padre Jacob Baegert, who served at Mission San Luis Gonzaga for seventeen years, wrote:

> They have no words to express whatever is not material and not perceptible to the senses and can neither be seen nor touched, no words to express virtues and vices or qualities of feeling. There are no terms which relate to social, human, or rational and civil life...It would be futile to look in a Guaycura dictionary, for instance, for the following words: Life, death, weather, time, cold, heat, world, rain, reason, memory, knowledge, honor, decency, peace, feeling, friend, friendship, truth, shame, faith, love, hope, desire, hate, anger, gratitude, patience, meekness, industry, virtue, vice, beauty, happiness...

The languages of the Guaycura of Loreto and the Cochimí of San Javier were entirely different. Generally they could only count to five. The Cochimí had words for the first four numbers: *tejueg, goguó, kombió, magacúbuguá.* To indicate "five," they said "a whole hand," *nagannná tejueg iñimmél.* After that, they usually just said "many," although some could count higher by using "one hand and one," "one hand and two," up to two hands and two feet. No one counted further than twenty.

There was no written language, and to illustrate that the Californios lacked even the concept of written language, the priests told the story of a young boy from San Javier who, during the first years of the Jesuit settlement, went to Loreto. The priest there sent him back to San Javier with a letter to Padre Juan Ugarte telling him the latest news and mentioning two loaves of bread he was sending by the same messenger. At that time bread was a rare treat, since it was only baked in Loreto and only when flour had been brought from the other side of the gulf. The boy tasted the bread during his long hike up the mountain, liked it, and sat down and ate both loaves. When Padre Ugarte read the letter from Loreto, he asked the boy to give him what they had sent him. The boy denied that they had given him anything. The priest reminded him that they had given him two loaves of bread. "Who says so?" the boy asked. "This," said the priest, showing him the piece of paper. Astounded that so small and thin a thing could speak, the boy said that if the paper said that, it was lying. Padre Ugarte knew what had happened, but he let it go.

Some time later, the same boy went back to Loreto, and the same thing happened. He was given some bread and a letter to Padre Ugarte telling him what was being sent. The boy wanted to eat the food, but he was afraid the letter would tell on him, so he put it behind a large rock and hid where it couldn't see him while he ate the bread. When he delivered the letter, Padre Ugarte asked him to give him the food, and again the boy denied that he had been given any. The priest told him he knew very well that food had been sent to him from Loreto. "Who says so?" the boy asked. "This," said the priest, showing him the letter. "Then it is lying," said the boy. "The last time it is true that I ate the bread in front of the paper, but this time I hid myself where it couldn't see me. If it says that I ate it, it is lying, because it did not see me eat nor does it know what I did."

In a report to the king of Spain in 1702, Padre Francisco María Piccolo summed up the missionaries' impression of the

Indians they had encountered in the area around Loreto:

> By nature they are very lively and alert, and they show this, among other ways, in jeering loudly any barbarism in use of their speech, as they did to us when we first preached to them. After being domesticated, they come to correct us of any faults we may have made in their language in preaching to them. When explaining mysteries contrary to their old errors, they surround the father, immediately after the sermon, reprimand him for what he has said, argue with him, and uphold their erroneous ideas with much reasonableness, but they soon calm down and yield to the force of reason. With these evidences of enlightenment, they show that they should not be counted among the brutes of that kingdom. Of these there are many and diverse numbers, some who live only to eat and enjoy themselves, others to beautify the fields and woods with their ingenuity.

The Indians quickly learned to read and write Spanish. By the end of the seventy years of the Jesuit stay, almost everyone was speaking Spanish, and in Loreto only a very few could still speak their ancient language. A few place names in the Guaycura dialect of the Monquí in the Loreto area is all that remains of that language. The Monquí called their area Conchó, meaning colored mangrove tree. To the south are Liguí or Malibat, Tripú or Tripué (now Tripuí), Nopoló or Numpoló, Notrí, Chuyenquí, and to the north Londó and Mulegé. In the Cochimí language the mountains west of Loreto were called Viggé, and the San Javier area was known as Biaundó.

Time
The calendar year of the Cochimí and Guaycura was divided into six parts. The Cochimí called the first part *meyíbo*. It included part of June, all of July, and part of August, and was a happy time because it was the beginning of the pitaya season. The second part was called *amadá-appí* and included part of August, all of September, and part of October. This season was a good one, too, because of the pitaya, other seeds which were gathered during this time, and the rains which turned the land green. The third season was *amadá-appí-gal-lá* and corresponded to our November and part of October and of December. The fourth, the coldest season, was called *meyihél* and lasted most

of December, all of January and part of February. The fifth, which included all of March and some time before and after, was *meyijbén,* and the sixth was called *meyijbén-maayí* and included part of April, all of May, and part of June. The word *maayí* meant "a bad thing," and it was probably given that name because it was the time of the greatest hunger.

They measured time by the moon, but had no name for this reckoning and only used it to indicate one or two months. For longer periods, they referred to the seasons or to the time when something had happened: "when we went to that place" or "when we gathered seeds."

The Jesuits and other priests declared that the people of the peninsula had no religion – and then went on to describe what were obviously religious practices and beliefs, although not Christian.

Religion

Padre Baegert wrote that he was told by one of his Guaycura about a god called Ema who met a bird and from their marriage arose human beings, that the first people came from the north, and also that all animals, wood, and stone had been human beings before. He dismissed this information as a foolish fable, and said that while maybe they believed something, they differed among each other "as the Calvinist from the Mohammedan because of lack of communication with one another."

The principal god of the Guaycura Monquí group of the Loreto area was called Guamongó. He lived in the north and long, long ago had sent another spirit named Guajaiquí to visit the peninsula in his name. On his journey along the peninsula Guajaiquí planted the pitaya cactus and created the good fishing places.

Guajaiquí traveled until he came to the mountains behind the harbor of Puerto Escondido. He remained there for awhile in seclusion and was served by other inferior spirits who brought him fresh fish and pitaya fruit. He made capes from human hair that was also brought to him, capes of the sort the medicine men were still wearing when the Europeans came.

The Guayacura believed that the sun, the moon, and the largest of the planets represented men and women. They thought that each day at sunset the sun fell into the sea and swam out the next morning; the moon and the planets swam out of the sea at night. They said that the stars were torches lighted in the sky by Guamongó, who re-lit them nightly after they were extinguished by the waters of the sea during the day.

The Cochimí of the San Javier area and northward believed that a Great Spirit lived in the sky whose name signified "He Who Creates All People." This was the principal spirit who made the sky, the plants, animals, man and woman. There were other spirits, also: one whose name signified "The Swift One" or "The Perfect One," and another "The Man Who Came From the Sky."

The Jesuits watched and described a feast for this latter spirit. On the selected day, a youth distinguished for his speed and agility would be dressed in plumage of the brightest colors and painted so that he could not be identified. Then, at an appointed hour, this representative of The Man Who Came From the Sky appeared at the crest of a high mountain back of Puerto Escondido. He shouted and came running at the greatest speed down into the valley, where a great feast had been prepared by the women in his honor. When the distinguished guest was prepared to make his run from the mountainside, the women and children were sent away, leaving the men to enjoy the feasting and dancing.

In 1684, a party of Europeans, under the religious leadership of the Jesuit missionary Padre Eusebio Kino and the military leadership of Admiral Isidro de Atondo y Antillón, attempted to establish a permanent mission at what is now Rancho San Bruno, about 12 miles north of Loreto. The attempt was a failure, primarily because of lack of water, but during the year they were there they met a man who was to prove helpful in the mission settlement of Loreto thirteen years later. He was a leader of the Guaycura Didiú band, and his name was Ibo (the sun). Ibo was an intelligent man who was interested in learning from the Europeans and was very friendly and of great assistance to them. The missionaries called him "Leopoldo." One morning, two soldiers, whose names were Sotomayer and Rodrígues, witnessed a harvest festival at what is now Rancho San Juan, which was led by Ibo/Leopoldo. Admiral Atondo, after making the two soldiers swear to tell the truth, recorded their account of the ceremony:

Some 2,500 Indians gathered to participate in the ceremony, hundreds coming down from the mountains to join with those of the valley. The central feature of the ceremony was the worship of a statue or idol representing a god of the harvest. The principal medicine man or priest was Chief Leopoldo.

On Monday, the 6th of November, about noon, while they were guarding the horses which were pasturing round about San Isidro (now called San Juan), they saw how an Indian captain of the Didiú nation, who we call Leopoldo, although he is not baptized, went up to the top of a hill dressed in a fiber net all covered with bunches of hair which covered him from his shoulders to his feet like a Turk. On his head he had a toque or little cap, made of feathers of various colors, which fell over his shoulders. In his right hand he carried a white stick a yard long and having two square holes in it. In his left hand he carried a bow and arrow. Climbing upon a rock which was on top of the hill, he gave loud shouts and made many gestures.

After he had been on this rock for a time, Leopoldo descended with such speed that he caused them surprise. Many Indians came out to receive him, and within an hour other heathen – there must have been about fourteen of them – went up the hill with the captain, dressed in the same way. Passing below the same rock, without stopping they descended to the ranchería.

About noon the next day, Sotomayor and Rodrígues:

...saw a great procession set out from the ranchería, led by Captain Leopoldo and others. Behind him was one of his wives, then followed an Indian and then another woman, and in this way they went intermixed, men and women, with canes in their hands and bunches of feathers on their heads, dancing and running and paying homage to a statue of the size of a newborn child. Its face was painted black. It had long locks and three bunches of white feathers on its head, the one in the middle standing up and the others hanging down a little.

This statue was carried by the last Indian in the procession, who went crouching with it till they came to a place where they had set up a pitahaya tree. On the tip of this tree were placed some wreaths, made of twigs of a tree which they call copale. Above them there were two wooden pennants woven of branches of the same tree and painted red, black, and white.

They put the image underneath a brush shelter raised a little above the ground, and at the foot of a large pile of seed which they call medesé. As soon as they had placed it there, the dance ceased for a spell. Afterward they resumed it and continued for two days and two nights in the following manner: In single file, men and women intermixed, they ran a long race. On coming to the end of the course, the captain and all his men would stop near the image and begin to talk, at the same time bowing down and making obeisance. After this they would rest for about a quarter of an hour and then repeat the same race and the same ceremony.

On the last day of the dance, a little before dawn, they gave such a loud whoop that they caused the infantry to seize their arms, thinking they were coming to attack them. At the same time the witnesses heard a great wailing among the women. Shortly after this, the Indians began to sing and continued all day, shouting and dancing, with pauses at intervals. At sunset they sat down in circles in various places and commenced to distribute the seed of the medesé which they had heaped up near the statue.

A few days after the festival, Leopoldo and another man went to the garrison to ask for food. When the corporal asked him about the statue his people had been worshipping, Leopoldo replied that it was the god who gave them their food, coming down from the sky when it rained to give them pitayas and medesé. Leopoldo added that the god had now gone back to the sky. He told the Spaniards that the idol talked to them in their language, that he had one foot and two teeth, one lower and one upper.

Spiritual Leaders and Healers   The priests representing the gods were called *guamas*. The missionaries thought these men were agents of Satan and had nothing good to say about them. From their writings, though, when the pejorative adjectives are eliminated, the guamas emerge as spiritual leaders and medical healers. They were a special caste, selected from the most intelligent and charismatic of the young men. The chosen ones were initiated into the mysteries and practices of the guamas during a long period of apprenticeship.

They were the men who planned and conducted all religious ceremonies, officiated at funerals, and cured the sick. The missionaries described them as great talkers. Padre Luis Sales, a Dominican who arrived in Loreto in 1783, wrote a description of a ceremony he witnessed:

> In some grove or barranca, hidden from the missionaries, sticks or poles are piled up to form a circle. A hut is raised for the exclusive use of the guama. The circle prepared, all gather there, the men gaudily painted and wearing on their heads a sort of diadem made of bird feathers. By a pole in the center of the circle stands the principal guama in his long cape made from human hair. Around him are gathered other old men, painted in black, wearing capes of deerskin secured by cords and carrying long staves in their hands. Some may hold the skulls of other chiefs killed in former wars.
>
> With great formality the principal guama calls for silence, then speaks to them of the purpose of the feast or ceremony. He goes on to tell of their ancient customs, tells of his own great cures and accomplishments, assuring them that he is on friendly terms with those people of the past of whom he speaks. Then he produces some wooden board or tablets which are painted with numerous ridiculous figures. These he interprets as telling the history of the famous men of the past, their bravest, their best runners, their great healers. Of all these he tells in a long eulogy, always ending by insisting that he, the present guama, is the greatest of them all. There are other wooden tablets about 33 inches in length, with a hole in the middle through which the guama occasionally thrusts his tongue, causing much laughter. When the principal guama retires exhausted to his hut, the general dance begins. Now and again the guama comes out of the hut, attired in his long cape of human hair, leaps several steps in one direction, then another, emits some loud shouts, which set all the others to howling. In this manner of orgy they would pass the entire night, pausing only occasionally for some refreshment that had been prepared by the women during the day. This feasting might be continued for twenty days or more.

The guamas presided over all burials. The dead were usually cremated, but sometimes they were wrapped in a deerskin and dropped into a shallow grave. Occasionally, a person in a coma would be buried alive, and a missionary wrote that he once saved the life of a girl about to be buried by giving her a good dose of chocolate. He said she lived for many years afterward.

A few days after the cremation or burial, the guama would call together all the friends and relatives, who came painted in black and yellow, the colors for mourning. The guama, dressed in his cape of human hair, carried a stick with some hair from the deceased tied to the end of it. He blew a whistle to recall the spirit of the dead and then talked with it, asking how things were in the North, where they believed the spirit had gone. He also asked if there was any person in that place as important as he, the guama, was, and the spirit always answered that there wasn't.

The guama then delivered a eulogy in praise of the dead, while the mourners wept and wailed through the night. At dawn, two old women, selected mourners, would sit apart and lament loudly. The guama invited all those present, except relatives, to join in a dance, saying that the deceased wanted to watch them dance one more time. The relatives cut off their hair and presented it to the guama, and he was given the choicest food. The guama then ran with the hair of the deceased on a stick to show that the spirit had now departed.

Besides conducting the funeral ceremony, the guama acted as healer for the sick. The guama painted his face a vivid red or smeared it with charcoal. He usually wore his cape of human hair and a headdress of sparrow hawk feathers. He carried fans made of feathers and his *chaquaca,* the carved stone pipe.

These medicine men used many plants to effect cures. Milkweed, *Ascelpias subulata,* cured rattlesnake bite. Mormon tea, *Ephedra californica,* was used as a sedative, a blood purifier, and as a treatment for kidney ailments, colds, stomach disorders, and ulcers. Old man cactus, *Lophocereus shottii,* also provided a tea to relieve stomach ulcers. Broom baccharis,

Baccharis sarathroidus, was chewed to relieve toothache, and the gum of the brittlebush *(incienso)* was also used for toothache and to relieve pain and infection. The sap of the lomboy blanco, *Jatropha cinerea,* was a topical dressing for hardening the gums, chapped or sunburned lips, superficial wounds and abrasions, to stop bleeding, and as a remedy for sore throats, ulcers, warts, and hemorrhoids. The young pods and bark of the mesquite tree were used as a tea for stomach problems. A tea made from the leaves and branch tips of the creosote bush *Larrea tridentata,* was also used for stomach pain, loose bowels, colic, coughs, and colds; tea made from the roots was thought to cure ulcers and to relieve arthritic pain.

The missionaries reported that the guama had another method of curing. Smearing his face with urine and putting a thorn in his mouth, he would approach the patient, carrying his pipe filled with wild tobacco smoke. After blowing smoke on the patient, he would extract the thorn from his mouth and wave it triumphantly as having been drawn from the patient and the cause of his illness. If this didn't work, the guama made an incision with his fingernail in the skin of a female relative of the patient and allowed the blood to drip on the body of the sufferer. Sometimes he would put his fingers in the patient's mouth and pull out a rock, which he had hidden in his hand, and claim he had extracted the illness.

If the patient fell asleep after the treatment, his relatives would hit him on the head with a rock to awaken him. If he died, the women shrieked and howled and punched their noses in grief. The guama was paid with small bundles of human hair, which he might be required to return if the cure was not successful.

The guamas received the finest fish and the best fruits and seeds of the season. Those who did not donate were made to do penance by fasting, or the guama might make tardy or reluctant donors the object of ridicule and invective in public. The people believed that guamas could not only cure but could also cause sickness if they became offended. They thought the breath of the guamas was very dangerous and were careful not to get too close.

There was a certain hazard, though, to being a medicine man. He was always required to attend the sick when called, and if the patient died, the guama was occasionally slain by the relatives.

European Perception of the Indigenous People

The severest critic of the Baja Californians was the German Padre Jacob Baegert. (Padre Baegert had very little admiration for Englishmen, Mexicans, Frenchmen or Spaniards either). He described the Indians as "stupid, dull, stubborn, dirty, uncouth, ungrateful, lying, knavish, extremely lazy, great gossips…a people who can never be tamed and who obey their natural instincts, like the animals."

But Baegert later reversed himself by saying, "They have reason and intelligence like other people, and in my opinion if they were directed from infancy by Europe…they would progress in manners, arts, and sciences." He went on to say of them:

> They live unquestionably much happier than the civilized inhabitants of Europe, not excepting those who seem to enjoy all the felicity that life can afford. Habit renders all things endurable and easy, and the Californian sleeps on the hard ground and in the open air just as well and soft as the rich European on the curtained bed of down in his splendidly decorated apartment. Throughout the whole year nothing happens that causes a Californian trouble or vexation, nothing that renders his life cumbersome and death desirable, for no one harasses and persecutes him, or carries on a lawsuit against him, neither a hail storm nor an army can lay waste his fields, and he is not in danger of having his house and barn destroyed by fire. Envy, jealousy, and slander embitter not his life, and he is not exposed to the fear of losing what he possesses, nor to the care of increasing it.

However, many of the Europeans who came to Baja California regarded the Indians as a lower form of human life. Europeans assumed that their advanced technology was proof that the Christian God favored their beliefs and way of life. Even the priests, most of whom sincerely believed that they were saving the souls of their charges from eternal hell fire and who loved and cared for them as their children, shared this view.

They never considered that great numbers of these rugged

people had managed to survive for thousands of years in this barren, rocky environment because of their way of life. They had managed to find enough food for their families to stay healthy and strong in spite of their meager diet (or perhaps because of it), and they enjoyed themselves enormously without the help of alcohol or drugs. Although they had no spare time to develop a complicated culture, their beliefs were poetic and reflected their experience and environment.

The first permanent European settlement in Loreto marked the beginning of the end for the indigenous people of the peninsula.

There was no census of the Indian population of the Jesuit area until 1760, after the Baja Californians had been subjected to the European diseases, but it was generally agreed that initially there were more than four thousand souls to be saved in the Loreto area. This included the coastal area from Punta Mercenarios to Agua Verde, about 80 miles, inland about 22 miles to San Javier, and the islands – about 2,500 square miles. The population of the entire peninsula was estimated at 45,000, or 1.5 persons per square mile.

In other parts of New Spain soldiers and other immigrants were encouraged to marry Indian women, and those women found that children fathered by European men survived because they inherited their fathers' immunity. But because of the isolation of the peninsula and the Jesuit desire to control the spiritual and physical lives of both the California Indians and the Europeans and Christianized people from the mainland who worked for them, this practice was discouraged.

From the beginning, the missionaries tried to gather the Indians into the mission centers and away from their nomadic life in order to supervise their conversion. They gradually accomplished this, partly through religious teachings, partly through fear of the superior forces of the soldiers, but primarily because the Indians could obtain food from the missions much more easily than they could by foraging in the desert wilderness.

It took the missions many years to develop an agricultural system, a system that was never completely self-sustaining but relied on a steady flow of supplies from the mainland. However, the padres managed to supply their neophytes with *pozole* (corn soup) or stew and other foods that the Indians came to depend on. A trip to the mission was easier than spending an entire day in search of food in the desert. Of course, they were required to work for this food by tending the fields and the cattle and building the missions.

Once the natives became used to living in the mission centers, the padres insisted that they wear clothes and live in houses, which many of the older people could not tolerate and died. The most dangerous unrecognized health hazard, however, was living in close proximity to Europeans, against whose diseases they had no immunity.

By 1700, the Loreto garrison included sixty persons, including seamen and Indians from the mainland. In 1704 two pearl fishing boats were wrecked, and the missionaries took care of 84 men. The following years saw more and more visits by pearl fishers, pirates, and adventurers of one kind or another. Padre Baegert wrote: "Every summer six or twelve poor Spaniards come over in little boats, such as discharged soldiers and others of similar description. They make very little and are always in poverty. They bring also some Mexican Indians to do the hard work." Padre Consag wrote that these adventurers from the mainland "steal their children and go to their rancherías to abuse their women, which makes the Indians most exasperated."

In 1698, Padre Salvatierra mentioned the first epidemic in Loreto. He wrote in a letter that "a certain Indian was infected in September of that year with a pest from which many died."

In 1709 and 1710 a violent epidemic of smallpox killed many adults and almost all the children. In Loreto some five hundred children died. Six or seven children were buried each day. Between one and two thousand died in all the peninsular missions.

From 1720 to 1723 about thirteen hundred Indians died of an undefined epidemic.

In 1729 smallpox rampaged again.

From 1742 through 1748 there were a series of epidemics, beginning with typhoid and malaria in 1742 and measles in 1748. At least four thousand died.

In 1762 typhus, malaria, smallpox, and measles continued.

It was reported that in 1769 the population declined by two thousand.

In addition to the epidemics, syphilis caused a reduced birth rate. A particularly virulent strain from the Philippines was introduced, probably by way of sailors from a Spanish galleon. California Indian families were always small; they rarely had more than five children. This disease brought their reproduction to a halt. A Jesuit missionary wrote:

> That which has most destroyed the mission Indians has been syphilis, which was introduced with such violence that after having annihilated all the people of the south, spread to the north, and in the most prosperous missions in which the Indians were counted by the thousands, they soon amounted to hundreds.

In 1768 Joaquín Velázquez de León visited the peninsula and wrote: "In Todos Santos there are scarcely one hundred individuals of all sexes and ages, most of them infected with syphilis, many entirely castrated and all contagious, since the children are born infected."

The Spanish Governor Pedro Fages wrote in 1786: "The missions of San José, Santiago, Todos Santos, San Javier, Loreto, Comondú, Codegones, Guadalupe, and Mulegé are making rapid strides toward complete extinction. The reason is so clear that it cannot be doubted. The disease ravages both sexes and to such an extent that the mothers no longer conceive, and if they do, the young are born with little hope of surviving."

By the end of the 19th century there were only mestizo descendents of the last Guaycura in Loreto and some Cochimís near parallel 28 to the north. At the end of the 20th century, the Guaycura and Pericú are extinct. There are less than a thousand descendants of the Cochimí, who mixed with the Kumiai, Cucapá, Paipai, and Kiliwa near the United States border.

Chapter Two

THE JESUITS IN LORETO
(1697 - 1768)

Imagine that you are the son of a prominent and wealthy European family. Raised in luxury and with years of the finest education available at that time in the world, you give up the promise of a prestigious career and a comfortable life in familiar surroundings to evangelize primitive people in a desert wilderness.

Most of the Jesuit priests who were the first successful settlers in California came from that kind of European background. But these men had no doubt at all that the heathen savages of this wild land were waiting to be saved and that it was their mission to bring the Christian religion to them. The religious discipline of the Jesuit order gave California a different history from the rest of Mexico and determined the course of its future.

The Society of Jesus was founded by Saint Ignatius Loyola in 1540. Loyola was a Spanish nobleman who had served as a military officer. His Jesuit organization had an efficient chain of command. It stressed discipline and fortitude in the military tradition. It welcomed young men of all nationalities and was particularly attractive to young intellectuals because it offered an excellent higher education and an opportunity for adventure and service.

In the seventeenth and eighteenth centuries, New Spain encompassed all of present-day Mexico as well as what is now the southwestern United States. Spain had explored and claimed the present Alta California, Nevada, Utah, Arizona, part of Colorado and Wyoming and Kansas, all of Texas and Florida. By the end of the 17th century, Spain had been weak-

North American territory claimed by Spain at the time of the missionary period in California.

ened by a long war for the succession to the Spanish throne and was practically bankrupt. However, it had three urgent reasons for exploring and conquering Baja California: the peninsula was thought at that time to be an island, possibly with a passage to the Pacific at its northern end which would provide a shorter route to the Far East; Spain needed a port of call for the Manila galleons, the trading ships that sailed from Acapulco to the Philippines every year; and Spain wanted a buffer state against the encroaching Russians from the north and the English from the sea.

Since the two unsuccessful attempts by Cortés to establish a colony in La Paz in the 16th century, the Gulf of California had been explored by a few navigators, but potential settlers on the peninsula had all been quickly driven out by lack of food and water and hostile natives.

Padre Kino's Settlement at San Bruno 1684

The first attempt to establish a European settlement in the Loreto area was made by the Jesuit Padre Eusebio Kino in 1684 at San Bruno, 12 miles north of Loreto. Kino was the religious leader of an expedition under the military command of

48

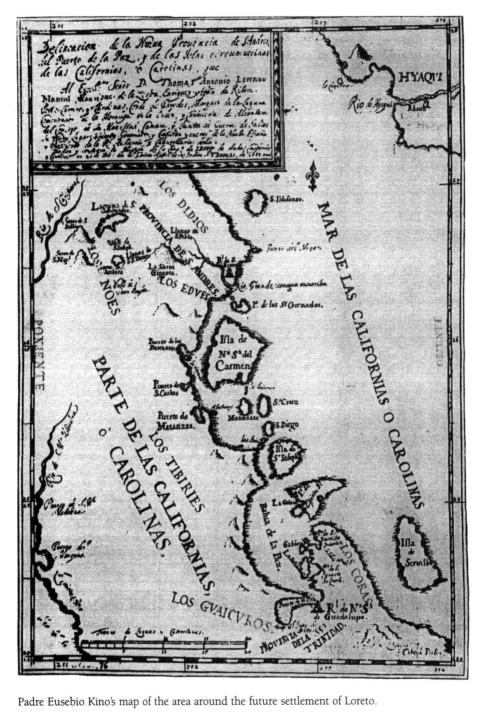

Padre Eusebio Kino's map of the area around the future settlement of Loreto.

49

Admiral Almirante Atondo y Antillón. The two leaders were accompanied by Padre Matías Goñi, fifteen soldiers, and thirty-eight civilian recruits, including peons, cooks, servant boys, female slaves, and a band of Mayo Indian laborers.

They had chosen the site at San Bruno because the explorer Captain Blas de Guzmán had described a *río grande* there the previous year. Unfortunately, Kino's group discovered that the "big river" was an arroyo that only had water in it during infrequent heavy rains. During their stay of over a year there, good relations were established with the Guaycura band called the Dedué of San Bruno, who roamed what is now Ranchos San Bruno and San Juan, as well as with the Monquís of the Loreto area. Padre Kino learned the dialect of the Monquí and Padre Goñi the dialect of the Dedué. Padre Juan Bautista Copart followed them on a later ship and wrote a grammar of the native language that was useful to the missionaries who followed. A small mission building was constructed, and Kino and Atondo led the first expedition across the mountains to the Pacific, which Kino mapped.

Only a few Indians were baptized, because Kino was unsure of the future of the settlement. He was right. The water supply was inadequate, they were unsuccessful in growing crops, and many of the soldiers died of scurvy. The remaining soldiers begged to be returned to the mainland, and so, once again, an attempt to colonize Baja California failed.

However, the area had been explored, maps made, Christianity introduced, and the way prepared for another attempt to bring Spanish rule and European civilization and religion to this wilderness.

Padre Kino was determined to try again, and he fired the imagination of his friend and fellow priest, Juan María Salvatierra. These two men, both from Italy, had met while working with the Tarahumara Indians in northwestern New Spain and together had explored the northwest coast looking for a land link to California. As a result of this friendship, Salvatierra became passionately determined to found a mission dedicated to Our Lady of Loreto in the California wilderness. Both Salvatierra and Kino had chosen the Virgin of Loreto as

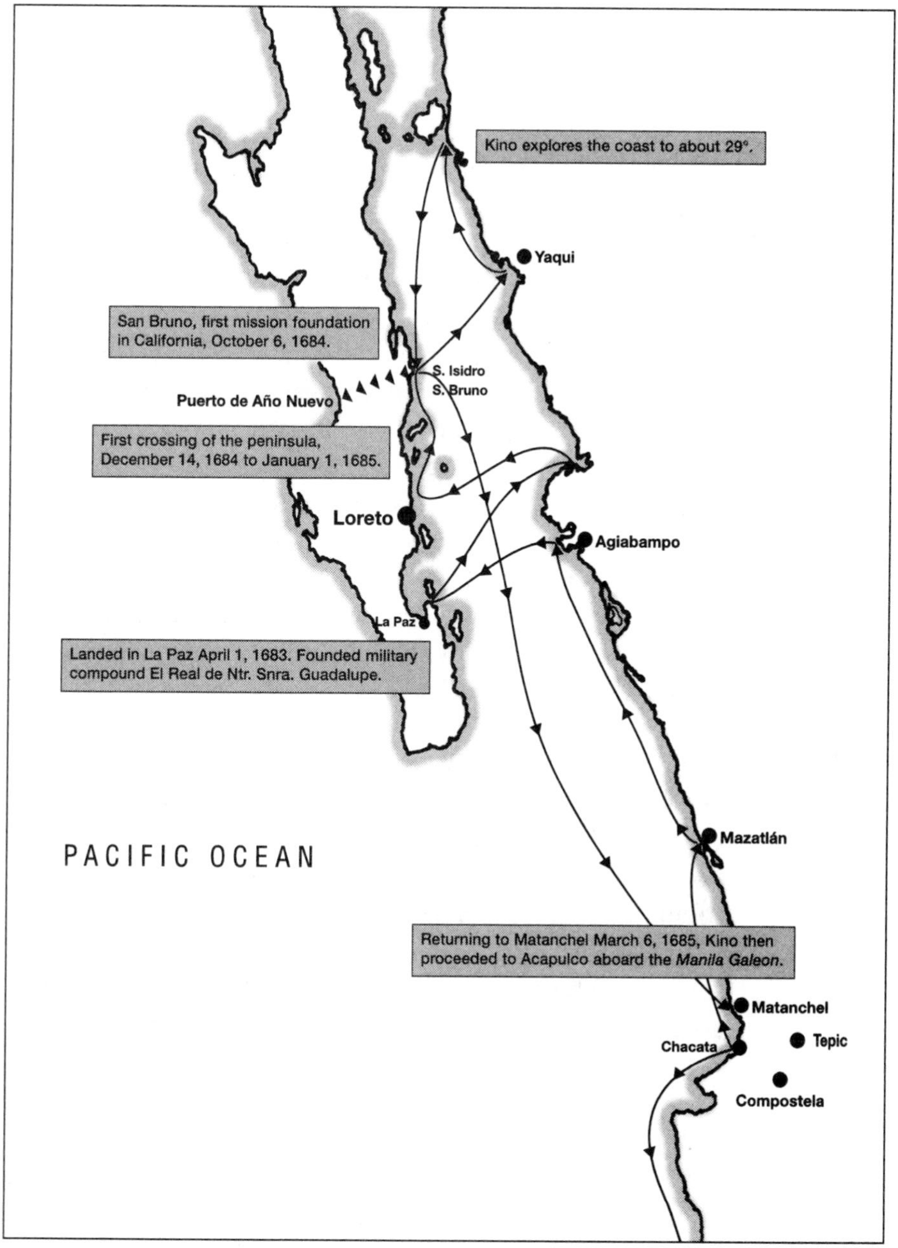
Kino explores the coast to about 29°.
Yaqui
San Bruno, first mission foundation in California, October 6, 1684.
S. Isidro
S. Bruno
Puerto de Año Nuevo
First crossing of the peninsula, December 14, 1684 to January 1, 1685.
Loreto
Agiabampo
La Paz
Landed in La Paz April 1, 1683. Founded military compound El Real de Ntr. Snra. Guadalupe.
PACIFIC OCEAN
Mazatlán
Returning to Matanchel March 6, 1685, Kino then proceeded to Acapulco aboard the Manila Galeon.
Matanchel
Chacata
Tepic
Compostela

The expeditions of Padre Eusebio Kino and Admiral Atondo from 1683 to 1685, including the settlement of San Bruno.

their patroness. Both had been inspired to become missionaries while praying in the same small church outside of Genoa in Italy which was dedicated to Our Lady of Loreto.

Worship of Our Lady of Loreto was based on the belief that angels had flown the house of the Virgin Mary from Nazareth to the little town of Loreto, Italy, in 1291. A cathedral was built around the house, and over the centuries people have made pilgrimages to the church and attested to miracles performed there.

While carrying out their missionary duties on the mainland of New Spain, Kino and Salvatierra planned and worked for thirteen years to return to San Bruno. They concluded that previous attempts to settle in California had failed because the expeditions were under the control of government and military rather than religious leaders.

The Pious Fund   In order to remain free of royal financial assistance and control, Kino and Salvatierra, assisted by Padre Juan Ugarte, professor of philosophy in the Jesuit Colegio Máximo in Mexico City, devised a plan. They approached wealthy patrons to tell them their dream of bringing Christianity to California, and asked for help. They promised their deeply religious benefactors the blessings of heaven if they contributed to the evangelization of these pagan people, and it gradually became a popular and prestigious cause among the elite of both New Spain and Spain. The money they received went into what was known as the Pious Fund. This fund grew over the years as Salvatierra, Kino, Ugarte and other Jesuits succeeded in persuading more and more benefactors to participate in their dream. They were so persuasive that their patrons donated money and ships and ranches on the mainland which would help to supply the new missions.

Salvatierra persistently requested authorization from the viceroy of New Spain for entrance into Baja California to establish missions there. Viceroy Conde de Moctezuma hesitated, because a royal decree of 1696 forbade any payments from the royal treasury without the specific approval of the king of Spain, Charles II. Salvatierra reminded the viceroy that they weren't asking for money, only authorization.

Finally, on February 5, 1697, the authorization arrived and with it a letter from the Jesuit *Padre General* approving the evangelization of the natives of California by Kino and Salvatierra. The viceroy's authorization indicated that the enterprise was to be undertaken solely with voluntary offerings and that nothing whatever was to be expected from the royal treasury. He authorized the Jesuit missionaries to take soldiers and sailors with them, as long as they were able to pay them. The officers were to be chosen by the Jesuits and could be dismissed by them if they did not perform satisfactorily. The missionaries could also name all civil authorities. The soldiers would have the same duties, powers, and privileges as those of the royal army in other presidios of New Spain, but they were to take orders only from the Jesuit missionaries. The land was to be claimed as a Spanish colony and the people were to become subjects of the king of Spain. This was a unique arrangement in the Spanish colonization of the American continent.

Just as Padre Kino was preparing to join Salvatierra for the expedition to California, a revolt broke out among the Tarahumara Indians with whom he had been working for many years in the present mainland Mexican state of Chihuahua. Padre Kino was ordered by his superiors to stay and control the situation there. To his sorrow, Kino never was able to return to his beloved California.

In order to understand why a wealthy educated man like Salvatierra wanted so desperately to go to the California wilderness, you have to know something about the times in which he lived.

Even the most educated and sophisticated men and women of the 16th and 17th centuries in Europe believed absolutely that the souls of innocent children and adults who had been baptized in the Catholic Church went to an eternal heaven. They believed that people in other parts of the world were waiting in a pagan darkness to be rescued by missionaries so their souls could ascend to the Christian heaven. Young men were taught that if they dedicated their lives to bringing the Catholic religion to these pagans, their martyrdom would absolutely guarantee them a place in heaven. All of the hardships of missionary work were seen as holy endeavors. Many of the religious men and women of that time literally had "the faith that could move mountains" and were able to overcome seemingly impossible odds to carry out what they believed to be God's work.

Padre
Juan María
de Salvatierra
(1648-1717)

Giovanni Salvatierra was born in Milan, Italy on November 15, 1648, the youngest son of Giovanni Salvatierra, who was descended from a prominent Spanish family. His father had named both his oldest and youngest boys "Giovanni" to ensure the continuation of his name, but both sons became Jesuit priests. His mother was the daughter of a powerful Lombard family, the Viscontis, which had ruled over Milan and its surrounding territory. The family spoke Italian and Spanish at home, and in school he added French, Latin, and Greek. At the age of twenty, Giovanni, who now called himself Juan and added the second name María, joined the Society of Jesus, and, after completing the rigorous education and training of that Catholic order, he was ordained a priest and sent to New Spain as a missionary. He continued his studies in Mexico City, where he also learned to speak *Nahuatl,* the Indian language of Central Mexico, which he spoke fluently all his life. From there, he was sent to work in the Tarahumara missions where he met and explored with Padre Eusebio Kino and learned still more Indian languages. He was next appointed as rector of the College of Guadalajara and then at Tepotzoltlán, but he continued to seek permission to go to California to save the souls of the people there.

The
Landing in
San Bruno

After months of preparation and after discovering at the last minute that Kino could not join him, Salvatierra sailed from a small port at the mouth of the River Yaquí on the *Santa Elvira* on October 11, 1697, accompanied by a launch, *El Rosario,* carrying supplies. The voyage started badly when the ship went aground on a sandbar at the mouth of the river. After strenuous efforts, it was freed, but they soon ran into strong winds, and the *Santa Elvira* was separated from the *El Rosario*, and both ships were blown off course. Salvatierra's ship put into Bahía Concepción for shelter, and it was here that he first set foot on California soil. When the wind calmed, they sailed

90 miles south to the site of Kino's settlement, San Bruno. Here, they found welcoming natives, but the water was scarce and brackish, and Kino's former mission site was a difficult journey from the beach. The captain of the *Santa Elvira*, Juan Antonio Romero, had sailed the area several years before and suggested they go a few miles south to a bay he remembered as having good water.

On October 18, 1697, Padre Juan María Salvatierra landed in Loreto, which the Monquí called Conchó, thirteen years after Padre Kino had arrived at San Bruno. In a letter to Padre Juan Ugarte, who was administering the Pious Fund in Mexico City, written a month later from Loreto, Salvatierra described their arrival and subsequent adventures:

The First Days in Loreto (1697)

> Captain Juan Antonio Romero insisted that in another bay very close by he had taken on water two years ago, and had found the water excellent and salt-free. The name of the bay was San Dionisio. As far as he could remember, the area was verdant and closer to the sea.

> It would be difficult to abandon San Bruno and continue to the bay of San Dionisio. Inasmuch as we were beset with difficulties on every side, we chose the Madonna as our patroness. In order to secure her assistance, we decided to cast lots in her name. The slip of paper drawn out bore the name of San Dionisio. Frankly, it was a severe blow to me for San Dionisio to be chosen. I preferred San Bruno since it would spare us having to travel farther.

> As soon as fortune favored San Dionisio, we weighed anchor at 3 p.m. on October 17 and sailed out of San Bruno Bay. We slept while resting at anchor close to the Islet of Coronados.

> The next day, early on the morning of Friday, October 18, we reached the bay shaped like a half-moon. As we viewed the area from the ship, it all appeared green. The bay must be about four or five miles across. I went ashore with the captain at the spot where the sailors thought that they had taken on water two years ago.

> Quite a few Indians with their wives and little children came to receive us. They knelt down to kiss the Crucifix and the Virgin. Their settlement was situated about half an harquebus shot* from the sea. We went with the natives to see the water

* A *harquebus shot* is about 50 yards.

Padre Juan María Salvatierra, Father of the California Missions

holes. We discovered them in a small valley flanked on the south side by a mesa, all flat and more than a pica** a high plateau on the west extends for the distance of an harquebus shot to the sea.

The site seemed ideal to me since we could easily entrench ourselves. The north side is protected by a high hill. The lowland of the valley where we were forms a small lake of somewhat brackish water but suitable for animals. Beyond the valley, on the other side, it spreads out into an extensive area covered by reeds, from which arrows shot at us would lose their force before reaching us, whereas our fire arms are effective at that distance. We can also graze our herds within sight.

At the time of our coming, the entire mesa was densely covered with mesquites furnishing us with good shade. While resting under their shade at siesta time, Captain Romero, Ensign Tortolero, and I measured the trunk of one and found

* A *pica* is slightly less than 13 feet.

that it was more than three varas* across. This amazed the captain, inasmuch as he had made a certified statement in Acapulco informing the Treasurer Don Pedro Gil de la Sierpe that he had seen no wood in California, and now he beheld these mesquites extending for miles!

Since it was already late and time to eat and to take possession of the land, I returned to the ship, most satisfied with what I had seen. But the Blessed Virgin wanted these solemnities to take place on Saturday; and, hence, when I got on board, the sailors began to express doubts that the harbor where we landed was the one where they had taken on water some years earlier. This latter place, they insisted, was better than the one just seen and was situated at the other end of the half-moon bay.

The party sailed south a few miles and went ashore but found that the water there was not as good, so on Saturday, October 19, they returned to their original landing place.

I went ashore with Captain Juan Antonio Romero, who took official possession of the land.

We worked until we had cleared the part of the mesa where the first settlement was to be established. All the animals were unloaded. Since it was all so new to the Indians, many of them gathered at the beach.

The next four days were spent unloading the ship with the help of the natives and constructing a fortification of thorny mesquite branches. Fearing an attack from natives, who were hungry for the food they had seen, they brought ashore and mounted a small muzzle-loading cannon, called a mortar.

The enemy did not immediately carry out the initial threat. That night, October 23, a downpour drenched us who were so sure that it never rains in California. The next day, we brought ashore the Holy Madonna, who found the ground all drenched. We recited with the Indians the Ave María in their language and sang the litany of Loreto. The Virgin was carried in procession to the *Real*,** Captain Juan Antonio Romero and others taking turns. She was received at the *Real* with more salvos. The tent of Don Domingo de la Canal was decorated as

* A *vara* is about 2.75 feet.
** A *Real* is a fortification.

57

a church. This tent and those of Don Martín de Zabalza and others take up the center of the compound.

The Indian men and women gave expression to their intense joy at the arrival of the sacred image which reached here Friday evening; and on Saturday, October 26, Mass was celebrated. Two days previously we had set up the Holy Cross surrounding it with many flowers; first, all the Spaniards and then many of the Indians insisted with me that they be permitted to kiss it.

Soon after the small group of Europeans arrived in Loreto, it became evident that the natives wanted all the food they saw in the mission settlement, and they wanted it immediately. Every day their actions grew more threatening. They stole cattle and food. The little missionary band was required to maintain constant vigilance. To demonstrate the effectiveness of their guns, called *harquebuses,* the men shot ducks and other animals and took turns shooting at a target to demonstrate that everyone in their little party could use these weapons. Salvatierra boasted that he also shot at the target and was one of the best of them all.

During this tense period, there was one hopeful occurrence. On October 29, 1697, an elderly native arrived who was obviously an important man. He asked about Padre Kino, Padre Goñi, Padre Copart, and other members of the earlier expedition to San Bruno. He turned out to be Ibo, whom the earlier padres had named Leopoldo. He was the leader of the religious ceremonies witnessed by Kino's soldiers at San Bruno. He had come to be baptized. He was very ill with a cancer that was described as "eating up his body." Salvatierra permitted him to stay in the compound with a few of his men, and Leopoldo attended catechism classes with, as the padre said, "evident signs of predestination." Salvatierra wrote that Leopoldo was the only native he had really been able to instruct or who understood the love and knowledge of God. Leopoldo's only drawback was that because he was such a big man, he had a huge appetite, and food was scarce.

The day after he arrived, Leopoldo told Salvatierra that the Monquís intended to kill the Europeans and take their food. The tension mounted daily. The natives began to throw rocks, and several struck the padre in the head. The soldiers threatened the natives with their guns but did not shoot. The besieged party got little sleep; they were surrounded night and day and had to mount a constant watch.

In the meantime, Leopoldo had grown steadily worse. The cancer had eaten through his whole body. On November 11, he was christened Manuel Bernardo. The next day, the newly christened Manuel Bernardo warned Salvatierra that hostile natives intended to carry off the supply of corn. The soldiers kept watch through the night and reinforced the weaker spots along the encircling trench.

Padre Salvatierra describes the dreaded confrontation, which occurred on November 13:

> While the soldiers were dining about four paces from the door with one of the lads acting as sentinel, armed with a sort of scimitar, a weapon we used as a halberd, many of the natives stood close to the door. When the guard tried politely to get them to move on, they refused to obey. One of the mischievous natives, a fellow of somewhat Spanish features from San Bruno, tried to wrench the scimitar from the guard. Ensign Luis, perceiving the insolence and peril, snatched the scimitar from the guard, blocked the door, and threatened to use the weapon on any who resisted, especially on the most rebellious among them.

> At other times such a show of force would have sufficed to get them to leave, but on this occasion they withdrew to re-form ranks. The natives gave orders for all of their own to leave, even those who were helping us – three lads of excellent character. One of them refused to obey and accordingly stayed alone with us.

> We then heard some shouting in the area of the reeds; the Christian Indian from Tepahui bravely drove the few escaped sheep and goats to the little corral within the compound. Inasmuch as the pigs were not far away, the ensign, another soldier, and a Sonoran Indian went out to bring them in. The men were so successful in their efforts that the animals – despite the arrows shot into them – came into the *Real* at our calling them.

> Arrows began striking our compound from every direction.

We were under attack from all four sides. Through the opening made by the valley below, one of the groups charged, protected from the rear by another contingent in case we should sally forth. The second group came out of the valley above us at the point where their settlement is situated; they also had another contingent to protect them from the rear. From the mesa heights they also had us encircled, on one side by the plateau that faces the sea and on the other by the river.

Our little group also took up its position. The ensign, or captain, Don Luis (Tortolero y Torres) and Bartolomé de Figueroa defended the most dangerous spot – at the juncture of the valley below and the mesa closest to the sea. At the center of the beach side, Marcos, a very courageous Sonoran Indian, took up his position and proved a most effective defender in battle. To the rear of Captain Luis stood Alonso, another Indian from Tapahui, and in the center below him, Andrés, a young mulatto from Peru. Along the strongest trench, at the least dangerous spot, on the last side of the mesa, the Portuguese Esteban Rodríguez took his place. Stationed near the gate, at the corner of the compound was the Maltese bombardier, Juan Caravana, who had served on the Manila Galleon. He was in charge of the mortar defending the entrance. On the other side, facing the beach, was the Sicilian Nicolás Márques, who had served our king for many years as bombardier.

I was also along the trench and tried to go from one place to another wherever the danger seemed greatest. My helper was an Indian lad from Ventitlán near Guadalajara.

The four groups of hostile Indians were from as many different tribes in the vicinity. On the two sides above us were the Laymonés from beyond the Giganta. The Monquís occupied the southern side. The Didiús and the Edúes held the heights and low areas toward the beach. All four groups made a concerted assault on our position. Besides shooting arrows at us, they began hurling into the trench rocks and sod from the heights on two sides. They kept up this barrage for some two hours.

Out of sheer exhaustion they finally stopped fighting for about half an hour, although even in this interval they kept shooting arrows at us from within the recesses of the mountain. When they thought that we had finally regretted our resistance, suddenly the groups, reinforced with more natives, made a second and more violent charge than the first.

No use had yet been made of the mortar, reserved for the final and desperate stand, many of the men having the greatest confidence in it. From time to time they would pretend to be on the point of firing it; each time the groups of natives would withdraw in fright from the junction or valley above.

Finally, the captain, compelled by this second charge, resolved that the Maltese bombardier should fire off the mortar. The most holy Madonna worked a veritable miracle in preserving from death me, the bombardier, and the two soldiers standing nearby, because the mortar burst with such violence that the surrounding wall was smashed to pieces, hurling part of it some six paces away; even the iron wedge was split into three pieces, each one flying off into a different direction. The mortar's magazine was hurled some nine paces with such force that it sailed almost directly above me. I did not notice it until I saw it lying several yards beyond me. The bombardier was knocked over by the mighty rush of air when the mortar exploded. He fell from his position to the ground below with such violence that he remained unconscious for a short while. Two blows brought him back to his senses, and we realized that he was not seriously injured. He snatched up his weapons and again took part in the battle.

We all regained courage to fight until death. The enemy also grew more insolent. Word was quickly passed to all the groups that, since the mortar caused no casualties, much less would the two little harquebuses. In virtue of this conviction, they closed ranks, coming from every direction, for the final assault, certain now of finishing us off and seizing the booty. They now approached with such insolence that I felt obliged to accost them on the side where the mortar was; and, standing before them, I warned that, unless they withdrew, they might be slain. Their reply was to shoot simultaneously three arrows at me.

In this desperate strait, God inspired me with conviction that it would be wiser to lend the men a hand. From the moment when the natives no longer obeyed the voice of their Padre, they were struck down from every side – some where injured and others were killed outright. Disheartened and terrified at our valor, they all withdrew simultaneously at about sunset.

The most absolute silence ensued.

About fifteen minutes later, Ibo/Leopoldo/Manuel Bernardo walked slowly into the compound. He was weeping and told them that three of the attackers had died. He was amazed to find the tiny contingent cheerful and apparently unhurt, although several of them had received minor injuries from arrows.

Not long after his arrival, a group of native women and their children came and sat down at the gate and pleaded for pardon. To prove their submission, they insisted on leaving their children with the Spaniards for the night. Salvatierra allowed only one of the children to remain and assured the women that the Spaniards were good and would not kill anyone except those "who tried to slay us and plunder our supplies."

As night approached, Salvatierra sent the women home. He noted that although many arrows had fallen at the foot of the Holy Cross that was set up at the entrance of the tent housing the statue of Mary, none had struck the cross itself. On the day after, many natives who had not taken part in the battle returned, one of them bringing a yucca root which the company welcomed as an addition to their diet, and the newly friendly natives told them deer and mountain sheep were to be had in the vicinity.

On November 21, the natives warned that another wounded Monquí had died and that his family intended to attack and were urging others to join them. This threatened attack did not occur because the Monquís received no support from the other bands and they were afraid of the harquebuses.

Two days after the battle, the El Rosario, which had left the mainland at the same time as Salvatierra's ship and which they had feared was lost, finally arrived with more men and supplies.

Calm returned, and many natives asked for baptism, inspired by the example of Ibo/Leopoldo/Manuel Bernardo. They were told that as soon as they learned the tenets of the faith they would be baptized. Only the two small sons of the old chief and two other children were baptized. They were given the names of benefactors to the Pious Fund.

On November 23, the *Santa Elvira* was sighted in the channel between the point of the bay and Coronados Island. A favorable wind brought the ship into the harbor in two days. Salvatierra was even happier when he found that the ship carried Padre Francisco María Piccolo.

Francisco María Piccolo was born in 1654 in Palermo, Sicily of a distinguished family. Piccolo was described as blond, blue-eyed, tall, and having a fair complexion. After receiving a good education, he decided to join the Jesuit order. He wanted to be a missionary and was sent to New Spain in 1684, and spent the next years among the Tarahumara in what is now the state of Chihuahua until he joined Salvatierra in Loreto. He came to California in place of Padre Kino.

Padre Francisco María Piccolo (1654-1729)

The Sicilian Jesuit was a welcome addition to the California missionary effort. Salvatierra wrote that Piccolo was "a veteran missionary who, after being visitor, and builder of mission churches among Tarahumarans for all his Indians, left his own flock out of obedience to God and king. Piccolo's mission was one of the best organized of that province of loyal Tarahumarans; yet he spontaneously abandoned all in order to start anew and accomplish as much among these poor California savages." He felt that Piccolo would assure the advancement of the California enterprise and that his arrival meant that "this time the standard of Christ will not be uprooted from a kingdom so vast that its full extent is still unknown."

The two Jesuits set themselves the task of learning the native languages. Salvatierra studied the Guaycura language of the Monquí, and Piccolo devoted himself to learning Cochimí. Workers quickly built a rock and adobe chapel with a thatched roof to house the altar and their few religious articles. Three rooms were attached: one would serve as the padres' quarters, another as a mess hall and captain's quarters, and a third as a small warehouse. Houses, made of branches daubed with adobe and thatched with reeds, were built for the soldiers. Some of the large mesquite trees that covered the mesa were used to support a stockade and to shade and hold sacks of food. Others were cut for logs for a palisade and their thorny branches used to discourage intruders into the corral that enclosed the newcomers and their possessions.

The Monquí, the Guaycura band which occupied the coastal area from about 10 miles north of Loreto to an area the natives called Ligüí, about 20 miles to the south, were drawn to the mission by the promise of food and protection from their enemies. One year after the Jesuits arrived, the total native population in Loreto was around four hundred, the highest it would ever be. The Monquí population of Loreto included hunter-gatherers who roamed the areas of Tuidú, Yeltí, Niodí, Bonú, Notrí, Chuenquí, Nopoló, Tripué, and Ligüí. Their manpower was needed to build and maintain the small settlement.

Life in Loreto continued peacefully for the next year in spite of the constant problem of getting enough supplies from the mainland. Work continued on the church, more children were baptized, and more adults were studying the catechism. Palm thatched structures were put up to provide shade for craftsmen working at necessary repairs and on the construction of housing and the church.

With the coming of Piccolo, the additional men in the garrison, and the establishment of peaceful relations with the natives, Salvatierra determined the time had come to establish more mission centers.

Some Monquí from Loreto and Cochimí from the mountains had been sent to the mainland to visit and see for themselves how the Jesuits provided for the converts there. They saw them being treated well and fed well, but they also saw them being punished with flogging for stealing cattle and other crimes. When they returned, they described all they had seen to their groups. Several men from the mountains told the priests that there were fertile lands up there where they could grow the maize they had seen the priests growing on the mainland. Many people of the Viggé, which meant "land high above the valleys," insistently invited the fathers to visit the area and see for themselves.

In February of 1698, six more soldiers arrived from the

mainland. Three were Spaniards, a Yaqui Indian, a mestizo, and Juan de Arce, whom Salvatierra described as "an Englishman brought up in New Spain who has served in the presidios of Sinaloa."

In May of 1699, it was decided that Padre Piccolo should lead the expedition into the mountains. The party of nine soldiers, the captain, and the priest set off on horseback, accompanied by natives on foot. The two missionaries had agreed ahead of time that if it became impossible for the horses to climb the rugged terrain, Piccolo would accompany his native guides on foot.

To their surprise, after they had gone about 9 miles, they came to an arroyo full of rushing water, which the horses crossed with some difficulty. Then they reached a hill so rugged and steep that it was impossible for the horses to proceed further. Captain Antonio García Mendoza, who had replaced the pioneer captain, Luis Tortolero, along with one or two of the soldiers wanted to turn back. Piccolo told them they were free to do so but that he intended to continue on foot. Inspired by his example, the soldiers agreed not to let the padre go alone and left the horses with Indian guards.

When evening came, the party stopped for the night near some gushing springs. Knowing that more hard traveling lay ahead, Piccolo talked to the soldiers, explaining the rewards awaiting them from God as they continued under the protection of the Blessed Virgin. The soldiers were so moved by his words that they resolved to continue until they reached the mountain heights.

The next day, after hearing Mass, they continued over terrifying cliffs and along the arroyo until they came to a patch of wild grapes that went on for a full league. This was the present Rancho Las Parras.

The climb up the mountain was exhausting and they were about to give up, when they discovered that the natives had thought they wanted only to climb the mountain rather than visit the fertile lands. They changed direction and at about four o'clock in the afternoon the vanguard shouted "Meadows! Meadows!" as a wide valley with groves and streams came into view.

Soon some natives came to welcome the missionary, and among them were several Christian children who had been baptized in Loreto and a young man who had been baptized and named Francisco Javier. This young man had been chosen to be baptized as an adult because of his unusually fine qualities. Now, seeing the deference paid to him by the natives, Piccolo assumed that his father was a leader and that the boy was destined to be a leader, too.

The padre gathered the natives together and explained the reasons for visiting their land. When he began to instruct them in the doctrines of the faith, he discovered they found his questions easy to answer. He saw that many of them already knew how to make the sign of the cross. Since most of them had never been to Loreto, he was surprised. When he asked, he was told that Francisco Javier had been instructing them in the tenets of the faith.

The party stayed in the valley, which was called Biaundó, four days. They explored the area and found fertile lands and learned that it rained there more often than it did in Loreto. Thirty small children were christened.

Many natives from other rancherías in the mountains came to visit as well as people from the west who were able to give the missionary information about the Pacific Coast.

After naming the place San Francisco Javier de Viggé Biaundó and setting up a cross and a simple shelter, the party returned along a shorter route and found the horses where they had left them. The return trip to Loreto took them only one day.

The success of the expedition to San Javier encouraged Salvatierra to head north to the area called Londó, which the party of Padre Kino had called Estancia de Don Isidro. Word was sent to the natives of the area that he was coming, and the message came back that many people planned to gather to hear him speak.

So, in that same month, Salvatierra set out accompanied by Captain Antonio García de Mendoza and nine horsemen. They needed many Loreto Monquís to carry the supplies of maize and other gifts, since they traveled without pack animals. To their surprise, they had many volunteers, because it was close to the season of the pitaya harvest, and the men wanted to harvest the fruit there and to attend the dances.

When they arrived, they found many children waiting to be baptized. They traveled around the area, inviting other rancherías to gather in Londó to attend religious instruction. Salvatierra sensed that the atmosphere in the area was not entirely friendly, but he returned to Londó and preached a sermon against worshipping the moon.

In the evening he baptized a dozen children. He was particularly pleased because one four-year-old girl, the daughter of a chief, behaved very badly before the ceremony and tried to run away. Her father held her firmly, however, and as soon as the sign of the cross was made on her forehead, she quieted down and behaved so well that even the natives were amazed.

While this was going on, some of the Monquís who had accompanied the expedition stole and butchered one of the expedition's two sheep in order to give it to Cochimí women they had been dancing with the night before. A sermon was subsequently preached against thieves and murderers, and the guilty Monquís ran away back to Loreto.

The Spaniards were still somewhat apprehensive about the intentions of the natives, and the soldiers were on alert for an attack. They heard an old woman shouting to summon all the natives for a meeting, and the soldiers took up positions and saddled their horses. For half an hour they waited in suspense and silence. Finally, eight young women came and sat down near them, which was their way of showing submission and pleading for peace. There was no further disturbance.

Once things had calmed down, it was time to return to Loreto to see that all was well there. Before leaving, it was decided that the mission formed from the settlements of San Bruno, San Juan, and the area at the foot of the mountain would be called San Juan de Londó to honor their great benefactor, Don Juan Caballero.

On the way back to Loreto, they stopped for the night some 15 miles south at a good water hole called Uhuahú. Captain Mendoza and his soldiers spent a couple of hours building a road over the only cliff difficult to cross, making it possible to travel the entire road at night on horseback between Loreto and San Juan de Londó.

The padres were anxious to build a road to San Javier, too, so they could travel by horseback to the rich lands Padre Piccolo had discovered and beyond to the Pacific Coast. It seemed an impossible task, but Captain García Mendoza owned and had opened a mine in the Sierra Madres and thought that the terrain to San Javier could not be much more difficult.

On June 1, 1699, Padre Piccolo, Captain Mendoza, and nine soldiers set out and, before noon, reached the place 10 miles from Loreto where the road became impassable by horseback. The captain and two soldiers went ahead on foot to survey the 5 miles of rugged cliffs and boulders. After inspecting the rocky areas along the arroyo and hills, they returned to the waiting men as evening approached.

Finding the soldiers reluctant to attempt to chisel a road out of this terrain, Captain García Mendoza rallied the soldiers to the cause with an impassioned speech, reminding them that their vows of service to God and the king and their personal honor made it imperative that they accomplish this difficult task. He promised they would receive the help of the Madonna of Loreto and her angels. He vowed that he would not turn back, and the soldiers all made the same vow.

Returning to Loreto, they informed Padre Piccolo of their solemn promise to work until it was possible to ride into San Javier de Viggé Biaundó. Piccolo was pessimistic about the chances of overcoming the difficulties of such a task and would not let them make such a commitment.

However, the next morning the enthusiastic group of soldiers set out with picks, axes, and hoes. The trail would have to serve for men, horses, and flocks, and the steep rocky sides of the mountain presented a challenge. Stakes were firmly planted to form a support for tree trunks and branches, and then the steep slope was filled in with rubble. On more level areas, the brush had to be cut and a trail made through loose and rocky spots, which sometimes meant digging down several feet to solid ground. Salvatierra reported that "so hard did they work that each ate the share of two men and all had soon worn out their shoes, with the result that it was necessary to send them pieces of leather to fashion sandals." Fortunately, even though it was June, the weather was cool, and all the men were in good health. Natives from Viggé came to help. Children came, too, to receive instruction from Padre Piccolo.

When they reached the part of the arroyo where they thought they would have to build a rock bridge across the stream, probably requiring more than a month of hard work, a Viggé native offered to show them an easier way along a narrow path over the hill. They were delighted with the discovery, since it would take them only three days to prepare a road along that route. They attributed this event to the intervention of Our Lady of Loreto and her angels and decided to name the native who had led them "Angel" when he was christened. .

On June 12 all the men mounted and rode through to the beautiful plains of San Francisco Javier Biaundó de Viggé. Captain García saw a very high hill nearby (what is now called El Pilón de las Parras or Loreto Peak) and promised the Virgin that he would climb it the next day to see what could be seen from it. The next morning the captain, accompanied by Esteban Rodríguez and another soldier, José Machuca, set out on foot to climb the mountain. Rodríguez was the first to reach the top. From the peak the three soldiers could see the two seas and all the land extending to the Pacific and thought they could also see Magdalena Bay, which Kino had mapped. They were so excited that they fired a salvo. The men below thought the shots meant that the explorers had been attacked by hostile natives, and they set out to rescue them. Everyone was relieved and happy that all the shooting was just to celebrate the discovery. They named the peak Cerro de Caballero in honor of their great benefactor.

After Piccolo visited some mountain families, said Mass and baptized several infants, the party returned to Loreto on Sunday, June 14. The men were all in rags and barefoot after two weeks of back-breaking work building the trail.

After a week of rest, these same soldiers, inspired by their accomplishment and by the enthusiasm of Padre Piccolo, began to clear the land where the church and house of the missionaries were to be built, replacing the improvised chapel. Padre Piccolo and Captain Mendoza marked off the area for the

Starting to Build the Loreto Mission

buildings, and the foundation of the mission church was begun in July.

Since materials and manpower were in short supply, adobe bricks were used on the stone foundation. Salvatierra realized that even this would take too long to build, so he commissioned a smaller chapel on the west side of the larger construction. This chapel was finished in 1700, and Salvatierra wrote that Our Lady of Loreto's image was "transferred to the new adobe house, all whitewashed and adorned with paintings, statues, an altarpiece, and a canopy. It resembles a veritable paradise." In the meantime, work continued slowly on the large church.

On July 2, 1699, ships arrived from the mainland, one bearing much-needed supplies of maize, rice, and other provisions, as well as the long-overdue salaries of the soldiers. The other ship carried six additional soldiers eager to serve in California. Even though he couldn't afford to pay them, Salvatierra enrolled them, saying that they were all "single, young, brave, and optimistic" and that he trusted that somehow he would be able to support them. These men brought the total to twenty-seven soldiers in the garrison.

The Arrival of Padre Juan de Ugarte (1662-1730)

In 1700, the third California missionary, Juan de Ugarte, arrived in Loreto. This priest was already a pillar of strength in the Jesuit enterprise in California. As a professor of philosophy in Mexico City, he had volunteered in 1696 to work with Salvatierra and Kino to raise money for the California missions. After the three padres had managed to acquire enough support to start the California enterprise, Ugarte was appointed to administer the Pious Fund. He set up a bookkeeping system and invested the donated funds in profitable cattle ranches. These investments allowed the Jesuits to independently establish and govern the California missions. Padre Ugarte was to spend the next thirty years devoting his unusual strength and intelligence to the California enterprise.

Juan Ugarte was born in 1662 in Tegucigalpa, Honduras to a wealthy Spanish family. He was educated in Guatemala City and came to Mexico City where he finished his religious education. He was a very large man with enormous energy,

Padre Juan Ugarte

enthusiasm, and ingenuity. He served as a missionary at Loreto in 1701, at San Javier in 1702, and again in San Javier from 1704 until he died there in 1730.

With Ugarte in California, Padre Salvatierra was able to leave Loreto in order to explore with Padre Kino the upper end of the Sea of Cortez for a long-planned attempt to prove that California was not an island but was connected on the north to the rest of New Spain. This would make it possible to supply the California missions by an overland route from the mainland. At that time, cartographers regularly showed Baja California as an island on their maps, but Salvatierra and Kino believed otherwise. After a difficult journey, they were able to reach a point where they could see the mountains of the upper end of the peninsula and establish that California was indeed a part of New Spain, although the waterless desert between made it a formidable area to cross. Salvatierra established a settlement at Guaymas on his return trip, as a port for the shipment of supplies to Loreto from the mainland.

After Salvatierra returned in 1701, Padre Ugarte went to San Javier to continue Padre Piccolo's work of building a mission and planting the fields, while Piccolo went to the mainland to try to raise more contributions for the Pious Fund and bring back urgently needed supplies. The problem of obtaining and delivering food to Loreto continued. More supplies and more ships to carry them were needed.

Juan Ugarte had his work cut out for him at San Javier. When he arrived at the mission with a few soldiers, none of the natives would come near it, and the area around it was empty. Suspecting it was the presence of the soldiers keeping the natives away, he sent them back to Loreto and remained alone at the mission.

Before long, a curious little boy visited him. The padre was kind to him and loaded him with presents to take back to his family, along with the message that the soldiers were gone. Soon the adults began to come to the mission, and the priest was able to set up a regular schedule of religious instruction and distribution of pozole. There was much work to be done to clear the land, build an irrigation system, plant corn, and build the chapel and house for the missionary. Ugarte realized it was urgent to make the mission self-sustaining. His great strength enabled him to work along side the Indians, winning their admiration.

The Cochimí men teased him, though. When he asked for translations of Cochimí words, they gave him obscene or wrong words and, when he used them, they roared with laughter. He learned to ask the small children for information. The congregation also thought Ugarte's description of hell was very funny. They said it sounded like a wonderful place to go, because there must be plenty of wood there and they could always keep warm.

Ugarte grew tired of their misbehavior and decided, since

they understood physical prowess, he would use it. He chastised one of the worst offenders by picking him up by the hair and bouncing him up and down. The others got the message.

Another feat gained him even more admiration. The Cochimí believed that mountain lions should not be killed, because then the killer would die. Lions in the San Javier area had been responsible for the death of many mission animals. One day, Ugarte came upon a very big lion asleep near a mountain path. He dismounted from his mule and killed it with a large rock. He had a struggle getting it on the back of his frightened mule, but finally returned to the mission to show it to the natives while it was still warm so they could see that he had killed it. When he didn't die and nothing else bad happened to him, they learned that it was safe to kill the lions themselves. From then on, the Jesuits rewarded anyone who killed a mountain lion with a bull from the mission herd.

1702 began badly in Loreto. The ship carrying supplies was delayed, and the little colony suffered a famine during June and July. They ran out of grain and corn, and Padre Salvatierra reported: "We were reduced to skeletons because our stomachs rebelled against the monotonous diet of lean meat." *Another Crisis in Loreto*

The previous year, Captain Antonio García Mendoza, dissatisfied with his status as subservient to the Jesuits, left Loreto and returned to the mainland. Among other reasons for his dissatisfaction, he complained that Padre Salvatierra was too generous with food to the Indians while neglecting the needs of his soldiers. Seventeen men went with him, leaving the Loreto, San Javier, and San Juan missions protected by only twelve armed soldiers.

At this critical time, a young soldier, José Pérez, almost caused another attack by the Indians. He had fallen in love with and married a young Cochimí girl from the mountains. All went well with the couple until the time of the pitaya harvest. The girl couldn't resist the fun of the harvest and the dances and ran off with her relatives to the celebrations. Against the orders of his superior officer, the distraught husband went in search of his bride, accompanied by a young Monquí friend. After several days of fruitless searching, Peréz and his friend came upon an old Cochimí in the mountains and demanded he tell him where the pitaya celebration was being held. The old man warned the soldier it was dangerous to interrupt the festivities and begged him to give up his search. They argued, and the angry and frustrated young man raised his harquebus and shot the elderly Indian. Cochimí nearby heard the shots and came running. When they saw what had happened, they drew their bows and shot arrows into Peréz, killing him. His Monquí friend escaped and ran to Loreto with the news.

The angry Cochimí men then went to the San Javier mission. Padre Ugarte was in Loreto that day, but several soldiers there managed to disperse the attackers, and no damage was done to the buildings. However, the Cochimí destroyed the corn crop, which was just about ready to harvest, and made off with all the goats.

Many of the aroused Cochimí then tried to organize a war to kill all the Europeans. The missionaries had done their work well, though, and the firebrands could not persuade the many Christianized Cochimí to join them.

That danger passed, but hunger remained a real problem. Salvatierra later said he hadn't been able to write any letters, because when he picked up his pen he was tempted to eat the feather. He proposed abandoning California, but the stalwart Ugarte persuaded him to hold on a little longer. Salvatierra agreed to stay but wrote that if Piccolo did not return with good news for the colony, he would dismiss all the soldiers, and he and Ugarte and Piccolo would remain alone. If they perished, they would be martyrs and insure their place in heaven, but California would have to be abandoned once again.

Finally, on July 22, 1702, a supply ship arrived. It not only brought food to feed the starving missionaries and their native charges, but also good news. The War of the Spanish Succession had ended, and the new king of Spain, the French Bourbon Philip V, had declared himself a friend to California.

Piccolo returned several months later, having received new private donations and, most importantly, news of a promise from King Philip of six thousand pesos a year from the royal treasury for the support of the California missions.

A fourth human rock on which the Jesuit missionary system in Baja California was built was not a priest but a soldier. Esteban Rodríguez Lorenzo was born in Portugal in about 1670. He emigrated to New Spain in his early twenties and worked his way up to majordomo on a Jesuit hacienda near Tepotzotlán. Padre Salvatierra met and recruited him there. Rodríguez accompanied Salvatierra on his arduous journey to the west coast of the mainland and helped the priest control an uprising by the Tarahumara Indians. Rodríguez was one of the soldiers who came ashore in Loreto with Padre Salvatierra in 1697 and was one of the defenders of the mission when it was attacked by the Indians. He was with the party that accompanied Piccolo to San Javier and helped build the road to the new mission. He climbed El Pilón with Captain García Mendoza and was the first to reach the top. When the dissatisfied Captain García left with seventeen of the soldiers stationed in Loreto, Rodríguez remained. He was chosen by the other soldiers to be their captain, and he remained in this position for the next forty-two years, from 1701 until 1743 when, too feeble to serve any longer, he was relieved of his command and was succeeded by his son Bernardo.

On a trip to the mainland in 1704, Rodríguez fell in love with the daughter of a prominent rancher near Tequila on the road to Guadalajara. In 1707, he returned to the mainland and married María de Larrea and brought her back to Loreto.

María adapted easily to the frontier life of Loreto, and everyone loved her. One Jesuit described her as "a woman of exemplary character and of great charity; she has devoted herself to teaching the Indian women how to perform the tasks incumbent on civilized women." Padre Piccolo said of her: "Ever since setting foot in this land, she has been serving as nurse for the Indians, both men and women, and caring for them in their rancherías. Her house is a hospital where the ailing from our missions gather, receive very kind treatment, and are much edified. She is teaching the Indian women not only to sew and to embroider, but even to read." In addition, María bore seven children, and Esteban and María Rodríguez became the founders of the first prominent pioneer family in Baja California.

Esteban Rodríguez Lorenzo

During his long years of service in Baja California, Rodríguez was not only a loyal military officer and supporter of the Jesuit enterprise, he also worked as a mason and supervised the construction of most new missions. As captain, his civil posts were governor and chief justice. As representative of the crown, he inspected the license of visiting pearl hunters and collected a fifth of their harvest for the king. He presided over hearings, settled disputes, carried out the laws, and meted out punishment in the civil community.

The California captain's powers and prerogatives, as listed at the time by the Jesuit chronicler Miguel Venegas, were imposing:

1. He shall be chief justice of all of California.

2. He shall be judge over the soldiers in military matters and also in matters political, civil, and criminal.

3. He shall likewise be governor and judge of all the other inhabitants such as sailors, the servants of the presidios and missions, and all the Indians.

4. He shall be the captain general not only of the land but also of the sea and coasts of California. Therefore, the chief ship of the presidio shall be called the "Capitana", and be entitled to enter all ports flying the flags proper to her rank. She shall omit to fly these flags only if she enters Acapulco when the Manila galleon is in port.

5. He shall be royal superintendent of all those who go to California to take pearls.

In Esteban Rodríguez, the Jesuits had found the perfect soldier for the job.

But all these duties and prerogatives were subject to the authority of the Jesuit administrators. The viceroy of New Spain was the final authority for all military captains, but no other captain had an immediate superior who watched so closely everything he did. The Jesuits gave up the power to appoint their captain in 1744 after Rodríguez died, but they continued to receive support from those who followed him, men who understood the religious nature of the California venture.

Rodríguez was faithful to the principles of the Jesuits in carrying out all his civil duties. He outlived Salvatierra, Piccolo, and Ugarte and in 1746 died, blind and feeble, in Loreto. He was the last survivor of the founding of the pueblo that he had helped to build.

Rodríguez was the best example of the kind of soldier the Jesuits sought to hire for California. He was, first of all, a European. They thought that only men from that culture could serve as good examples to the natives.

Since it was difficult to find Europeans willing to serve on this remote frontier, the padres were forced to employ many half-castes, or mestizos. These men found military service to be their best chance of achieving a respectable position and a secure existence. They were attracted to California because the Jesuits there provided better pay, although it should be noted that they were never paid in money but in goods. This was common throughout New Spain, because the Jesuits believed that money led to gambling, of which they highly disapproved. In other parts of New Spain, it was common practice for officers to use their men as servants and to siphon off part of the soldiers' pay for their own use. This practice was not allowed by the California Jesuits. California service was also less dangerous, because there were fewer natives, they had no modern weapons, and they were not as belligerent as those on the mainland.

Nevertheless, the turnover in soldiers was great, because many young men did not like the restrictions imposed by their religious employers. Their moral conduct had to be above reproach. They had to attend religious services daily; they could not use the natives as slaves or treat them with disrespect; they had to work hard at any tasks they were assigned; they had to obey the priests instead of the generals; and they could not appropriate land or raise cattle. If they did not conform to all the moral demands of their religious employers, they were dismissed and sent back to the mainland.

The number of soldiers in the Loreto presidio varied from twelve to as many as sixty during the seventy years between 1697 and 1768 of Jesuit rule. The soldiers were presented to the California Indians as representatives of the king of Spain who, the Europeans told them, was now their supreme ruler.

In addition to protecting the mission against hostile attack, the soldiers' duties included chasing down natives who had committed crimes against the mission and bringing them in for punishment. These punishments were public. The Jesuit chronicler Venegas described how they worked:

> Before any sentence is carried out, whether at the criminal's mission or at the presidio of Loreto to which he has been brought, measures are taken to make certain that the Indians of his pueblo or such of them as are in Loreto shall be present at the execution of the sentence. In this way, news of his punishment may be spread abroad among his people and may serve as a warning to the rest. To this end, through an interpreter, the reason for his arrest is made public along with the crime or crimes which have been proved against him, and the punishment to which he is condemned in consequence. In this way, the offender is chastised for his crime, and the other Indians are warned by his chastisement. This justice is executed by the captain, or, at his orders, by the soldiers. Thus, the whole country is held in subjection, and all the Indians are submissive and obedient to the man whom they recognize as His Majesty's officer.

From the first, California soldiers were required to be jacks of all trades. Harry Crosby in *Antigua California* describes a California soldier's life:

> In spite of its small garrison, Loreto was the workshop for the entire conquest. The tiny body of men incorporated virtually the entire range of basic European technologies needed to sustain Hispanic life on the frontier. Survival depended on constant maintenance or replacement of every article that distinguished the newcomers' culture from that of the natives. Manufactured articles were not only slow, uncertain, and expensive to replace, but parts and even raw materials were lacking for long periods. As a result, there was a continual process of planing, carving, chipping, cutting, forging, riveting, grinding, punching, and stitching as the people of Loreto repaired their vital gear or manufactured replacements. Arms were overhauled, boats were scraped and caulked, pots and pans were soldered, tools mended, clothing darned and

Illustration of a California soldier by Padre Ignacio Tirsch.
Tirsch illustration: Courtesy of Glen Dawson.

patched, and riding and pack gear restitched and gradually replaced.

Padre Jacob Baegert described the gear of California soldiers:

> Their weapons are a sword, a musket, a shield, and an armor of four layers of tanned, white deerskin, which covers the entire body like a sleeveless coat. Otherwise, they wear whatever they like; they have no uniforms. They serve on horseback or on mule, and because of the rugged trails, each man is obliged to keep five mounts. The soldiers have to buy these animals as well as their weapons, clothing, ammunition, and all their food.

In addition to the small group manning the presidio in Loreto, one or more soldiers were sent to assist the padres and guard the individual missions as they were founded throughout the peninsula. The sophisticated padres did not always enjoy their ignorant soldier companions. "We cannot live with them, and we cannot live without them," Juan Ugarte joked. However, on the whole, the soldiers tried to please the padres and were useful. After the expulsion of the Jesuits from Baja California, Padre Miguel del Barco wrote:

> ...The captains always took care to select, for the missions in which padres had to stay alone, those soldiers who showed the best judgment and conducted themselves in the most honorable Christian fashion....The captains made such careful choices that, for the most part, the soldiers at the missions performed well and honorably and gave much relief and comfort to the padres.

Padre Salvatierra described one soldier's bravery. In 1704, he and Padre Pedro Ugarte, Juan Ugarte's younger brother, were going from Loreto to Ligüí where they hoped to establish another mission. The two priests were accompanied by the soldier Francisco Javier Valenzuela and several interpreters. Just before they arrived at Ligüí, some Monquí men jumped out of hiding and shot at them with arrows. The soldier never hesitated. He charged at the Monquí, firing his musket and waving his sword. This angry, noisy monster so frightened the Monquí that they threw down their bows and lay flat on the ground. The padres forgave them, gave them gifts, and successfully established themselves in Ligüí.

California Sailors

Esteban Rodríguez is also listed as the first commander of Loreto's principal ship, which made the major supply run from Loreto to Acapulco or Matanchel every year and sometimes brought beef from Soñora. Rodríguez made this trip in 1707, when he went to the mainland to get married. During the Jesuit period, there were eight commanders of this vessel.

For Loreto's first forty years, a number of sailors were employed. They had the dangerous task of sailing the small launches that kept the colony supplied and also carried out journeys of exploration. The number of sailors varied over the years; in 1733, thirty-nine sailors manned two ships, but by 1751 the number had decreased to eighteen. Most were Filipinos, Yaqui Indians from Soñora, native Californians, or mestizos from the western coast of the mainland.

A crew of craftsmen to maintain the ships lived in Loreto. These consisted of a master blacksmith, a master carpenter, and a master caulker. Each had a crew of two or three assistants.

They built shelters made of forked trees and palm roofs, called *tinglados,* on the beach. One tinglado was for the smithy, another the carpenter shop, and the third, nearest the sea, held the caulkers' tools. A bench vise from the carpentry shop, made of mesquite and capable of holding wood used in small craft construction, can be seen in Loreto's Museum of the Missions. The craftsmen were almost all mestizos, and they usually stayed a long time. Many of them founded families, and their names, like Romero, Murillo, and Márquez, are still very common in Loreto and other parts of Baja California.

Reports from the survivors of Cortés' first expedition to Baja California in 1533 of an abundance of pearls in the Sea of Cortez inspired many expeditions to these waters over the next few hundred years. *Pearl Fishing*

The Jesuit historian Francisco Javier Clavijero described the methods employed during that time to fish for pearls:

The best season for this fishing is from the first days of July to the last of September. As soon as the pearl diving outfitter (the person at whose expense the fishing is done) has the boats ready and has provided all the necessary things, he goes to the eastern coast of California and there selects a port near the pearl beds, provided there is water for drinking there. During the three months which diving lasts, the boats and the divers go out daily and return to ports.

The fishing begins two hours before noon and continues until three hours after midday, because the sun, being more perpendicular then, greatly clears up the bottom of the sea, and it makes visible the shells which are there. They do not fish during the remainder of the day, nor when the day is cloudy. The oysters are fished at a depth of up to 50 or 60 feet, according to the skill of the diver. They dive, each one taking a net tied to his body to hold the oysters and a well-sharpened stick to defend himself from mantas and for other uses. As soon as they have filled the net or cannot hold their breath any longer, they come out of the water and return to the boat either to empty the nets or to take a few breaths, because the fatigue which they suffer is quite considerable on diving to the bottom as well as coming up. When the catch of the day is ended they return to the port where they count and the division of the oysters is made.

Every day the counting and distribution are made in this manner: If the diver is on salary, four are taken from the entirety of all the oysters for the pearl outfitter and one for the King. If the diver is not on salary, the first is taken for the outfitter, the second for the diver, the third for the outfitter, the fourth for the diver, and the fifth is set aside for the King; and so they go on counting in this manner until the pile is finished.

After they have made this division, they open the oysters to take out the pearls. Some oysters have absolutely nothing; others have one, and frequently some have two pearls or more. The outfitters buy those which fall to the divers, or they trade them for merchandise which those who undertake pearl fishing usually bring with them for this purpose.

The entrepreneurs who sent boats to search for these treasures used natives to dive for them, in many instances exploiting them both physically and economically. Salvatierra was determined to protect the neophytes of his missions from such exploitation and did his best to make it difficult for would-be pearlers to obtain licenses. He also absolutely forbade soldiers and sailors in the employ of the Jesuits to engage in pearl fishing. Those who did were immediately dismissed. When they complained, Salvatierra replied that he did not pay pearl fishermen but sailors and soldiers. He told them that when they were employed they had contracted never to be employed in pearl fishing, and if they were not content with that, they were free to leave and go ask the viceroy for permission to do the fishing they so much desired.

Salvatierra's antipathy toward pearlers was reinforced in September of 1703 when a storm drove two pearling vessels onshore at Loreto. The boats were badly damaged, but the seventy men survived. A few days later, fourteen more starving survivors of a sunken pearling craft paddled into Loreto. The little colony, already existing on short supplies, now had eighty-four extra hungry men to feed. Padre Piccolo had gone to Soñora to obtain supplies. His return in mid-October with not only food but craftsmen who could repair the pearlers' ships was a godsend. After two months, the unwelcome guests were finally able to leave.

By 1705, the missions at Loreto and San Javier were operating, and it was time to explore promising sites for new missions.

The Jesuit plan was to explore the California wilderness and contact the natives until they had incorporated all the human population into the Catholic Church. The enormous struggle to accomplish this goal – raising money, getting supplies across the sea, learning new languages, difficult exploration of the rugged land, recruiting and disciplining soldiers and sailors – the missionaries gladly undertook, because they believed it was God's will.

San Juan Londó, the site of Kino's mission and Salvatierra's first expedition, had become a visita, or chapel, served by the Loreto priest. Half of the native population of Loreto had died in a smallpox epidemic in 1704, and many people from the San Juan area were moved to Loreto to replace them.

In 1705, Padre Pedro Ugarte, Juan Ugarte's brother, founded Mission San Juan Bautista at Ligüí, and a small church was built there. This mission was abandoned in 1721 when its native population was moved to another mission, again because of the decline of the natives from diseases to which they had no immunity.

Also in 1705, it was decided that a self-sustaining mission could be established north of Loreto by the river at Mulegé. Padre Juan Manuel de Basaldúa was assigned to develop the mission Santa Rosalía de Mulegé in that area.

Three years later, Julián Mayorga, a brilliant Spaniard who had been educated at the court in Madrid before entering the Jesuit order, had arrived in Loreto directly from teaching philosophy at the Imperial College. He was assigned to establish a mission at Comondú in a valley in the mountains north of San Javier. Several years earlier this area had been explored by Salvatierra who thought Comondú a promising agricultural site. Padre Mayorga arrived in California in poor health, and Salvatierra gave him time to recover. In 1708, Mayorga was escorted from Loreto to his new post by Padres Salvatierra and

Juan Ugarte and soldiers and helpers led by Captain Esteban Rodríguez.

Twelve years passed before the founding of more missions. In 1720, La Purísima Concepción de Cadegomó was established by Nicolás Tamaral, and Jaime Bravo was assigned to develop La Señora de la Paz Airapí. Both priests were from Spain. A German Jesuit, Everardo Helen, founded the mission of Nuestra Señora de Guadalupe de Huasinapí in that same year. The following year, Clemente Guillén established Nuestra Señora de los Dolores Apaté, and the Italian Ignacio María Nápoli was sent to develop Santiago el Apóstal.

In the years between 1728 and 1737, four more missions were established: Nuestro Señor San Ignacio Kadakaamán by Juan Bautista de Luyando; San José del Cabo Añuití by Nicolás Tamaral; Todos Santos, where two successive missions were located, Santa Rosa de las Palmas, followed by Pilar de la Paz which moved there in 1749; and San Luis Gonzaga Chiriyaquí, established by the German Lamberto Hostell.

In the final fifteen years of the Jesuit presence in Baja California, only three more missions were founded, all to the north. In 1752, another German Jesuit, Jorge Retz, established Santa Gertrudis de Cadacamán. The Bohemian Wenceslao Linck built San Francisco de Borja Adac in 1762, and in 1767, two Spanish Jesuits, Victoriano Arnés and Juan Diez, were sent to build Santa María Cabujakkamung.

San Juan Londó was moved to the jurisdiction of the mission at San José Comondú in 1717 after the death of Salvatierra, because the priest at Loreto was too busy with administrative duties to serve it properly. A rude chapel had been built originally, and some work had been done on it over the years. The remains of this building can be seen not far from the highway on what is now Rancho San Juan. In 1754, the Londó people were moved to San José Comondú after an epidemic there decimated most of the population at that mission.

During the seventy years of Jesuit rule between 1697 and 1768, eighteen missions and one visita were founded and fifty-six priests served in Baja California. In addition to the Hispanic priests, there were Bohemians, a Croatian, an Alsatian, Italians,

The establishment of the Jesuit
missions of Baja California

Santa María

San Borja

Santa Gertrudis

San Ignacio

Guadalupe

Santa
Rosalia

MAR DE CORTES

La Purísima

San José
Comondú

Loreto

San Javier

Bautista

Dolores

San
Luis

OCEANO

Pilar

Todos
Santos

Santiago

PACIFICO

San José del Cabo

Germans, a Scot, Austrians, and a Sicilian.

Months and years of exploration and trial and error preceded the establishment of each mission. It was hard to find a location on this desert peninsula with enough water and soil to raise crops to feed the native converts. Exploration, planning, and organization were all carried out from Loreto, which gradually evolved from a mission settlement to the headquarters of a theocracy, a religious government, ruled by the Jesuit priests.

Loreto became, as Harry Crosby wrote in *Antigua California,* "the heart of the colony, the mother church, the government, the presidio, the seaport, the general store, and the only place where all elements of California society could meet."

Since the Renaissance, popes had glorified Rome with richly built and decorated churches. The Catholic Church believed that to create faith in its teachings, its authority should be displayed in majestic and beautiful buildings. The church in Loreto, which was begun in 1699 by soldiers and native converts, was finally dedicated five years later. It had been impossible to obtain the long roof beams that would eventually be covered by tile and adobe, so the new church had only a thatched roof. However, the statue of the Virgin and other religious decorations of the chapel were installed with great ceremony and Padres Salvatierra, Juan and Pedro Ugarte, Piccolo, and Juan Manuel Basaldúa solemnly presided over the first service. The Guaycura and Cochimí beheld a church which was as impressive as any in the area of Spanish conquest.

In 1705, Salvatierra was recalled to Mexico City and appointed *Padre Provincial* (head of the geographical area of the Jesuits of New Spain). He was able to visit Loreto only once during the next two years. While Salvatierra was gone, Juan Ugarte was in charge. He continued the building program of the pueblo. A new and larger house for the padre and a smaller one for visiting missionaries were built. Instead of adobe, these structures were of stone and mortar. Since a limestone deposit had been found on Coronados Island, Ugarte was able to make cement. He imported the roof beams for the new buildings from Sinaloa, and roofed them with adobe tiles. A garden orchard was planted, which had its own well.

Even after Salvatierra returned from his assignment on the mainland, Ugarte directed additions to the pueblo. He built a small house on the south side of the mission for his own use when he was in Loreto, and this closed in all four sides of the mission complex. Finally, the long cedar beams were brought from Sinaloa to cover the 17 foot nave of the Loreto mission church. A flat roof, composed of beams, a layer of fired tile, several inches of adobe covered with tile and sealed with a mixture of pitch, tar, grease, and oils, replaced the palm leaves.

Padre Ugarte was eager to educate the new converts, and he established a school where boys were taught religion and morality as well as introducing them to the tools and skills of the Europeans. Children were sent to Loreto from all the missions to be taught Spanish, writing, and religious music. Orphans, especially little children, were brought to Loreto to be taught "the kind of work appropriate to their sex." *Loreto Schools*

Outside the mission complex, toward the mountains, two long rows of adobe huts, facing each other, were built to house the native converts of Loreto. A well about 9 feet deep was dug in the center of this neophyte settlement. Francisco "Pancho" Barreño, employed at the Museum of the Missions, remembers that in about 1950, when some pipes were laid and the street in front of the mission widened, the well was uncovered. It was found to have had a circular stairway with twenty-three steps that wound down to the water level. It was covered again when the work was finished.

The homes of the married Hispanic soldiers and artisans were spaced at a distance from each other wherever they chose to build. Padre Jacob Baegert described these houses shortly before the Jesuits were expelled: *Loreto Homes*

> About two to three and a half dozen mud huts were scattered over the sand, without order, looking more like cowsheds of the poorest little village than homes, and usually containing but one single room. These are occupied by the married soldiers, the few sailors, the one and a half carpenters and equally numerous blacksmiths, and their wives and children, and serve as lodging, living room, storeroom, and bedroom.

Each house probably also had a thatched roof addition

where the cooking and, in hot weather, most of the family life was carried on. Because of the climate, this kind of outdoor living is still common at the end of the 20th century. Floors were of packed earth, as some still are, which are easy to sweep and comfortable to bare feet.

Beds were made of wood, often palm logs, which were strung with strips of rawhide to form a lattice. These beds are still being made and are in use in most of the ranches. A soft skin and pad of mescal fibers were thrown over the lattice for comfort. Other furniture – tables, chairs, chests – was made of wood, although some families used whale vertebrae for chairs.

An example of the adobe stoves used in the 18th century, and still being used on many ranches, can be found in the Loreto museum. They measure about 5 feet long, 3 or 4 feet wide, and 2 or 3 feet high. The framework is filled with tamped earth so the top is solid. More adobe brick are placed on top to make three or four open fire-boxes, each 1 foot wide by 2 feet deep. A line of larger bricks at the back keeps pots off the flames. Mesquite twigs are used to build fires in the boxes and iron rods are placed across the top of the fire-boxes to support pots and pans or comals to make tortillas.

The Loreto Presidio   On the east side of the mission, near the beach, stood the presidio. The original hastily-erected fort was gradually replaced. The Loreto presidio was never as large or well fortified as the presidios in Alta California, because there was no need for protection from a hostile population or invasion from other European powers. Padre Piccolo, in 1702, wrote: "the fortification consists of an entrenchment laid out in the form of a square large enough for a military plaza and soldiers' quarters. The building material of...the soldiers' quarters is good adobe with tile roofs." These roofs were the first to be tiled to avoid being attacked with flaming arrows. While Ugarte was directing building in Salvatierra's absence, a large stone-and-mortar warehouse was added, the soldiers' quarters were expanded to house thirty men, and the wall surrounding the presidio was strengthened. Inside the wall, there was enough space to parade and to load and unload animals. All the rooms incorporated the peripheral wall as one side. After Ugarte's improvements, apparently no changes or additions were made to the presidio until 1751, when a new guardhouse was built to replace the old one which had been destroyed by a storm. The new building was of stone and mortar and served as a barracks for unmarried soldiers and guardroom for men on watch.

A Wall for Protection from Flooding

At times the region sees little or no rain for as long as seven or eight years, but when the rain does come, it runs off the mountains, which do not have enough soil to absorb it, and down through Loreto to the sea. In 1750, the Jesuits began to build a wall around the mission compound to protect the church. It was completed in 1752. Parts of this wall, which was rebuilt from time to time by Franciscan and Dominican missionaries, can still be found. Houses, though, had to be built on high ground to survive the flash floods.

Loreto Women's Work

Houses were a good distance from the water sources, and fetching water from the village spring was an all-day chore. Clothing had to be carried down and washed at a waterhole, and firewood had to be collected further and further from home as the local supply diminished. Women did all the cooking, washing, sewing, child tending, and housekeeping – the traditional occupations of European women.

Sewing took up a great many hours of a woman's day. Fabrics arrived from the mainland on the annual supply ship, and the women were responsible for cutting and sewing most of the clothing for both sexes. The hard work and rough environment meant that a great deal of patching and mending had to be done as well. Some ready-made clothing was also imported but was usually saved for special occasions. Both European and native women dressed in skirts and blouses, petticoats and stockings. They wore shawls or ponchos in cold weather and always wore scarves over their heads in church. Both men and women wore hats made of felt or woven of straw or palm leaves for protection from the hot sun.

The soldiers' wives taught the neophyte women to sew and embroider, to knit and weave stockings. Indian women, who had embraced Christianity in the beginning as a relief from their daily search for food, found that while they had gained a few skills and more leisure time, they had also lost their importance and status as providers of food for their families.

Separation of Indian Men and Women

The Jesuits, who placed great emphasis on chastity, considered it very important to separate the sexes. Unmarried men and women slept in separate quarters, guarded by a house mother or father who saw to it that they didn't slip out during the night. Married neophytes were assigned to the small adobe houses built for them close to the mission.

Loreto Cattle, Sheep, and Goats

Although the desert outside the oasis of Loreto did not permit the growing of crops, the Jesuits raised increasing numbers of cattle, eventually over a thousand head. Because of the barren terrain, the animals had to forage over a vast area. Every bit of every animal was put to use. Hides were salted, hoofs and bones used to make soup, and jerky (*tasajo*) was prepared by cutting the meat into thin strips, salting it, and hanging it to dry in the sun. This was a great favorite of the soldiers and vaqueros, and the men of Baja California were often teased about their addiction to tasajo. Padre Baegert wrote a good description of the many uses of the animal products:

> Cattle, sheep, and goats had to supply the meat for the healthy and the sick, but they were also needed for their tallow, used to make candles and soap, and in caulking ships and boats. They also furnished the fat used to prepare beans. In California, as well as elsewhere in America, the beans are not prepared with butter churned from milk, but with the rendered fat and marrow of the bones. For this purpose, every time a well-fed cow or ox was killed, a rare occurrence, every bit of fat was carefully cut from the meat, rendered and conserved in skin bags and bladders. This fat was used for the preparation of food and for frying the very lean or dried meat. Some of the hides were tanned for shoes and saddles and for bags in which everything was carried from the field to the mission or anywhere else. Other skins were used raw to make sandals for the natives, or were cut into strips for ropes, cords, or thongs, which were used for tying, packing, and similar tasks. The natives used the horns to scoop up water or to fetch food from the mission.

Health and Healing

The health of the Hispanic population was generally very good, although, as we have seen, the native population quickly succumbed to the diseases brought by their conquerors. A room was set aside with a few beds for attending to the sick, who were nursed by a priest assisted by Indian helpers. Local remedies, such as the dried bark of palo blanco trees, jojoba, and the pulp of the cardón cactus, were used. Baja Californians still rely to a great extent on these natural curatives. Some liniments for use on people and animals were brought in, and the laxative castor bean was introduced.

In Loreto, as in all the missions, the process of "civilizing" *Daily* the Indians to adapt to the European way of life was carried out *Activities* through a system of organizing daily activities so that everyone was kept very busy every moment.

A typical day began at daybreak when the church bells tolled the Ave María and the entire population gathered at the church to join in prayer and sing the Alabado, a hymn of praise to the Eucharist. Those without early morning duties remained to celebrate Mass.

Padre Ignacio Tirsch illustration of a ram and a mountain lion.
Tirsch illustration: Courtesy of Glen Dawson.

91

Worshippers left the church to attend to their assigned tasks. Some prepared breakfast, which consisted of *atole* (a corn soup) for most of the mission people, or *pozole,* a thicker corn soup with added beans, bones, and perhaps meat for the field workers, the sick, and the old. Because of the poor soil and lack of water, it was always necessary to import dried food from the mainland. Thus, with only minor variations, the diet remained the same at every meal, day after day. The padres blessed the food and ladled it out to those who had attended church.

After breakfast, accompanied by a soldier or majordomo, some native men went to work with the animals or on construction, well digging, and other projects. Native women helped with food preparation, but the men cooked for the community. At ten o'clock, the mission bells tolled, and the boys and girls, segregated by sex, went to church to study the catechism.

At noon, everyone reassembled at the church, prayed to the Virgin, and sang the Alabado. A noon meal, again atole and pozole, was served, followed by a siesta until two o'clock, when work was resumed. At five o'clock, the church bell called the children to church to recite the Angelus and the catechism and sing the Alabado.

In the evening, bells tolled the Ave María, and everyone knelt to the Virgin. Following a supper of the same food, everyone attended church and recited the invocation and responses of the Rosary and Litany.

Recreation   The Jesuits encouraged their flock to have fun, too. Fiestas were held on all the special days of the Catholic Church with music and dancing, games and contests. Of course, the missionaries hoped these celebrations would attract the unconverted. Salvatierra described the first Loreto Christmas fiestas in 1697:

> The month of December now began. During this month we celebrated with great solemnity the Feast of the Immaculate Conception and the feast of our patron, San Francisco Javier. Since the launch *San Francisco Javier* was in the bay within sight of the real, we sent powder down to it and two small guns, and in this way the salutes fired on land were answered from the sea. The whole launch was hung with lanterns and was made beautiful with lights. Rockets were sent up, both on

sea and on land. The water was very calm, and the lights were reflected in it.

On Christmas day, hundreds of neophytes came to the festivities and more than a hundred of these New Christians performed native dances. These dances are very different from those of the tribes on the mainland coast. These Indians have more than thirty dances, all of them different. They are performed in costume, and they are designed to give instruction in various pursuits and occupations, such as making war, fishing, carrying babies, packing loads, and other things of this sort. The boy of three or four years of age prides himself on properly playing his part in the dances. These children act as if they were already mature, skilled performers vying with one another.

Both the Europeans and the Indians enjoyed dancing, and they had fun competing with one another. The soldiers taught the converts their dances, and Salvatierra wrote that he joined in the dancing, too.

Storytelling was, and still is, a primary source of entertainment in Loreto. As the center of activity on the peninsula, Loreto was the place where stories of adventures on land and sea and gossip and rumors were recounted.

Storytelling

Many stories were told of the exploits of Padre Juan Ugarte: how he killed a mountain lion with a stone; how he clung to a rock for twenty-four hours in the middle of a raging stream during a hurricane in 1717; about this former professor of philosophy's great physical strength as an explorer, pioneer farmer, log-splitter, mule driver, builder, and his spiritual strength as a leader and priest.

They told how he built the best ship Loreto ever had, the *Triunfo de la Cruz*. In 1720, Ugarte learned from some Indians of a stand of good trees in the mountains 200 miles north of Loreto. He went there with four men from Loreto and gathered a crew of natives to help fell the trees, shape the logs, and transport them through ninety difficult miles of ravines and rocks to Mulegé, a Herculean task. On the beach at Mulegé, under the direction of Ugarte and Guillermo (William) Stafford, an English shipbuilder, the ship was constructed. This sturdy ship, *El Triunfo de la Cruz*, served for many years to bring supplies and people to Loreto from the mainland.

Another famous Ugarte story was the one about the copper pots. Once, when Ugarte was visiting the mission at Mulegé, some Indians from the north came to visit and noticed the large copper pots used for making pozole. They said they had some like that in their land. Ugarte sent his soldiers to investigate. They found the Indians reluctant to bring them out. Finally, they led them to where the pots were buried in the sand. When they had first been discovered on the beach, the Indians thought the pots had magic properties and had taken them to a cave and placed them with their mouths facing out. Some time later, though, there was an outbreak of disease, and the leaders of the tribe decided that it had been caused by emissions from the mouths of the pots. Their mouths were stuffed with mud and weeds, and they were returned to the beach and buried. Their origin remains a mystery, although Ugarte guessed that a ship, perhaps a Spanish galleon, had sent a boat into shore to look for water. He thought the sailors had probably been surprised by the natives and had fled back to the ship in such a hurry they had left the pots on the beach. Leaving one pot in Mulegé, Ugarte took the other four back to San Javier where they were used for the rest of the Jesuit period as vessels for making wine.

The story of the demon of San Miguel de Comondú was probably a favorite, too. Padre Nicolás Tamaral reported that a disgruntled guama had summoned a demon to stalk the area. The demon was reported to have horns, cloven hoofs, and a human shape covered with hair. It seized a young boy, Juan Bautista, in church and threw him down in a field. The people said it emitted a noxious vapor at night and made loud and scary noises, sounding like the grunting of a thousand pigs. At the urging of the natives, Padre Tamaral held an exorcism ceremony. With the inhabitants of San Miguel in procession, he carried the statue of the Virgin to the hill overlooking the fields, where he prayed for protection of the mission settlement. This took care of the demon.

A Spartan Life   Tobacco was available in Loreto, and many of the Hispanic men, including the padres, smoked cigars and pipes.

94

The padres kept their wine and brandy locked up, and the wine that was sold was too expensive to constitute a problem. Making or distributing any alcoholic drink, such as *pulque,* made from meszcal, was strictly forbidden. Anyone who used profanity had to pay a fine of a pound of chocolate or its price, and the money was used to decorate the church. Gambling was also forbidden, and the soldiers and sailors who enjoyed it did so out of sight of the padres.

Unlike other frontier settlements in the Americas, life in Loreto was sober, Spartan, and disciplined. Many people left, but those who remained formed a community whose values persist to this day.

In 1717, Padre Salvatierra was sixty-eight years old and suffered from a severe kidney ailment. At that time, a new viceroy had arrived in Mexico City from Spain and wanted to confer with him about the possibility of royal support for the California missions. In spite of his infirmity, Salvatierra set out in March on the difficult journey from Loreto to Mexico City, accompanied by Brother Jaime Bravo. He collapsed in Tepic, and volunteer relay teams of natives carried him by litter 100 miles to Guadalajara. He was cared for there in the Jesuit College, where he had served as rector twenty-five years before. He spent the last weeks of his life preparing Bravo to meet with the viceroy and then died on July 17, 1717.

Salvatierra was succeeded as *Padre Visitador* (father superior) of the California Mission by Juan Ugarte, who served in that position from 1718 to 1722. During his tenure, a mission was founded at La Purísima in 1719 with Padre Nicolás Tamaral in charge. Then Ugarte decided it was time to establish a mission for the difficult natives at La Paz. He chose Jaime Bravo, who had recently been elevated from brother to priest. Bravo had proved his competence as assistant to Salvatierra and as *procurador,* or administrator of supplies and funds for the mission system. Ugarte then sent Padre Clemente Guillén to establish Mission Señora de los Dolores between Loreto and La Paz. He closed Mission San Juan Bautista at Liguí, where many people had died of diseases, and moved the survivors to this new mission.

The California pioneer missionary, Francisco María Piccolo, served as Padre Visitador from 1723 to 1725. During his jurisdiction, two more new missions were established, Mission Santiago in the south in 1724 and San Ignacio in the north in 1725.

Four years after completing his term as Padre Visitador, Francisco María Piccolo died on February 22, 1729 at Loreto. He had lived to be seventy-five. Piccolo had arrived in Mexico from Sicily as a young man of "fair complexion, blond, blue-eyed, tall" and spent thirty-six years in the service of the California missions. He had been sent to Loreto in place of Padre Kino, helped Padre Salvatierra establish the mission in Loreto, explored and founded the San Javier mission, and wrote a report of California that was instrumental in getting support of the Jesuit effort there. He established a mission at Guaymas where Salvatierra had founded a settlement and port to supply the needs of California. After two years in Guaymas, he was appointed Padre Visitador of the Soñora missions. In 1709, Piccolo returned to California and was the padre in Santa Rosalia de Mulegé for eleven years until he returned to Loreto as the father superior of all the peninsular missions. He is buried in the Loreto Mission.

On December 29, 1730, the last of the founding fathers of the mission system in California, the remarkable Juan Ugarte, died at San Javier at the age of sixty-seven. During his final years he had an asthmatic cough, which prevented him from sleeping, and an infection from an open sore, which made him feverish. Padre Clemente Guillén, then Padre Visitador, urged him to stop working and traveling, but Ugarte replied: "Rest and quiet makes me suffer more, and from this you may judge that traveling and laboring is for me a relief." Ugarte had been a teacher, missionary, and administrator. He was an explorer and builder, a farmer and cattleman, and a source of strength, support, and inspiration to his fellow priests and all who knew him. He is buried in the altar area of the San Javier church..

Since the mission system was expanding and the administrative burden had grown, it was decided that a new Padre Visitador would be appointed every three years from among the Jesuits working in California. Just one of the duties of the Padre Visitador was to visit each mission twice a year, an arduous journey on horseback. Padres Clemente Guillén and Sebastián de Sistiaga alternated as Padre Visitador of the California missions for the next twenty-one years, from 1726 to 1747. Guillén was the missionary at Los Dolores, and Sistiaga worked with Padre Consag at San Ignacio. During the administration of Padre Sistiaga, in 1730, Nicolás Tamaral was again sent to found a new mission, this time at San José del Cabo, to meet the royal demand for a mission in that area to supply the Spanish galleons on their yearly trips to the Phillipines. In 1733, while Padre Guillén was Padre Visitador, he sent Padre Sigismundo Taraval to found another mission in the south called Santa Rosa, for the Pericú at Todos Santos.

In January of 1734, the galleon from the Phillipines arrived at Cabo San Lucas, and Padre Tamaral rounded up pitaya fruit and fresh meat for the men, many of them seriously ill with scurvy. This promising event, which showed the Spanish government the importance of the California mission effort, was quickly followed by a violent revolt of the Pericú tribes of the area. By October 1734, Padre Nicolás Tamaral at San José del Cabo, Padre Lorenzo Carranco and two servants at Santiago, and a guard at La Paz had been killed by rebellious natives. *Rebellion in the South*

There were only twenty-five soldiers at the presidio of Loreto, and eighteen of those had been assigned to individual missions. Captain Esteban Rodríguez had petitioned as early as 1731 for an additional presidio in the south. He pointed out that with only seven men in the presidio at Loreto he couldn't protect the peninsula safely, especially since most of these seven had to escort the Padre Visitador over 500 miles of trails every six months. Rodríguez' petitions traveled through a Spanish bureaucracy which was becoming increasingly suspicious and hostile to the Jesuit order, and Spain did not respond in time to avert the death of the missionaries and the destruction of the southern missions.

The attention of Spain was caught, however, when the galleon put into Los Cabos in January of 1735. By then the Pericú tribes were in control of the region, and they intercepted and killed the landing party of thirteen men.

Bernal de Huidobro, the Governor of Sinaloa, and an open adversary of the Jesuits, was appointed by the viceroy, who shared his dislike of the California missionaries, to subdue the rebellion in the south. When Huidobro arrived in Loreto with forty men in December 1735, he conferred only with Esteban Rodríguez, whom he treated with contempt, and he refused to have any dealings at all with the missionaries. Huidobro stayed in Loreto until February when he moved his troops by boat to La Paz and conducted a leisurely campaign from there. It took him two years to finally end the rebellion.

Before he left the peninsula in 1737, Huidobro installed the southern presidio that had been requested six years before by Esteban Rodríguez. The new presidio's captain and troops were not to be under Jesuit control. Bernardo Rodríguez, Esteban's son, was appointed captain but was soon replaced by Pedro Antonio Alvarez Acevedo, a protege of Huidobro. As a result of a Jesuit campaign, Alvarez Acevedo was recalled to the mainland in 1742 and control of the presidio of the south returned to the Jesuits. Pedro de la Riva, who had been a soldier at Loreto for many years and was married to one of Esteban Rodríguez' daughters, was installed as commander of the troops in the south.

However, the rebellion had ended California's isolation. Soldiers and entrepreneurs from the mainland discovered that there was attractive land and water available in the southern part of the peninsula in addition to silver mining operations and pearl fishing. The pioneer Jesuits were all dead, and the California Jesuits had to deal with a new threat to the dream of Salvatierra and Kino of establishing a theocracy in this wilderness.

From 1730 to 1744 Padre Jaime Bravo acted as *Padre Procurador* in Loreto. Brought to Loreto in 1705 as a young Jesuit brother, not yet qualified as a padre, Bravo had learned this job under the tutelage of Juan María Salvatierra. Salvatierra turned over to him the increased responsibilities of keeping books, paying the hired help, ordering supplies, reporting to higher authorities, and maintaining inventories. Salvatierra grew to depend on the competent Brother Bravo and had entrusted him with negotiations with the viceroy after his death. Bravo carried these out successfully.

After completing his training and becoming a priest, Bravo founded the mission at La Paz in 1720 and developed the *visita* at Todos Santos in 1725. Padre Bravo then returned to Loreto and again undertook the duties of Padre Procurador and managed the practical affairs of the California missions for the rest of his life.

Around 1740 Bravo enlarged the church in Loreto by extending the old one to the north, and his stone church stands today, although rebuilt and modified over the more than 250 years since it was finished in 1744. Padre Visitador General Juan Antonio de Baltasar, who visited Loreto from México City that year, described it:

Jaime Bravo (1683-1744) Enlarges the Loreto Mission

> Padre Rector Jaime Bravo...has just finished building a structure that resembles a school. It surpasses anything we have in our missions this side of Guadalajara. Neither Chihuahua nor Parras can boast so fine a building, whether church, residence, barn, or warehouse. It is so sturdy, firm, and solid that all are amazed.

When finished, the church was 150 feet long. It was less than 20 feet wide, since that was the width of cedar beams that could be shipped to Loreto, but the walls were raised 28 feet to increase the dimensions.

While he had the artisans and materials in Loreto, Bravo also built a house on the southwest corner of the square across the street from the church. This stone-and-mortar building, 67 feet long and 31 feet wide, had walls 3 feet thick and 10 feet high. It was meant to be the residence of the padres and came under severe criticism from Padre Baltasar, who wrote:

Bravo's House

> ...the doubt arises whether the presidio and houses for the captain and the soldiers (of which there is almost nothing) should not have been built from these profits (from supplies and food sold to the soldiers at double the purchase price by the Jesuits). If the profits belong to the soldiers, then they are justified in protesting on seeing how comfortably the Padres are housed while they are so neglected. This matter must be satisfactorily corrected.

Bravo wrote a defense of his project but died in the same

year, so no action was ever taken. His "mansion" continued to serve to house padres and then governors until the end of Loreto's reign as capital of Baja California in 1829. Rebuilt after major earthquakes and hurricanes, the southern half of the house is still a residence, and the northern half is rented for commercial enterprises.

Manuel Ocio

Although Captain Esteban Rodríguez had devoted his life to the Jesuit enterprise, several of his sons-in-law were instrumental in undermining the Jesuit power in Baja California. His daughter Rosalía had married Manuel de Ocio, the first successful California entrepreneur. This former Loreto soldier had founded his fortune selling pearls and used this capital to supply provisions and equipment to other pearl seekers and open a silver mine in Santa Ana. Ocio knew the area of Santa Ana well since he had visited it often as a soldier. He knew that the fierce Uchití tribe, who had been leaders in the Pericú rebellion and who still roamed the hills and mountains south of La Paz, were a danger. Ocio proposed, therefore, that another Rodríguez son-in-law, Pedro de la Riva, in charge of the southern presidio, join him in his enterprise. Riva, married to María Rodríguez, was an ambitious man with no loyalty to the Jesuits. He and his troops killed a significant number of Uchití men and women, and the two brothers-in-law continued to try to bring a civil government to Santa Ana and get out from under the control of the Jesuits.

The Old Soldier Dies

Esteban Rodríguez, born in Portugal in 1665, died in Loreto at age eighty-one, after almost fifty years in Baja California. He is buried in the Loreto church near Padre Piccolo, the only civilian to have received that honor. Padre Miguel del Barco wrote in Loreto's book of burials: "On the fourth of November 1746 died Don Esteban Rodríguez, captain commander and one of the first conquerors of California. He received the Holy Sacraments and was buried in the church at the place where the captains are accustomed to sit."

Captain Rodríguez, the fourth rock, with Salvatierra, Piccolo, and Ugarte, on which the California Jesuit mission system was built, had lived on for sixteen years after Ugarte's death, growing increasingly feeble and nearly blind. Padre del

100

Barco wrote that Rodríguez continued to be an active participant in services in the Loreto Mission, and although his voice grew cracked and quavering, most listeners were moved rather than annoyed. As a result of the growing animosity in México City toward the Jesuits, Rodríguez was never awarded a pension for all his years of service, so the fathers continued to pay his salary while his son, Bernardo, took over his duties. Bernardo was not in good health and died before his father. Rodríguez had been given the privilege of running cattle in the area near La Paz, and in his last years the Jesuits paid him a thousand pesos to buy back this privilege.

In July 1751, Fernando Javier de Rivera y Moncada was installed as captain of the Loreto presidio. He was only twenty-six years old. Born to a prominent Spanish family in Compostela, Rivera joined the California military at age eighteen and served for six years under Pedro de la Riva in the southern detachment of the presidio of Loreto. Although he was young, Rivera was educated and literate, intelligent and plain spoken. His experience in the south had familiarized him with the ambitions of Manuel Ocio, and although he was loyal to his Jesuit employers, he also understood the needs of the people struggling to make a living in California.

Capitan Fernando de Rivera y Moncada (1725-1780)

Rivera's first years were a severe test for the young captain. Manuel Ocio filed a constant barrage of accusations and demands against the Jesuits, and in his capacity as judge and administrator of civil affairs, Rivera had to deal with them. Despite his youth, Rivera acted in a fair and creditable manner, and for the remainder of his captaincy managed to hold Ocio off and maintain a relatively peaceful period in California.

Captain Fernando Rivera wanted to marry, but was too busy to return to Compestela to court his future wife. His brother Basilio acted as his proxy and even stood in for him at the marriage ceremony in Compostela which united Fernando Rivera with María Teresa Dávalos y Patrón. Basilio Rivera escorted the bride to Loreto where María already knew some people, since many of the soldiers and their wives were from Compostela. The couple's four children were born and baptized in Loreto.

In his first year as captain, Rivera explored the upper gulf with Padre Fernando Consag of Mission San Ignacio in search of sites for new missions. With renewed confidence, the Jesuits had determined to push the mission system to the north with the hope of eventually expanding as far as Monterey in Alta California. The German Padre Jorge Retz was sent to establish the mission at Santa Gertrudis in that year, after Padre Consag had prepared the way for him.

In 1753, Rivera and Consag again undertook an arduous exploration to Bahía de los Angeles and then northwest through rugged mountain country. They were forced to return without having found a suitable location. However, they had discovered that the Cochimí in the north were ready for conversion, and a cooperative tribe at Bahía de los Angeles was available to help establish missions to the north by carrying supplies which could be shipped by boat to the bay.

In 1762, Padre Wenceslaus Linck founded Mission San Francisco de Borja Adác, following preparation of the area by Rivera. The captain supervised the building of the mission and explored the surrounding country to find water and grazing land. Twenty miles southeast of the mission he found a place now called Las Cabras, and over six hundred cattle and some breeding mules were brought in.

During this period, Rivera explored further to the north with Padre Linck to scout new mission sites. They discovered a suitable area at Santa María Cabujakaamung. There the last Jesuit mission was established by Padres Victoriano Arnés and Juan José Díaz in 1766. Rivera also scouted the site further north at Velicatá that would serve as a *visita* for Santa María.

Miguel del Barco (1706-1790) Builds the San Javier Church

From 1751 to 1754 and again from 1761 to 1763, Miguel del Barco was Padre Visitador of the California mission system. Padre del Barco was another of the brilliant men attracted to the Jesuit order. He was born and educated in Spain and began his ecclesiastical training there. He volunteered to serve in the New World and, after finishing his studies in New Spain, was ordained a priest and sent to California in 1738.

Most of Miguel del Barco's thirty years in California were spent at Mission San Javier where he worked among the

Cochimí Indians and built the remarkable stone church that still stands. He began building the church in 1744. Built of vesicular basalt called *tezontle* that was quarried nearby, it was the first California church to have a vaulted roof. It was not finished until 1758, because del Barco had difficulty finding a master builder who would travel to so remote a land to train and supervise the native workmen.

Padre Jacob Baegert described the process of building a church in California:

Building material, like workable stone, limestone (and the necessary wood for burning it) is difficult to find at most missions. It takes much effort to transport these and many other materials to the proper places. However,...time, industry, hard work, patience, and a large number of donkeys and mules will overcome all difficulties. Many California natives learned stone masonry and brick laying. A missionary, a carpenter, or a competent soldier supervises the construction, or a master builder from another place is engaged for pay. The common labor is performed by Indians who, while the building is under construction, do not have to roam the fields in search of food. For scaffolding, any kind of rough lumber and poles will do. Should some pieces be too short, then two or more of them are tied together with strips of fresh leather; also the trunks of palm trees are used for scaffolding....Except for the three missions in the south, the land is full of common building stones. It is therefore possible to construct within a few years and with little expense such a respectable California church as would do credit to any European city.

During his years in California, del Barco was an acute observer of the natural life of the peninsula and the customs and language of the native people. After his retirement, he spent the rest of his life recording his invaluable observations in his *Natural History of California*.

As Padre Visitador, Padre del Barco had to endure the growing conflict with Manuel Ocio and other entrepreneurs hostile to the Jesuits. During his first term, he was responsible for the wise choice of Fernando de Rivera as captain of the California soldiers. Rivera was able to help him in his relations with the growing unrest of these ambitious men of the south, since he had served in that area and understood the problems.

During his second term, in 1759, the new California supply ship *El Aguila,* built in Nicaragua at royal expense, was wrecked on the gulf coast south of Mission Santiago on its maiden voyage. This left the California missions with nothing but small sailing craft to supply their needs. The Spanish government, short of funds as always, did not offer to build another ship, so Padre del Barco decided the Jesuits would have to build a ship at Loreto, as Padre Ugarte had done before. He knew a Filipino sailor, Gaspar de Molina, who had served in Loreto since 1733 and had shown a talent for building small boats. Del Barco brought Molina out of retirement in Sinaloa and commissioned him to build a large, ocean-going supply ship on the beach at Loreto. Wood was imported from Matanchel, salvaged parts from *El Aguila* were used, and mesquite wood from the present Rancho San Juan was adzed and carved. The workmen were sailors from the Loreto presidio. The ship was designed by Molina. In August 1761, *Nuestra Señora de la Concepción* was launched from the Loreto shore. The ship was 48 feet long at the keel, and the Jesuits reported that it had been built at only half the cost of *El Aguila,* ten thousand pesos, although it had actually cost twice that. They wanted to prove to the viceroy that they were prudent and thrifty and not a burden to the crown. *La Concepción* was seaworthy and served long and well. Ironically, it was to be the ship that carried del Barco and his fellow Jesuits away from California and brought the Franciscan Order to Loreto.

Later, Molina was commissioned to build another, slightly smaller ship on the beach at Loreto, *Nuestra Señora de Loreto,* which was launched before 1768, and *La Loretana,* as it was called, served even longer on the Sea of Cortez than her sister-ship.

Another notable Jesuit, who is remembered chiefly as a commentator on life in Baja California, was Jacob Baegert. He was born in Schlestadt, Alsace in 1717 to what must have been a very religious family, since all three of his brothers also became priests. After receiving the usual rigorous education

The mission church at San Javier. Photo: Leland Foerster.

required of Jesuits, he was sent to Baja California in 1751. He was described at that time as "of poor physique, fair skin, corpulent, thin beard, and thick lips."

After a three-day journey across the gulf in a small hollow-tree canoe, Baegert landed in Loreto. He later described the frontier settlement he found there:

Loreto lies only a stone's throw from the California Gulf. The dwelling of the missionary is a small quadrangle of not more than one story, of unburnt brick and having a flat roof. One wing of the quadrangle, which alone is partly built of stone and lime, constitutes the church. The other three wings contain six apartments, each alone about 20 feet square, and having each one an opening towards the beach or sea; these serve for sacristy, kitchen, and a small store-room from which the soldiers, sailors, and their wives and children, procure buckles, straps, ribbons, combs, tobacco, sugar, linen, shoes, stockings, hats, and similar goods.

Near the quadrangle are four other walls in which are kept very lean beef, also tallow, lard, soap, unrefined sugar, chocolate, cloth, leather, wheat, corn, several millions of black bugs which are generated in the grain, and other articles. In addition to these structures one sees at about the distance of a musket-shot a kind of shed, which serves for guard-house and barracks for the unmarried soldiers. The whole garrison of the Loreto presidio, including the captain and his lieutenant, sometimes consists of six or eight, but never of more than twelve or fourteen head.

Moreover, towards the setting sun one sees two rows of huts made of mud, in which, when big and little, men and women, are all together, dwell about one hundred and twenty natives. Furthermore, one sees, here and there, scattered about the sandy waste, without any order, about two dozen or two dozen and a half cabins constructed of earth, which resemble the poorest village cow-stable rather than a house, and generally having only one apartment, which serve the married soldiers, a few sailors, and their wives and children for shelter, dwelling-room and sleeping-quarters. Finally there is a structure made of poles and covered with brush, which constitutes the arsenal or ship-yard. All this forms Loreto, the capital of California.

The church is large, but consists only of the four walls without art, and only covered with a flat roof formed of nicely-worked beams of cedar wood. On the other hand, none equals it in the number of paintings and in the costliness of the vestments.

Padre Baegert spent only two weeks in Loreto and then went to his assigned mission, San Luis Gonzaga. This mission is located southwest of Loreto in a small oasis surrounded by miles of barren desert. Padre Lambert Hostell had established the mission in 1737, and Baegert found the tiny church in ruins. During his years there, Baegert built the sturdy stone church, which is still standing. On October 4, 1754, in a letter to his brother, Baegert described his impression of the land to which he had been sent:

...It appears to be certain that in the beginning God did not create California; it also did not come out of the great flood. The first can be proven by the following: there are rocks and hills, also parts of the land in the plains and valleys, which have petrified or stonelike shells and 'snail houses' scattered all through them.

My suspicion is that California arose long after the great
flood out of the salty ocean water by and through the force of
an underground fire....It is certain California is a pure coagula-
tion of thousands of things and materials, of which the least is
soil and hardly any water.

And yet, he wrote: "I have not yet had a sad or melan-
cholic hour and pray to God for his care in sending me to this
place instead of other Spanish missions."

In 1761, he composed (in Latin) and sent to his brother
the following poem:

> Huge land, California, and pressing on a great sea;
> But greater the earth to which it lies subjected.
> It is cultivated by a small people: smaller than the people
> Is that harvest of joy which it renders to the cultivator.
> Choice soil and choice sky, and breastband, the dweller has,
> Small portions of wool over the flesh, and hide over the bones,
> A bow with darts, and all equipment is short;
> And one labors to and return hither and thither.
> Living on garbage; drink evil smelling and standing water;
> Alas, how badly are thirst and hunger drivers for these!
> No spring, no rain flowing from the sky,
> They wholly gather hard rocks and only thorn-buster.
> But there is doubt, and it cannot
> Be said, which is more covered –
> The land with thorns or the people with vices.
> If perhaps there is some defect in quantities, forgive,
> For here is no step to Parnassus.

Yet Padre Baegert cried when he was expelled from
California in 1768, and he spent the rest of his life missing and
writing about the land which "God did not create."

In 1766, while Lamberto Hostell was Padre Visitador, a *Charges*
series of charges against the California Jesuits was presented to *Against the*
the court at Madrid and then forwarded to Mexico City. The *Jesuits*
charges probably originated with Manuel Ocio, and a copy of
the document was made and sent to Loreto. There were seven
accusations:

First: that the soldiers are paid only in merchandise and
that at excessive prices ordered by the padres.

Second: that the Señor Capitán does not actually command

the troops and that the padres fill all the vacancies, hiring and firing at their arbitrary wish – on which account the soldiers do only the father's bidding.

Third: that the padres hinder work at the mines, that they obtain the silver which is taken out because the miners have to buy corn and other supplies necessary for their existence from the missions at excessive prices, etc.

Fourth: that the padres secretly work the mines on their own account.

Fifth: that with the silver thus obtained, the padres engage in commerce with Manila galleons and with Dutch ships which are accustomed to arrive on these coasts.

Sixth: that the Indians work hard for the padres' benefit and are paid only with cooked corn.

Seventh: that the padres prevent the entrance of españoles to the missions because they wish to keep the Indians in ignorance of the fact that they have a king and so that they will continue to believe that they have no superiors other than the missionaries themselves.

These charges were refuted by Padre Hostell and Captain Rivera, but the tide of sentiment against the Jesuits was too strong to stop.

Events in Europe Determine The Fate of California

Changes in Europe exacerbated the Jesuit's problem. Emerging from the Middle Ages, European nations were developing technologies enabling them to conquer foreign lands and import their riches. With the Age of Enlightenment, scientific and technical studies were encouraged, piety and scholasticism began to fall out of fashion, and people began to be less concerned with preparing for the next life than with profiting during the present one. This new philosophy began to erode the power of the Catholic Church.

The Jesuits had become a successful, wealthy, influential, and powerful order. Royal governments began to view the Jesuits as a rival for temporal power. As the stature of the order grew, it became the object of gossip and slander all over the world.

In 1759, the Bourbon Carlos III was crowned king of Spain. That same year in Portugal all of the wealth of the Jesuits was confiscated, and they were expelled from the country and from all Portuguese colonies. At the same time, France also began the process of expelling the Jesuit order. After the disastrous Seven Years War (1756-1763), for control of Germany and supremacy in colonial North American and India, Carlos III urgently needed to replenish the Spanish treasury, and the wealth of the Jesuits in Spain and its colonies was a tempting source of riches. The governments of both countries appropriated the wealth of the Jesuits, which went into the national coffers.

Books were written and gossip circulated throughout Europe and New Spain, charging the Jesuits with just about everything imaginable. Although never explicitly written in the accusations against them, the Spanish government resented and feared the foreign priests who were in charge of missions in their colonies. In California at that time, eight of the sixteen missionaries were middle European, from Germany, Austria, Bohemia, Bavaria, and Alsace.

One advisor told the king that the Jesuits questioned his legitimate right to the throne of Spain. This was the last straw, and the king, encouraged by his ministers, decided to expel the Jesuits from the Spanish realm.

Word of the growing Spanish animosity reached California, and the padres responded by offering to turn over some or all of their missions to another order so that their native charges could continue to receive Christian supervision. In the previous four years, plagues of locusts had wiped out the few crops and fodder for the animals; no money had been forthcoming from the royal treasury; and drought on the mainland had cut off available supplies from that source. The thought of giving up the struggle against such great odds could not have been entirely unwelcome. There was no response to the Jesuits' offer to give up their missions.

In 1765 King Carlos appointed José de Gálvez, a petty nobleman and judge in Madrid, as Visitor General to New Spain. This new position outranked the viceroy. Gálvez was answerable only to the king, which gave him enormous power. He was commissioned to carry out the economic and governmental reforms in New Spain which the king had instituted in

Spain. Gálvez approached his task with zeal. He had two qualities that were valuable to the king: tremendous energy and fanatic loyalty to His Majesty.

Early in 1767, Carlos III finally initiated the procedures to expel the Jesuits from Spain and all its possessions. In México City, on June 24, 1767, the viceroy of New Spain, the Marquis de Croix, in the presence of the archbishop of México and high officials of his court, opened a sealed packet from the king which called for the immediate arrest and expulsion of the Jesuits from New Spain. His order was carried out secretly and efficiently by Visitor General Gálvez and the Spanish bureaucracy. The next day Jesuits were arrested in nearly all parts of New Spain. In many areas, they were put in chains and treated cruelly by the soldiers, and some lost their lives. They were all marched to Vera Cruz and put on ships to be taken to Italy where, King Carlos said, "the pope can take care of them." California was too remote for the Jesuits there to be a part of this initial expulsion. When the king's orders arrived in New Spain in June of 1767, Captain Gaspar de Portolá, a thirty-year veteran career officer, was appointed governor of California. Portolá was ordered to proceed to the port of Matanchel and then to California to complete the mission of expelling the Jesuits, bringing Franciscans to replace them as priests, and installing a civil government.

A Mysterious Ship In Puerto Escondido

In September of 1767, travelers from Loreto saw one of Manuel Ocio's ships in Puerto Escondido. When they approached the ship they recognized some sailors, but there were also five strange men in military uniforms aboard. These strangers refused an invitation to come ashore and would not answer any questions about their purpose or their destination, although they did reveal that a new governor, appointed to direct California affairs, would arrive soon with Franciscan friars for California missions. Then the ship sailed away.

This incident fueled much speculation in Loreto and among the California missions. The padres theorized that perhaps the viceroy had accepted their offer to give up all or part of their missions. Maybe, they thought, the Franciscans were to replace some of the Jesuits, and a new governor had been appointed because otherwise the Franciscans would not be given command of the presidio. Or perhaps the California Jesuits would be allowed to expand the mission chain northward or would even be transferred to other mission fields. They still had no idea of what was about to happen to them.

Captain Portolá made two attempts to cross the gulf in July and August, but the winds were unfavorable. In September, one advance party of soldiers did get to California – the mysterious ship in Puerto Escondido – but when Portolá didn't join them, they returned to the mainland.

Portolá finally set out in October of 1767, but the winds blew the ship south, and he spent forty-four days at sea before sighting the peninsula at Cabo San Lucas in December. Everyone was glad to finally go ashore, but the captain was uncertain of his reception in California. He had heard the stories circulating about the wealth and power of the Jesuits there and was prepared to meet with organized, armed resistance. Padre Benno Ducrue, the last Padre Visitador, later wrote in his *Account of the Expulsion,* "the governor had come with no little fear. He had heard that the California neophytes were equipped with ten thousand muskets and a vast amount of powder in order to resist any attempt to invade their country."

Gaspar de Portolá Arrives in California

Portolá was relieved when Padre Ignacio Tirsch rode in from the mission at Santiago to Cabo San Lucas with a small, unarmed group, greeted him with courtesy, and offered to help him in any way he could. Even when the captain told him that he had been sent to arrest and expel the Jesuits, Padre Tirsch accepted the news calmly.

Captain Rivera happened to be nearby and was invited to join the conference. Miguel del Barco later wrote of their meeting:

> After having talked with the Santiago missionary and much more with Capitán Rivera – who knew the Jesuits to the core, their sentiments and their loyalty – (Governor Portolá) became entirely persuaded that he had nothing to fear from the padres, not the slightest thing, and that they would obey the king's orders to the letter even if no troops accompanied them, even a single communication from the Lord Viceroy declaring His Majesty's decision would have been sufficient...Captain Rivera

was able to give those assurances with the security of knowing about the Jesuits' offer to renounce all their mission provinces and especially California. Furthermore, this same captain knew full well that, in case this universal renunciation was not accepted, the California missionaries had attempted shortly after to give up at least the two southern missions (San José del Cabo and Santiago), those with the best land and most fame for their riches.

Padre Tirsch sent to Santiago for horses for Portolá's party, and a rider was sent to Loreto to request additional horses and saddles to be started south to meet the party on its twelve-day journey to Loreto.

Portolá, who had believed the rumors that he would find the padres' coffers overflowing with gold and pearls, was startled at the poverty of the first mission he saw at Santiago. There were no armed natives waiting to repel any threat to the Jesuit government, and he realized how dependent these people were, both spiritually and physically, on their priest. He appointed a soldier to supervise mission activities in the absence of the padre, as he would do in all the other California missions, until the arrival of the Franciscans.

The trip north to Loreto was an education for the new governor. He rode with Captain Rivera who was able to give him an idea of the practical problems of his new responsibilities. Portolá saw for himself the barren land and the great distances between habitable locations. He experienced the heat, the thorns, the rocks, the lack of water. They marched for ten hours a day and arrived in Loreto on December 17, 1767.

His Spanish soldiers suffered greatly on the trip, and Portolá later sent half of them back to the mainland. He wrote to his superiors:

...they are incapacitated by so much fatigue and work. This is not the case, I assure you, with the Californias, for I found both men and animals in very good condition...It is certain, Sir, that in order to carry out the service in this country, it is more necessary to have a cowboy than a soldier to care for so much livestock by day and to guard it by night. For this reason, I find it necessary to retain as many soldiers as possible from said company and even, temporarily, the two officers who serve as captain and lieutenant.

When he arrived in Loreto, Portolá presented himself to the Padre Procurador Lucas Ventura. He commandeered for himself the house that Jaime Bravo had built opposite the church, and sent a letter to Padre Benno Ducrue, who was then acting as superior of the California missions from his post at Misión de Guadalupe, 150 miles north of Loreto. Padre Ducrue had been born in Bavaria and was described as "tall, slim, fair skinned, with two moles on his cheek." Portolá asked him to come to Loreto immediately, because he was too tired to travel any further. After sending messages to the other padres notifying them of Portolá's arrival and telling them to leave their missions and come to Loreto as soon as possible, Padre Ducrue said a sad final goodbye to his native charges and set out the next day for Loreto.

Padre Ducrue arrived in Loreto on Christmas Eve. Governor Portolá waited to present the royal decree until after the religious ceremonies of that night were performed. Ducrue (who always called himself Father Visitor in his reports) wrote:

The next day out of regard for the feast nothing was said about the decree, but instead a letter written by the Viceroy of Mexico was handed to the Father Visitor. It informed him about the coming of the new Governor, asking that the missionaries receive him well and see to it that their Indians did likewise. This was done in accordance with the orders received.

The next day, the Feast of Saint Stephen, all the missionaries were summoned after the sacred functions. The following were present: Father Visitor (Padre Benno Ducrue), Father Rector (Padre Lucas Ventura) and his companion (Padre Javier Franco), also a lay-brother (Juan Villavieja); a royal ensign, his secretary and a sergeant. The royal decree containing the order of our expulsion was read and immediately signed by those present.

Among other orders imparted by the royal decree, one forbade our fathers to celebrate Mass publicly or participate in any other ecclesiastic functions. Immediately after the reading of the decree, they were to be locked in their rooms and guarded by soldiers until they could set out on their voyage. The Governor, however, saw fit to dispense from such a rigorous measure. His motives were the failure of our successors to arrive and especially, as he told me several times, to prevent unrest among the people.

The only part of the order which he put into effect was to take over the keys and henceforth take charge of the presidio, which up to that time had been administered by us. Further, he requested an account from the Father Treasurer (Padre Ventura) and received from him the immense riches which our enemies claimed we had hidden in California. The treasure in the form of gold and silver amounted to about seven thousand pesos; it belonged in part to the presidio and in part to the various missions. The rest, owned by the presidio, derived from the annual allotment to pay the salaries of the soldiers...and amounted in value to sixty thousand pesos...It was in the form of linen, silk cloth, and other goods and tools used by people in such circumstances. Excluded from this reckoning is the meat and wheat of which at the time there was a negligible amount in the Loreto warehouse, so much so that the Governor immediately ordered a supply of such brought in from the neighboring missions. These were the vast riches which had been promised to the king – no less than the equivalent of four million pesos. Then the Chaplain (Don Pedro Fernandez, a secular priest accompanying Portolá), in the name of the Bishop, took over the goods and keys of the Loreto church.

The Expulsion   After the decree was signed and the process of inventory and transfer of goods started, it was five weeks before the expulsion could be completed. It took time for the padres to travel from their distant missions to Loreto. At San Borja an epidemic had struck the native population, so Padre Wenceslaus Linck was allowed an extra week to nurse and administer last rites to the stricken. At Santa Gertrudis, Padre George Retz, who was overweight and had difficulty traveling at any time, had badly injured his foot and had to be carried on a litter by teams of his neophytes over the more than 200 miles to Loreto.

On February 3, 1768, the time had finally come to leave. Once again, Captain Portolá ignored his orders and allowed the priests to celebrate Mass. Padre Ducrue's account of the last day is touching:

Before committing themselves to the sea, Father George Retz celebrated the Mass and Father Visitor (Ducrue) preached to the assembled people. Nearly all received communion. Father Lambert Hostell, a most zealous missionary of California for nearly thirty-three years, held a second religious ceremony in honor of Our Lady of Sorrows. Father Hostell had not only won many souls to God, but had behind him the memory of a most virtuous life. On this occasion, the Mexican missionary, Father Juan Diez, renowned for the innocence of his life and zeal for souls, preached the sermon. Thus was the divine assistance and protection implored. The day was taken up until night came.

Governor Portolá thought it would be wiser to have the Jesuits embark at night when there might be fewer spectators. The strategy didn't work. Ducrue wrote:

We took a light supper and then visited the church again, praying for California and imploring God's mercy and assistance. As we returned to the shore, behold we were surrounded on all sides by the people, the Spanish soldiers among them. Some knelt on the sand to kiss our hands and feet, others knelt with arms outstretched in the form of a cross and publicly pleading for pardon. Others tenderly embraced the missionaries, bidding them farewell and wishing them a happy voyage through loud weeping and sobbing. This sad spectacle moved the Governor to tears. This royal official had come prejudiced against the Jesuits by the most serious accusations. But now he saw the very opposite of the calumnies spread against us, and could see with his own eyes how false they were. He never ceased to deplore the lot which befell him and to sympathize with us. And although he could not reverse the orders given to him, he did make clear as far as he could how reluctantly he carried them out. And hence we should be grateful to this Catholic gentleman and discrete judge that through his compassion he lessened our suffering, whereas other royal officials (contrary to the orders of the king) gave free rein to their inveterate hatred for the Society of Jesus...The Governor not only treated us at all times with kindness as the king ordered, but even generously provided us with everything necessary for our journey.

It is time for our departure. The Indians gladly carry on their shoulders the missionaries to the waiting ship in repayment for having been brought by them to Christ. Farewell, beloved California; farewell, beloved Indians. We leave you not of our own free will, but by a higher decision. True we are separated physically, but we shall always preserve the memory of you in our hearts, which neither time, nor forgetfulness, no, not even death itself, will ever efface...We go with joy in our hearts, because we have been held worthy to suffer contumely for the name of Jesus. We helped you as much as divine providence allowed, bringing you along the paths which lead to life eternal.

Such were the words of the missionaries as they boarded the launch. We recited the Litanies of Our Lady of Loreto until at midnight we went aboard the ship at a distance in the harbor.

Instead of leaving immediately, the missionaries were forced by lack of wind to spend another day becalmed off the shore of Loreto gazing back at their beloved California. Finally, on February 5th, a favorable wind sprang up, and *La Concepción,* which had been built on that shore by Padre Miguel del Barco, sailed him and his fellow Jesuits away forever.

Chapter Three

FRANCISCANS, DOMINICANS, AND SPANISH GOVERNMENT IN LORETO

The departure of the Jesuits from Loreto was the beginning of a period marked by conflict between church and state, the deterioration of the peninsular mission system, and acceleration of the extinction of the original inhabitants of Baja California.

THE FRANCISCANS – 1767-1773

In 1219, Saint Francis of Assisi founded the Franciscan Order of missionary priests. The order was dedicated to the conversion of nonbelievers to Christianity. Like the Jesuits, the Franciscan priests were sent all over the world, and by 1535 there were seventy Franciscan monasteries and nunneries in New Spain.

In 1767, when the command was received in New Spain from the Spanish king to expel the Jesuits, his Visitor General José de Gálvez invited the Spanish Franciscan priests of the College of San Fernando near Mexico City to go to California. They were to take over the present mission system on the California peninsula and, more importantly, to expand that system to the north in order to prevent further inroads from the Russians and English into Spanish Alta California. At that time, Spain claimed most of the western half of what is now the United States.

Again, a remarkable man was to lead a California adventure. Gálvez appointed a priest with the religious zeal and leadership qualities of a Salvatierra or Kino as head of the Franciscan missionaries in California. Junípero Serra was born on the Spanish Island of Mallorca in 1713. He was educated on

Padre Junípero Serra (1713-1784)

119

Junípero Serra. Copy of an original painting, now lost, by Rev. José Mosqueda. Preserved in the Santa Barbara Mission.

Mallorca at the Lullian University of Palma and for fifteen years taught philosophy there. He welcomed the opportunity for active service in New Spain. After a voyage that lasted ninety-nine days, he and eighteen other priests landed in Vera Cruz in December of 1749.

Vera Cruz, on the east coast of Mexico, was the port of entry to New Spain for all the European missionaries. In his enthusiasm for his mission in this new land, Serra insisted on walking from Vera Cruz to Mexico City. During his arduous journey of over 200 miles to the central plateau of New Spain, an insect bit his leg, and the bite became infected. The wound went unattended and never healed properly. He was to suffer constant pain in this leg for the rest of his life,

Padre Serra and his friend and former pupil in Mallorca, Padre Francisco Palóu, volunteered for the missions in the Sierra Gorda in northern New Spain and spent eight years there. When they were returned to the College of San Fernando, Padre Serra became known as an eloquent and ardent preacher. In the pulpit, he illustrated his sermons by striking himself on the chest with a stone or applying a burning torch to his chest and shoulders or scourging himself with a chain.

After nine years at the college, Serra gladly accepted the challenge of replacing the Jesuits in California. The group of sixteen Franciscans, led by Serra, with Palóu as second in command, proceeded to Tepíc where they were delayed for many months because of storms at sea and a misunderstanding with the viceroy.

While Serra and his group of sixteeen Franciscan missionaries were waiting in Tepic for a ship to take them to Loreto, the commissary general of the Franciscans apparently misunderstood their situation and asked the viceroy to send another party of Franciscans from Jalisco to Baja California. The Jalisco priests left on October 19, 1767, on one of Manuel Ocio's ships from the port of Matanchel, at the same time that Portolá sailed to deport the Jesuits. However, the Franciscans were blown south and spent eighty-eight days at sea before finally coming ashore near Cabo San Lucas. Their leader, Padre Manuel Zuzárregui, appointed a priest to each mission as they walked to Loreto, where they arrived on March 12, 1768.

The First Franciscans Arrive in California

Two weeks later, on April 1st, Serra's contingent of Franciscans arrived in Loreto. Serra's group had finally left from San Blas on March 14, 1768, on the *Concepción,* the ship that had transported the Jesuits from Loreto, and they crossed the sea directly to Loreto in only two weeks. They arrived on the evening of Good Friday and went ashore on Holy Saturday. Governor Portolá met them on the beach, and they proceeded directly to the church to give thanks for their safe arrival.

Padre Serra carried orders from the viceroy, which

declared that their group was to be in charge of the California missions. The viceroy's order recalled the Jaliscan priests to serve in Sonora. There must have been at least some grumbling from the Jalisco friars who had endured three months at sea in a small boat followed by the arduous trek from the tip of the peninsula to Loreto, only to be told they had been victims of a bureaucratic mistake. They sailed away from Loreto on April 10th, having been there less than a month.

Conditions in California Upon Serra's Arrival

On the day they arrived, Governor Portolá read a letter from the viceroy to Padres Serra and Palóu ordering that all the churches, sacristies, and furniture of the Jesuits must be turned over to Serra's group, but he stipulated that the management of the missions be left in the hands of the soldiers whom Portolá had appointed after the Jesuits left. Padre Serra accepted the order without argument, but Padre Palóu recognized that this disposition of control would make it difficult or impossible to administer the missions. Portolá explained that he had turned the missions over to the soldiers to protect the property from destruction by the natives. He believed then that when the king's representative José de Gálvez arrived in California, as he was expected to do in a few months, full control of the missions would be restored to the Franciscans.

On Easter Sunday, April 3rd, Padre Junípero Serra preached the sermon to the assembled congregation of native converts and Hispanics in the Loreto mission church. He told them that the Franciscans had come to labor among them, as far as possible, in the same manner as the Jesuit padres had done. Two days later, Serra designated Padre Fernando Parrón to remain with him in Loreto and assigned the other padres to their respective missions. Padre Francisco Palóu was assigned to San Javier, and the other priests accompanied him there and then proceeded to their own missions.

The Franciscans were to be the spiritual administrators of thirteen missions with a neophyte population of 6,585 souls. In addition, they were given spiritual charge of the presidio in the south as well as of the presidio and capital of Loreto, which at that time had a population of four hundred, including native converts, sailors, soldiers and their families. At each mission the soldiers turned over to the missionary the church and sacristy with all the vestments, religious articles, and furniture, the dwelling, and the household goods, except in Loreto. There, the Spanish governor retained the house that had been built by Jaime Bravo, and Padres Serra and Parrón were obliged to board with him.

By the time the Franciscans arrived, the missions they had inherited were in deplorable shape. The soldiers left in charge were untrained and uninterested in maintaining the missions or their native charges. They didn't have the skill or energy to cope with the lack of water, plagues of locusts, and other problems of supplying food in a barren and rocky land. Many of them had sold off hundreds of cattle and what agricultural products there were to line their own pockets. The padres could no longer offer food and security to the natives, and their loss of power cost them respect. It was clear that unless the Franciscans could regain control of the temporal authority of the missions, it would be only a few years before the seventy years of labor and sacrifice by the Jesuits would be undone.

1768 was indeed an eventful year in Loreto. In February the Jesuits had departed after seventy years in California. On March 12th the first group of Franciscan friars had arrived and departed quickly when the second group, headed by Junípero Serra sailed into port on April 1st. Then, on July 5th, the most powerful man in New Spain, Visitor General Gálvez, came to Loreto to see what could be done with California.

José de Gálvez came to Baja California to carry out the *José de* orders of the king of Spain, orders which had an impact on the *Gálvez in* history of Loreto and Baja California that lasted for more than *California* a century. He had been sent to New Spain by King Carlos III as his direct representative, empowered to make decisions and initiate programs in the king's name. As a result of years of war in Europe, Spain was in desperate financial straits and needed more revenue from its colonies. The rulers of Spain had learned that the cheapest and most effective way to conquer new territory was to send missionaries instead of soldiers. The main purpose of Gálvez' visit to California was to initiate expeditions to Alta California to establish a mission system there.

Gálvez was born in Spain in 1720. He was an energetic man who took his responsibilities to Carlos III very seriously and raised more income for the royal coffers from the Spanish colony of New Spain than had ever been done before. Gálvez was also severely mentally unstable during several periods in his life.

After touring the missions and seeing for himself the results of the mismanagement and dishonesty of the soldier commissioners, on August 12, 1768, Gálvez issued a series of edicts. One edict ordered the soldiers to turn over all mission property to the missionaries and to send in their accounts through the padres, who were to examine and sign them. This order, returning absolute control of the missions to the Franciscans, was executed everywhere except at Loreto. Loreto was to be the headquarters of Spanish administration and for the established mission system in Baja California and the colonization and development of missions in Alta California, and therefore it would be considered a government center rather than a mission.

Gálvez and Serra Work Together

Gálvez then turned his attention to carrying out the orders of the king to send expeditions to San Diego and Monterey in Alta California. He was in Santa Ana, a silver mining town south of La Paz, in October of 1768, and he sent for Padre Serra to leave Loreto and join him there to confer on the steps to be taken to accomplish this expansion of Spanish sovereignty to the north.

Gálvez informed Serra that he planned to send two ships and two land expeditions to San Diego and Monterey in Alta California to insure the success of the enterprise. Two royal packet boats, the *San Carlos* and the *San Antonio*, were expected soon in La Paz. Padre Serra immediately volunteered to join one of the expeditions. In order to cut down on the expenses of the expansion, they decided to take what they could from the old missions. Together they collected vestments and other church articles from the southern missions and packed them aboard the *San Carlos,* which had arrived early in December, Gálvez boasting that he was a better packer than Serra.

On January 6, 1769, Padre Serra blessed the ship and

Padre Fernando Parrón, who was to be its spiritual leader, and on the 10th the *San Carlos* sailed from the harbor of La Paz for Monterey.

Serra then left for Loreto, collecting goods from the missions on the way for the next expeditions. Padre Palóu wrote:

> So great was the zeal of the illustrious lord inspector (Gálvez) that he wished to adorn the new missions as though they were cathedral churches, because, as he said to the Rev. Fr. Presidente (Serra), it was proper to decorate them as much as possible, and that the vestments should be of the richest, in order that the pagans might see how God, our Lord, is worshipped, and with what splendor and cleanliness the holy Sacrifice of the Mass is offered up, and how the house of our God and Lord is ornamented, so that this itself might move them to embrace our Holy Faith. To this end he charged the Rev. Fr. Presidente, as soon as he arrived at Loreto, to take from the government warehouse whatever should be necessary, and also from the sacristy of Loreto, and to order everything made

Impression of a Spanish Governor and his Lady, by Padre Ignacio Tirsch. Tirsch illustration: Courtesy of Glen Dawson.

which he deemed suitable for the church in the missions, and on passing through the missions of the north to take from them whatever he thought they could spare.

Padre Serra found absolutely nothing in the Loreto warehouse, so he turned to the church. Padre Palóu listed the things he took from the sacristy of Loreto:

...five yards of scarlet damask, five of China silk, three of blue taffeta, two cinctures of gold cloth with tassels, five yards of green cloth with gold flowers for a chausible, and the necessary lining of scarlet taffeta, gold lace and fringe of the same for a cape, a sash and its lining which he ordered made, some more of the same for another cape with another sash which was made over, and a copper-plate with an engraving of the Immaculate Conception in tortoise-shell frame.

Serra Sets
Out for Alta
California

On Easter Sunday of 1769, Padre Juniper Serra preached his last sermon in the Church of Our Lady of Loreto and three days later left Loreto for good, accompanied by two soldiers and one servant. His diary tells it best:

I left my mission and the Royal Presidio in California, having previously visited the missions of the South.

I departed from Loreto on the 28th March 1769, the third day after Easter. I had performed all the ceremonies of Holy Week with all solemnity and every devotion possible. On Easter Sunday, together with the High Mass, I had preached my farewell sermon, exactly one ecclesiastical year from the day I had first preached in this church and had taken charge of the administration of spiritual affairs of this mission.

On each of the two following days, I recited Holy Mass in honor of Our Lady of Loreto, praying for her protection on this very difficult journey. After the mass of the third day (Tuesday), I sallied forth upon the trail.

The first day's travel was to bring me to the mission of San Francisco Javier de Biaundó. Nothing worth noting occurred to me on this journey, and as everyone is familiar with this route, I shall say nothing about it.

March 29, 30, 31.

I remained at this station for a variety of reasons. To justify this stay of three days the first cause is quite enough, namely, the love of us two, Fray Francisco Palóu and myself, an ancient and enduring love.

The Padre Minister of this station was my pupil. He is a faculty professor and Commissary of the Holy Office. He was chosen by our College to succeed me as Presidente of these missions, in case of my death or lengthy absence. This last circumstance, therefore, is a second and very sufficient reason to prolong my stay. It was necessary to agree upon the measures to be taken by him – under the responsibility which he assumes which my departure necessitates – in order to assure the stability of these missions. It was likewise urgent to brief our plans for the coming visit to Loreto of the illustrious Visitor General.

The third motive – the one that I should like to underscore and call particular attention to – is this: When I left Loreto I took for my entire journey of this long jornada absolutely nothing but a loaf of bread and a piece of cheese! During my entire year at that place, as regards temporal affairs, I was simply the passing guest of Señor Trillo, the Royal Commissary. His generosity at the moment of my departure provided me with a cheese sandwich!

Happily, the Reverend Father at this mission has, by his loving providence, amply supplied my indigence. He was so generous with food, with clothing, and with other articles for use on my journey, that I could scarcely describe them in detail, much less refuse to accept them. Even so – sinner that I be – I must confess that I enjoy my creature comforts. May God recompense him for his great benevolence!

Concerning the overland expedition, His Eminence commissioned Don Fernando Rivera y Moncada to arrange for everything that was required. Captain Rivera had been stationed in California from the time of the Jesuits.

On September 29, I celebrated a votive Mass in honor of St. Joseph, who was chosen as Patron of both expeditions, maritime and overland. Two days later, Rivera issued his requisitions and started his trek to the California Ports, as the King had commanded. On leaving Loreto, he stopped first at San Javier.

Proceeding without the least variation, he began there and

continued in the others to draft everything worthwhile that they possessed. Although his requirements were exorbitant, it was all for God and King.

Rivera's party of twenty-five experienced soldiers from the Loreto presidio and about forty natives from the missions of Santa María and San Borja scouted the best land route to San Diego. Along the way, they stripped the northern peninsular missions as Serra had done in the south and arrived in San Diego with more supplies from the peninsula for the Alta California missions.

Padre Serra left San Javier on April 1st. His friend Palóu urged Serra to let him go in his stead because of the painful condition of Serra's leg and foot. After many years Serra still suffered the result of the insect bite he had incurred on his arrival in Mexico. Palóu wrote:

> Seeing the sore and swelling on his leg and foot, I could not restrain my tears as I considered all he would have to suffer from the rough and dreadful roads which are known as far as the frontier, and on those that were unknown and to be discovered later, with no other doctor or surgeon than God, and with no other protection for the foot than the sandal; for he never used shoes or stockings or boots on the roads of New Spain or of the two Californias.

Serra replied that he had "placed all my confidence in God, through whose goodness I hope to be permitted to reach not only San Diego to plant and establish the standard of the holy Cross at that port, but Monterey as well."

Anyone familiar with Alta California history knows Padre Serra carried out his plans.

Gaspar de Portolá Leads the Second Land Expedition

Governor Portolá's party left Loreto on the second trek to Alta California on May 15, 1769. They followed the route scouted by Rivera, and on July 1st all the parties were reunited in San Diego. The two ships that reached San Diego had lost most of their crew to scurvy, and the land expeditions lost most of their Baja California natives to desertion.

Gálvez in Loreto

On April 22, 1769, Inspector General Gálvez arrived in Loreto from the south.

He saw at once that Loreto, the capital, was in sad shape.

Without regular supplies from the mainland and with little land or water to grow food, many families had left. Because of its history, its harbor, the presidio and warehouses, Gálvez resolved to restore its prosperity and population. He designed an elaborate plan for the reconstruction of the California capital, with a native settlement and a Spanish town. He ordered that one hundred native families be sent to live in Loreto when the settlement was finished. The plan was never implemented. After Gálvez left, Padre Palóu settled twenty-five native families at Loreto, and this was all that was ever accomplished to carry out the Visitor General's project. Gálvez had failed to consider that there were no resources available to build or support the beautiful capital city of California that he had envisioned.

In his decree of August 12, 1769, Gálvez offered California land to Spanish colonists of good character on the condition that they make improvements and pay a small annual tax to the king. A few discharged soldiers and sailors of Loreto took advantage of this offer, but there were not many other takers for the next fifty years.

The legislative decrees that Gálvez wrote during his stay in Baja California were utopian but unrealizable, although no one questioned whether it was possible to impose the Spanish colonial system on the fragile land of the peninsula. It quickly became clear that Gálvez' reforms collided with the reality of Baja California, and the mission system entered an irreparable process of decay. The missions had begun to lose their Indian populations during the Jesuit period. With the expulsion of the Jesuits and the temporal administration of the soldier-commissioners during the governorship of Gaspar de Portolá, this process accelerated.

Gálvez wrote, at great length, many other suggestions to the Franciscans for improving the missionary system. Even though he spent time in Baja California and traveled over the barren terrain, he failed to grasp that methods that were implemented in the rest of New Spain were impossible and impractical in the peninsular desert. Most of his edicts were never carried out, but the attempt to do so left a legacy of strife between the missionaries and the governors who blamed each other for not being able to accomplish the impossible.

Gálvez also reduced the soldiers' pay and raised the price of goods sold at the store, creating an even heavier burden on the missions. After issuing another flurry of orders, all of them impractical, Gálvez left Loreto on May 1, 1769. He had accomplished the king's orders to begin the settlement of Alta California, but he left the peninsula in an even poorer condition than when he arrived.

Padre Palóu as Head of Baja California Missions

Padre Palóu turned Mission San Javier over to Padre Juan Escudero and moved to Loreto with twenty-five families who had volunteered to accompany him. Palóu wrote:

> As soon as I took charge, I discovered that the mission at Loreto could not subsist and that all the others in a short time would decline, because, owing to the new price-lists, the value of meat, tallow, fat, figs, wine and brandy had very much decreased, and these articles were the only products of the missions, and from the sale of which the Indians were provided with cloth to cover themselves, and with corn in those years when none was harvested, which harvest generally does not yield enough. Despite my misgivings, I tried to await the results, so that with the experience made I might approach the inspector-general for relief, though I well knew that it would be difficult to obtain it while the pay of the soldiers was reduced.

Palóu's task of maintaining the Baja California missions was further complicated by a series of epidemics which wiped out more of the native population.

On October 23, 1769, a new royal commissary, Antonio López de Toledo, arrived in Loreto with an order from Gálvez that was almost the last straw for Palóu. The royal commissary told Palóu that Gálvez had ordered him:

> In the work of taking out salt to the wharves of Carmen Island and in other work in the service of the king, the commissary should employ the Indians of Mission Loreto, and from the other missions others that might be needed, and to give them on account of the royal treasury the usual subsistence, without other wages, because all subjects who are truly such, have the obligation of serving the king.

Palóu wrote:

Gálvez told the commissary that he should populate the salt works of Carmen Island with enough people, erect a warehouse there for the storing of salt, and take precaution that all the barks which had to return brought the salt to San Blas. The commissary intimated these instructions to me and said that he would soon have to execute them, and that the Indians should, therefore, quickly make ready, and that, as there were few at Loreto, I should ask the missionaries of the neighboring missions to send laborers for the royal service which must have a sufficient number. Hearing this, and considering that in the adjoining missions the Indians had become very scarce on account of the epidemic mentioned before, that they were needed for necessary work, and that, if the land were not cultivated, they would have to purchase corn from the warehouse at so high a price, that to the discredit of the missionaries great damage, if not the destruction of the missions, must result therefrom. I wanted to prevent it. For that reason I asked the royal commissary what wages would be given to the Indians? He answered: "None; that as the inspector had commanded in the instructions, only rations would be allowed to those that worked and during the time of that work." I asked him further, who should have to support their wives and families? Who should have to give them clothing, and who should have to maintain them if they were sick? To all of which he replied, "The missions." Well, if the missions have to maintain and clothe them, it is necessary that they work for the missions; and therefore, as long as they are not paid the six dollars a month for their labor, as the inspector has ordered in the price-list which he left, I cannot furnish a single Indian, because I am convinced that the said instructions are erroneous, if not fictitious, for in them no mention is made of the wages which a few months before have been assigned them, and therefore he should suspend the execution of the regulations which he claimed to possess.

Palóu conferred with the Governor-elect Matías de Armona, who had arrived in Loreto on June 12, 1769. Armona tried to help where he could. However, the new governor had already sized up the situation in California and determined that it would be impossible for him to govern effectively and would probably end his political career if he tried. He had already petitioned to return to the mainland, and his request was granted.

Palóu then sent a list of fifteen petitions to Inspector General Gálvez. Among them, he asked that the natives be paid six dollars a month, as had been promised, instead of having to work for rations only and that payment be made from the Pious Fund to clothe the natives:

> The tenth petition is that the governor and commissary should not meddle with the temporalities entrusted to the Fathers by his Lordship; for the royal commissary, Antonio López de Toledo, came with the impression that everything that existed at the missions was at his disposal, and that the Fathers were his inferiors; and he said another thing, that if the Fathers did not send him what he wanted, he would come with soldiers and would take off the lock from the granaries and would carry away the contents by force.

> The eleventh petition is that, as to the garden which his Lordship has added to the temporal property of Mission Loreto with the obligation that the Father take care that its fruits are delivered to the governor and to the royal commissary, he should order his obligation revoked, because from it might result much friction between those gentlemen and the Father, as to whether he took good care or not, whether or not all that it produced was delivered; besides no Father stationed there would take charge if the said gentlemen are the first who must be regaled with what the garden produces.

(The garden had two fig and six olives trees, some old grape vines, some cotton plants, and a few pomegranates.)

He also asked that the governor and the commissary be given separate quarters from the priests, since the annoyances of the temporal and spiritual factions sharing the same quarters were mounting daily. All the other petitions were related to the welfare of the native converts whose condition was steadily deteriorating.

Gálvez by this time had gone mad and was locked up in a mission in northern New Spain. He claimed to have direct communication with Saint Francis of Assisi and called himself king of Prussia and sometimes king of Sweden. He proposed to end insurrection by bringing six hundred gorilla apes from Guatemala, put them in uniform and send them to fight against insurgents. He remained sequestered, at times in a wooden cage, for six months. He did not read Palóu's petition or grant any of the requests.

A new governor of California, Felipe Barri, was appointed and arrived in Loreto in March 1771 with letters from the viceroy announcing that new missionaries were being sent to California and that money to support them and build new missions was being sent out of the Pious Fund. The viceroy also noted that he was donating a rich vestment to the Loreto church.

The funds for the establishment of the missions in Alta California and the maintenance of the missions in Baja California came, not from the Spanish government, but from the Pious Fund which had been established by the Jesuits.* Relations between the new governor and the Franciscans began well but worsened swiftly under the pressures of the impossible tasks both had to carry out. The conflict grew to the point that Padre Palóu offered to turn over the administration of the mission at Todos Santos to the governor. In a report to his Franciscan superior, citing the aggressively hostile behavior of Governor Barri to the Franciscans, he suggested that one solution to the existing problem would be to turn some of the missions over to the Dominican order.

The Dominicans had already applied to the king of Spain for permission to send some of their missionaries to California, so Palóu's suggestion came at the time when this option was being discussed in Spain and New Spain.

In January of 1772, Palóu received an order from the head of the Franciscan missions in New Spain to send him a complete report on the status of all the peninsula missions. Palóu's report was extensive, and his description of Loreto at that point in its history is valuable. He wrote:

* An historical footnote: The Fund lost money over the years as the government appropriated large sums, and, in 1842, General Santa Anna withdrew the Pious Fund from the administration of the Bishop of California and gave the remaining funds to General Valencia, chief of staff of the Mexican army.

This was the first mission founded on the peninsula, and began on October 25, 1697, on which day possession was taken of the peninsula in the name of His Majesty and the first Mass was celebrated by the venerable Father Juan María Salvatierra of the Company of Jesus.

In the year 1698 Don Juan Caballero (a wealthy Spanish patron) endowed this mission with $10,000, like the foregoing. It was in charge of the Fathers of the Society of Jesus from its foundation until the beginning of February, 1768, when they left the peninsula. During this time, as is clear from the books, there were baptized six hundred and forty-six children and adults, Spaniards and Indians, and three hundred and twenty-nine were buried, while ninety-two marriages were celebrated, including Spaniards and Indians.

The College took charge on the first of April, 1768, the first missionaries being the Rev. Fr. Presidente, Fr. Junípero Serra, and his companion, Fr. Fernando Parrón. They controlled the spiritual affairs only, however, until they left for Monterey, when the Rev. Bachelor Pedro Fernandez, chaplain of the Guaymas expedition, came and took charge. He remained until the first of May 1769, when the mission returned to the care of the College, which administered it by order of the inspector-general in both temporal and spiritual affairs. From the departure of the Jesuit Fathers until the last of December 1771, there have been baptized seventy-six children of either Indian or Spanish parents. There have died one hundred and thirty-one persons; and twenty couples were married.

On the side of the mission towards the gulf is the royal presidio, and it alone separates the church and colegio, which are constructed of masonry with flat roofs, from the mission. At present the town is occupied by women and children of the soldiers only, because most soldiers are now at San Diego, Monterey, and the frontier. In front of the town is the suburb for the royal sailors, which likewise generally has only women, because their men are in the ships. The mission is situated in a beautiful and sufficiently extensive plain, which for want of water as well as for the scarcity of rain cannot be cultivated at all, wherefore to avoid the expense they provide themselves with water from wells which are tolerably wholesome. During the visitation which the inspector made, he found the mission deserted by the Indians, so that only nineteen families could be found; he therefore ordered the number to be increased to a hundred families by drawing 25 away from San Javier and the rest from other missions in the north. I put the decree into execution (partly) at once by taking 25 families from San Javier, but I suspended the removal of the rest, because there was not wherewith to maintain them.

The mission is comprised of forty families having one hundred and sixty persons. It has a rancho for cattle which are all scattered so that their number cannot be known, but it has no tame ones. It has thirty-two mares, fifty-four horses and fillies, seven mules, but neither sheep nor goats. It has no other revenue upon which to subsist and with which to clothe the Indians than the cattle which it can slaughter at the ranch. It is distant from San Javier eight leagues, the road over which for five leagues runs to the west and for three to the south; from San José de Comondú it is eighteen leagues, of which five run to the west and the rest towards the northeast, the greater part of which road goes over rough hills. From Santa Rosalia de Mulegé it is forty leagues traveling north and going up the coast of the gulf; within this territory are the cattle of the mission, which extends to the borders of that of Mulegé.

In the same report he described the sad state of affairs at San Javier, which had suffered a plague of locusts, lasting over a year, followed by drought. At that time, there were sixty families and seven widows living there.

Palóu reported that in all the thirteen missions the Franciscans had received there were only 5,094 natives, while at the beginning of their administration there had been over seven thousand. "It will be found then," he wrote, " that they have decreased by as many as two thousand and fifty-five by reason of the epidemics that have occurred in the three years and four months, and if they continue to decrease in that degree, Old California will be wiped out."

Answering a question from his superior about the orders Governor Armona had issued for the welfare of the Indians, Palóu replied:

As to the last orders, which Governor Armona issued for the welfare of the Indians, are carried out, I have to say that not even his name can be uttered before Governor Barri; for he says that he came to ruin the peninsula; and in the presence of Fr. Juan Escudero, who may have already reported it to Your Reverence, he said to me that he wanted no harmony with me, lest he perish like Armona had perished; and so, unless the information about said orders is demanded by his Excellency, there is no hope of seeing them executed; for I do not speak, because I consider it is time lost to increase the resentment.

It was probable that the isolation and heat of the peninsula, plus the knowledge that his career would no doubt end in this remote outpost, had worsened the paranoia and depression of Governor Barri to the point that he had become completely unreasonable. He hated the missionaries and did everything he could to make their lives miserable. Instructions from the viceroy to help the Franciscans only exacerbated his anger, because he thought they were prompted by complaints from the missionaries. He was right about that. In a report to his superior, Palóu had begged that he "...urge His Excellency to restrain the governor, so that he do not meddle any more with what does not concern him, and that he let us civilize, educate, and correct these poor neophytes, for otherwise the peninsula is on the point of destruction, and then it will not be possible to repair the damage."

Relief from the tensions and difficulties of dealing with a hostile governor and the accelerating decay of the lower California missions finally arrived for Padre Palóu and his fellow Franciscans. A royal decree from the king of Spain, dated April 8, 1770, commanded that Dominican priests be sent to lower California to replace the Franciscans there. The king thought it best not to have all of California under the control of one religious order, and so granted the petitions of the Dominicans to come to Baja California.

THE DOMINICANS – 1773-1854

The Dominican order was founded by Saint Dominic in 1215 and, like the Jesuits and Franciscans, was devoted to bringing Christianity to what they considered to be the uncivilized parts of the world. Like the Franciscans, the Dominican priests in New Spain were all Hispanic.

On October 14, 1772, the first ten Dominicans finally arrived in Loreto on the packet boat *La Loretana* and were warmly greeted by the Franciscans. However, their leader, Padre Juan Pedro Iriarte, was still at sea, and the newly arrived Dominicans had no authority to relieve the Franciscans until his arrival. Ten days after landing in Loreto, one of the Dominicans died. In order to lessen the expense of feeding the remaining nine in Loreto, two were sent to San José Comondú and two to San Javier. *The First Dominicans Arrive*

The two Dominicans in San Javier shortly discovered a plot by Governor Barri to cause a revolt among the neophytes there in order to harass the newly arrived Dominicans. The priests were able to warn Padre Palóu, who immediately recalled the Franciscan priests from that mission to Loreto. Padre Palóu wrote:

> On the very day on which the Fathers left, the Indians came to ask the Dominicans, who had remained, for permission to go to Loreto; and though at first they said they went on business, they at last explained that they went at the request of the governor to demand that the Franciscans be removed and the Dominicans be put in their place. The Dominicans showed them that there was no necessity for this as the Fathers had already gone away, and the Fr. Presidente had asked them to take charge of the mission, and so there was no reason to go. Nevertheless, they insisted on wanting to go to Loreto; for if they did not show themselves there on the morrow, for which day the governor had called them, he would punish them. "He will not do that; what you have to do," the Dominicans advised them, "is to write a letter telling that, since the Fathers had already gone away, you would not molest him about it, when you may be assured that he will say nothing" With that the revolt was quelled before it took shape; and though one of the

Dominican Fathers came and begged me to return the Fathers, as all was then quiet, or that I go, I could not go, nor allow the Fathers to go, not even when one of the ringleaders wrote to me asking pardon in his name and for the rest, in order to avoid the risk that anything should result therefrom, and I only permitted Fr. Murguía to go at the proper time to transfer the mission.

Padre Vicente Mora Appointed Dominican President

Almost five months later, on April 7, 1773, a ship arrived in Loreto bringing the news that the Dominican superior, Padre Presidente Iriarte, and two other Dominican priests had been in a shipwreck and drowned. Padre Vicente Mora received unofficial notice at the same time that he had been appointed presidente of the Dominican missionaries. He did not want to accept the responsibility until the official papers appointing him arrived, but in the meantime Padre Palóu gave him a complete accounting of all the possessions of the Franciscans in Baja California. Governor Barri had told the Dominicans that the Franciscans had robbed the missions of goods and cattle, and these meticulous accounts were to demonstrate to the Dominicans that the governor was, once again, trying to cause trouble for the Franciscans.

The Franciscan Accounting

Palóu's report included a description of the Loreto church:

A stone church 56 varas long and 7 wide, faced with brick, with a beamed roof; its choir of wood, and under it a baptismal chapel; and on the epistle side next to the baptistry, a chapel of Our Lady of Sorrows, also of stone, 27 varas long and 6 wide. Its iron-bar door faces the prebytery as does that of the Chapel.

A main altar of wood overlaid with gilt in the old style; it has three sections: in the first is the patroness of Our Lady of Loreto in her niche, and on the sides two canvases of Saint Joachim and Saint Ann.

In the second a canvas of the Virgin with Saint Ignatius, and on the sides two canvases of Saint Francis Borgia and Saint Francis Xavier.

In the third a canvas of the Holy Trinity, and on the sides two canvases of Saint John Nepomucene and Saint Thomas Martyr. Under the niche of the patroness is the tabernacle of gilt wood with a portrait of Saint Joseph framed in silver on the door. On the sides there are two small elongated canvases; one of the Three Martyrs of Japan; and on the other, Saint Aloyisius Gonzaga and Saint Stanislaus.

Side altars, presbytery, baptistry, chapel of Our Lady of Sorrows, sacristy, treasures (chalices, etc. of precious metals), ornaments, vestments, musical instruments, statues of our Lady of Loreto, Our Lady of the Rosary and two of Our Lady of Sorrows with their adornment and vestments and the offices are inventoried and described in detail as part of the Church.

Inventory of the house and utensils therein: A living area next to the Church, cloistered of stone and mortar, with its roofs, which has thirteen rooms on the ground floor and two above, and another small room with a door to the outside, and two small adobe corrals: one for chickens, which has a small room for them, and another for a pigeon roost; another corral next to the kitchen, with its little font for water and an oven for baking bread.

This list also contained a catalog of the 190 titles contained in the library, a listing of archives and registries, and an accounting of furniture, dishes, kitchen utensils, tools for the gardens, shops and pasture, and the launch and boat owned by the mission.

Finally, on May 12, 1773, a ship arrived in Loreto bearing eighteen Dominican priests and the official papers appointing Mora as presidente of the Dominican missionaries. After the priests were dispersed to their respective missions, the process of transferring the administration from Franciscans to Dominicans began. *Eighteen More Dominicans Arrive*

On May 24th, Padre Palóu was finally able to leave Loreto to join his friend, Junípero Serra, in Alta California. In addition to his accounting, Palóu left Padre Mora with a mass of elaborate instructions issued by Gálvez for the governor of the missions, plus all the decrees of the California governors and the formal petitions from the viceregal court, a list of cattle taken by Gálvez to sustain the new settlement of Alta California, and the inventory of all the missions and the royal storehouse which amounted to only ten thousand pesos. To the last of his days in Loreto, Palóu continued to be harassed by Governor Barri, and for two additional years the vindictive governor was successful in preventing the Franciscans from receiving their personal possessions, which were to have been sent to the north.

In 1775 the Dominicans built Mission Santo Domingo on the northern frontier and took charge of the rest of the missions. This was a difficult assignment. The natives were gradually dying off. At the same time, the viceregal government was sending its aid in droplets and with evident lack of interest in their fate.

Padre Mora Takes Over

The first Dominican presidente Padre Vicente Mora was born in the province of Cordoba in Spain in 1740. He served in Loreto from 1773 to 1781, when he retired due to poor health. Padre Mora tried initially to cooperate with Governor Barri, but the governor's spiteful behavior toward missionaries continued after the Franciscans had left. Mora was characterized by the government officials who complained about him as an enterprising man, jealous of his authority over the missions, not very agreeable, fond of high living, a womanizer, authoritarian, and endowed with good knowledge and writing ability. Barri complained that: "In the time that I governed the peninsula and had to deal with the Dominicans, my experience was that he was despotic and authoritarian...He wanted to be independent and not recognize the secular administrators and was totally disobedient, taking it so far as to threaten excommunication."

The conflicts between the presidents of the missions and the California governors dated back to the Gálvez decrees, each agency accusing the other of not being able to carry them out. Padre Palóu criticized the unfriendly Felipe Barri, and there was real animosity between Junípero Serra and Governor Felipe Neve, so the governor's evaluation of Vicente Mora should be taken with a large grain of salt.

Governor Barri Goes Too Far

Governor Barri tried to intimidate the Dominican presidente as he had Palóu. Padre Mora reported in a letter to Padre Serra that Governor Barri had twice appeared at the door of the Dominicans' quarters with his armed soldiers, charging the Dominicans with scandalous behavior. He announced that he would hang anyone who would not take up arms with him against the enemy, implying that the Dominicans were the enemy.

Barri had finally gone too far, and in October 1774, he was relieved of his office. Ex-governor Barri set sail for San Blas on October 26, to everyone's relief.

The new governor Felipe de Neve, major of a Querétaro regiment of provincial cavalry, arrived in Loreto on March 4, 1775. Governor de Neve lost no time in complaining to the viceroy that the country was destitute of everything and that ships, horses, soldiers, clothing, and arms were desperately needed. He found the southern missions impossible to support or develop, because they had been abandoned by the natives and had no crops and only wild cattle. He noted that Gálvez' elaborate rules for managing the king's revenues could not be carried out because the missions' annual income was only two hundred dollars.

Felipe de Neve Appointed Governor

Governor Neve did carry out Gálvez' order to build a warehouse and commissary in Loreto next to the mission church. The building was constructed from materials of the region: stone, lava rock, brick, lime made from seashells, mesquite, ironwood and palms. The palms were brought from Rancho El Palmarito 40 miles away. It was abandoned after the missionaries left and then served over the years as a shelter for families, a prison, a primary school, a junior high school, and a boarding school for children from remote ranches and fishing villages. It is now the Museum of the Missions.

Padre Mora wrote two letters in February 1776 answering the charges of Governor de Neve that he was not fulfilling Gálvez' orders. These letters illuminate the conflict between church and state, and also provide a valuable picture of a time in Loreto's history that is not well recorded. Mora wrote that he would have carried out the decrees if it had been possible, but that de Neve must have noticed the decrease in population of the missions in the south and the fact that, except for Todos Santos, not enough food was grown to maintain the natives and what little was left, they sold to friends. The Dominicans had tried to develop the land and water resources of the three southern missions, but the lack of laborers and the inexperience of the Dominican padres had not permitted the advance-

Padre Mora's Answers to Neve's Accusations

141

ment that, with more understanding and experience, they might have been able achieve in several more years.

Mora repeated, as the Franciscans had written, that it was not possible to relocate more Indians to Loreto. Mora wrote that the peninsular Indians were not interested in working their lands or becoming vassals of the king or accepting the guidance of the missionaries. Although some Indians from the south had been transferred to missions Santa Gertrudis and San Borja, there were many Indians the missionaries were simply unable to maintain. He did not believe the king had ever found, nor would ever find the Indians of Baja California of much use as vassals. Many natives were afraid to go into the missions because their relatives, who had been forced, either died on the long trek, or from one of the various epidemics that ravaged the more populated settlements. Mora wrote that despite their fears, the natives had not lost their Christian religion; even the fugitives in the desert and mountains came to the missions once a year to confess and receive communion. He also wrote that even if the natives accepted the orders peacefully and came into the pueblos of the missions, most of them would die of contagious diseases and the rest would become too debilitated to work. Those who stayed in the mountains and deserts were strong and healthy.

Regarding Loreto, Padre Mora wrote that the soldiers in the presidio had only corn and beans with water and salt to eat, and their families had even less. This left nothing for the Indian workers who were supposed to build the pueblos. The land around Loreto was so bad that the orchard of the government house that year produced four cantaloupes, six watermelons and a few pomegranates, and it required the services of one native to water it. Some missions were poorer than others, but even the best missions were poor and stocked only urgent necessities. In Loreto it was no different. Neither the families that had been moved from San Javier nor those already there had enough food, and those who returned to the mountains survived better. Gálvez had given Loreto only one cattle ranch; the natives living there were the only ones who were living peacefully with enough food to maintain themselves. He himself was so poor, he said, that he had to tear pages from books in order to write letters.

In San Javier the natives were barely able to produce enough food for their families due to the small amount of arable land and water available. The ranches of Primer Agua and San Vicente had been abandoned, because they cost more to farm than they were able to produce.

Mora concluded by saying the Dominicans had tried to carry out the orders of Gálvez, "but the results were so contrary to the pious ends of this project, the effects so unfortunate, as described, that, in truth, if we carry them out we will ruin the work already done, reduce the livestock, leave the people without comfort and have great difficulty being able to recover from this backwardness."

In his second letter, Mora protested the accusation of Governor Neve that the Dominicans were not loyal to the king. They were loyal to God and the king, he wrote, but they were not the servants of Governor de Neve.

In 1776, the Spanish government decided to change the seat of government of the Californias from Loreto to Monterey in Alta California. Loreto lost its importance as the center of administration of the two Californias. From that time on, all peninsular activity was directed from Monterey, although Loreto was still the nominal capital of Baja California. Governor de Neve was appointed governor of both Californias, with headquarters in Monterey. He was succeeded in Loreto by a familiar face.

Government of California Moved to Monterey

Fernando Javier Rivera y Moncado had started his career as a very young soldier under the Jesuits at the Loreto presidio. He had been promoted to captain by Padre Miguel del Barco, led the first land expedition to San Diego, and had served twice as governor of Alta California. However, he had incurred the animosity of the Franciscans in disputes over jurisdiction and was excommunicated by a Franciscan priest, a severe blow to this religious man. He was sent back to Loreto in 1776 as captain of the presidio and lieutenant governor, replacing de Neve.

Captain Rivera Returned to Loreto as Governor

This soldier, who had spent most of his youth working happily with the Jesuits, didn't get along any better with the

Dominicans than he had with the Franciscans. In 1780 he was sent across the gulf to recruit soldiers and settlers for Alta California. On the way up to Monterey, his group was attacked by hostile Indians near the present city of Yuma, Arizona, and he was killed defending his charges. His widow was never reimbursed for his back pay and was left destitute in Loreto.

Soldier Settlers

In 1781, only ten former soldiers or sailors were listed as cattle ranchers in the Loreto area. They were: Felipe, Ignacio, and José María Romero at Rancho San Luis; Juan, Francisco, and Julián Murillo and Jaime Carillo at Rancho Primer Agua; Diego Pérez at Rancho El Chuenque; and José de la Cruz and Juan de Osuna at Loreto.

The Dominican Heritage in Baja California

On the orders of the government, the Dominicans established eight new missions in the northern part of the peninsula to serve primarily as way stations on the road from Loreto to San Diego. Between 1775 and 1791, they founded missions Nuestra Señora del Rosario, Santo Domingo, San Pedro Martir, San Vicente Ferrer, Santa Catalina, San Miguel, Santo Tomas, and Guadalupe. None survive intact today.

During the Dominican era in Baja California, the native population continued to decline, the missions deteriorated, and the conflict between church and state increased. The indigenous people resented being transferred from their home territory to missions in other parts of the peninsula, and they bristled under the strict discipline of the Dominican priests. H. H. Bancroft in his *History of Texas* wrote:

> The fact is, the Dominicans were harder task-masters than either the Jesuits or the Franciscans, and administered severer punishments, and the natives were weary of excessive labor and the lash. An example had to be made, however, and several of them were tried at Loreto, found guilty of rebellion, severely flogged, and the leaders were also banished to the south.

The harsh treatment of the native Californians by the Dominican missionaries reflected the attitude of the Spanish, who regarded them as conquered peoples who should supply the labor necessary to advance Spanish colonization. When the natives rebelled, the Dominicans, who had been given the dif-

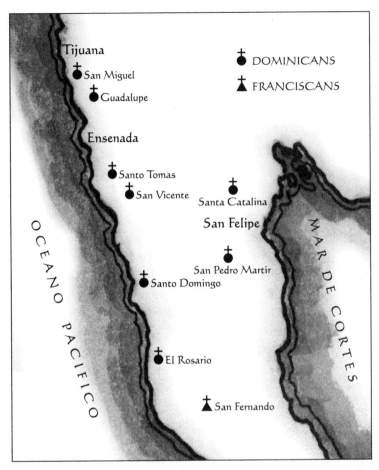

Missions founded by Dominicans and Franciscans in Baja California.

ficult task of managing this labor, felt free to use the lash or any other method of keeping the labor force submissive.

In 1781, there was an especially severe outbreak of small-pox. Many of the natives fled to the mountains to escape the disease, but the epidemic raged for over a year and thousands died. In the same year Padre Mora retired as presidente of the Dominican missions because of ill health, and Padre Miguel Hidalgo was sent to Loreto to take his place.

Padre Miguel Hidalgo Replaces Padre Mora

To add to the problems of the Dominicans, in 1781 their supply ship was lost and only a small launch was left to bring goods from the mainland. In that year neither money nor supplies were received, very little arrived in 1782 and none in 1783. It was reported that in Loreto, the soldiers wore any kind of attire they could find and many families could not attend church because they didn't have sufficient clothing. The supplies of food in the warehouse dwindled to almost nothing.

Report of Governor Pedro Fages

In 1786, Pedro Fages, then governor of California, reported:

> That the missions have deteriorated is beyond question...All the Indians of California are alike lazy, incapable, and stupid. Their only aspiration is to rove about the country. The women do some weaving and knitting, but under the supervision of the missionaries. The grain which is harvested scarcely suffices to maintain the inhabitants. Diving for pearls is the principal source of wealth, but it does not prosper for want of people. If the Indian had the land to himself, he would not be capable of cultivating it, so lazy is he.

Fages described the rapid extinction of the natives and also reported that there were no cattle except at two missions and very few crops. No missionaries had come to the peninsula for the last fifteen years, although many had died and "some had lost their reason", so that at that time there were only twenty-one priests in charge of sixteen missions.

Loreto at the End of the 18th Century

In 1793 the Dominicans reported that the church in Loreto was richly decorated. The house of the missionaries, built of masonry and with a tile roof, had a reception room 12 varas long and 6 varas wide and another room measuring 6 by 7 varas. The library contained 466 volumes. In 1794, to protect the foundations of the church, the yard was paved. In 1795 a primary school was started. By 1800 the Loreto population was about six hundred, mostly Hispanic. Only thirty-seven indigenous people were reported living in Loreto in 1798.

Dominican Scandals

The later years of the Dominicans in Baja California were marred by the scandalous conduct of some of the priests. In 1802, Padre Rafael Arviña came to Loreto as vicar and presidente of the missions. He learned that many of the missionaries were being accused by the natives of extreme cruelty and were lashing their charges unmercifully. Presidente Arviña circulated an order limiting the number of lashes to five and rebuked the padres for their harsh treatment. Nine Dominicans in charge of northern missions were incensed when they received this order and joined together, refusing to obey. They not only rebelled, but they accused the presidente of flagrant immorality. Their letter said that although they might or might not have been overly harsh, at least they hadn't been behaving as badly as the presidente who, they charged, was behaving scandalously with the ladies of Loreto. They wrote:

To the small extent that His Very Reverend Paternidad conforms to our sacred rules, we beg him that instead of passing so much time amusing himself with Estefana, Martína, and other Spanish females and instead of taking part in the fandango so often, he should devote a little more time to reading the Dominican Constitution. In that way he will not be guilty of such absurdities, nor will he be the white one in the province, nor will he lament our honor, as he does now, by communicating to individuals what is much better concealed.

When news of the affair reached Dominican superiors in Mexico, Padre Arviña was removed in January 1804. Padre Gabriel of Loreto was removed some years later for abducting Indian wives, and, still later, a Padre Cabellero committed the same offense. Padre Antonio Berraguero, the Dominican missionary in Mulegé, was noted for drunkenness and general licentious behavior.

The religious zeal of the Dominicans had not been enough to overcome the difficult task of bringing their ideal Christian civilization to a land and people that did not welcome it. The Dominican order withdrew from Baja California in 1854.

SPANISH GOVERNMENT IN LORETO

The governors appointed to serve in Loreto were not enthusiastic about the position. Some became irrational as did the first governor Felipe Barri, and they all repeatedly petitioned for other posts. Especially after the center of jurisdiction of California was moved to Monterey, Loreto was not considered a prestigious appointment or one that would advance one's career.

Spanish Govenors

Fourteen Spanish governors had served in Loreto from the time the Jesuits were deported in 1768 until the citizens of

Baja California took the oath of allegiance to the independent government of México in 1822. They all lived in the house that had been built by Jesuit Padre Jaime Bravo across from the church.

In 1804, a royal order declared that Alta and Baja California were to be separated. Monterey would be the capital of Alta California and Loreto the capital of Baja California. Felipe de Goycoechea, the commandante to the Santa Barbara Presidio, was appointed governor of Baja California and arrived in Loreto in July of 1806 to take up his new position. He lived in Loreto until 1814, when he was replaced by José Dario Argüello, the last of the Spanish governors in Baja California.

The War of Independence from Spain

In 1808, Napolean Bonaparte invaded Spain, and the desperate Spanish were stripping their colonies to finance their war for survival. This caused great hardship in New Spain, and a movement grew to throw off Spanish domination. In 1810, the king of Spain Ferdinand VII was imprisoned in France, and the Mexican priest Miguel Hidalgo y Castillo issued the call for the War of Independence against Spain.

For the next twelve years, while fighting continued on the mainland, the Baja California Peninsula remained isolated. Supplies and communication from the mainland were cut off. In 1813, Morelos convoked the first Mexican Congress. Between 1815, when Morelos was executed and 1821, when Augustín de Iturbide declared himself Emperor of Mexico, not much is recorded regarding Baja California or Loreto.

The movement for independence from Spain had little effect on Loreto except to increase its isolation from the rest of the world and to force the people remaining there to rely on their own resources. The Dominican missionaries and the soldiers of the Loreto presidio could not receive their salaries. Governor Argüello could not collect his salary either, and he and his family had difficulty surviving. The missionaries and authorities of both Californias were stubbornly against the independence of Mexico from Spain and ignored their orders to accept it.

There are very few accounts of life in Loreto during these years. One of the few is from Captain James Smith Wilcocks who arrived in Loreto in 1817 on the American ship *Traveller* loaded with grain from San Diego. He reported that when he arrived in the poverty-stricken port, a treasury officer seized his ship and stripped it of all valuables before releasing it.

In February of 1822, the isolation of Loreto was broken. Another foreigner, this time an English admiral, entered the annals of Loreto history. Thomas Cochrane, the tenth Earl of Dundonald, was a former member of Parliament and ranked among the greatest of British seamen. He had been invited by Chile in 1817 to command its fleet in the War of Independence against Spain. His naval feats contributed greatly to the independence of Chile and Peru. While considered a naval hero in England; the Spaniards called him a pirate.

A Pirate Attack on Loreto

Admiral Cochrane sent two ships from the Chilean navy to Baja California to help the peninsula achieve independence from Spain. They went first to La Paz, where it turned out that the Chilean sailors interpreted "help" to mean a license to sack the town. When one of the ships, the *Arancano,* under the command of Robert Simpson appeared outside Loreto, its reputation had preceded it. Many people fled to Comondú, including the priest and Governor Argüello, who left in such haste that he didn't take his silver plate, which the raiders seized. The Chilean sailors also desecrated the mission church and stripped the Virgin of Loreto of her pearls. Since at first no resistance was offered, the sailors also established a slaughter yard and started killing cattle.

Ensign José Mata of the Loreto presidio took charge and organized a small force, which attacked and imprisoned the invaders. Captain Robert Simpson sent for help, and, on March 4th, another of Cochrane's ships arrived in Loreto to rescue the Chileans. Ensign Mata, to prevent the recurrence of such an invasion, proclaimed the loyalty of Baja California to independent Mexico a few days later.

Independence from Spain is Declared in Loreto

In April of 1822, Emperor Iturbide sent Rev. Agustín Fernández de San Vicente, a canon of the cathedral of Durango, as his emissary to Loreto to obtain an oath of allegiance to Mexico. Canon Fernando de San Vicente also laid down regulations concerning the treatment of the native people and

149

appointed commissioners to each mission to see that they were well treated and not over worked. The canon's regulations were well meant but were based on ignorance of the land and conditions in Baja California.

When Canon Fernández de San Vicente arrived, the last Spanish governor José Argüello hastily resigned and was replaced in October of that year by José Manuel Rúiz, commander of troops on the frontier, who was given the title of Jefe Politico. Not long after he arrived, Rúiz wrote protesting that the missions couldn't afford to feed the government commissioners appointed by the canon.

The First Loreto Municipal Government Is Elected

On July 2, 1822, the bells of the Church of Our Lady of Loreto rang out early in the morning, and a salvo of gunfire from the troops called the people to Mass. When Mass was concluded, the missionaries, led by Canon Fernandez de San Vicente, took the oath of allegiance to Mexico in the presbytery of the church.

In the stone house in which Jefe Politico Rúiz lived, which still stands on Calle Francisco Madero in Loreto, a transcription of the Act of the First Government in Baja California states:

The neighbors gathered at 7:00 in the morning for the purpose of naming parochial electors who will designate those individuals necessary to compose the Government that will be installed and having discussed by secret scrutiny the rules of election that originate in the Constitution of Spain (where they may be adaptable) propose the names for electors of the citizens.

The people chose Miguel Mesa, Juan Higuera, Juan Ibañez, Cecílio Peña, Domingo López, Anastacio Arce, and Enrique Arce as electors. The electors then voted among themselves and chose Juan Higuera, mayor; Anastacio Arce, alderman; Enrique Cota, second alderman; Luis de Cuevas, deputy. The newly elected officials took the solemn oath of office.

Speeches were made, church bells rang, and the soldiers marched to the sound of drums followed by a procession of joyful citizens. A ball was held that night in the house of the first mayor of Loreto, Juan Higuera.

Chapter Four

THE ISOLATION OF LORETO

In 1823 a rebellion led by Antonio López de Santa Anna forced the abdication of Emperor Iturbide. On October 4, 1824, the first Constitution of independent Mexico was formally established, and Santa Anna became president for the first of eleven terms. The constitution declared Baja California to be a federal territory, with a governor appointed by the president of Mexico and a Territorial Legislature elected by the people. The territory was divided into the four districts of Cabo San Lucas, Loreto, Santa Gertrudis and San Pedro Martir.

Although still nominally the capital of Baja California, Loreto remained relatively untouched by events in the rest of the new republic of Mexico. It was a long way from Mexico City, and communication with the rest of the world took a very long time, sometimes years. Many documents of the period have been lost in natural disasters and through human carelessness. Descriptions of Loreto during the next century can be found mainly in the published accounts of visitors.

In July of 1826, Lieutenant R.W. H. Hardy, a representative of an English pearl fishing enterprise, visited Loreto and wrote his employers a valuable description of the capital of Baja California:

Visitor Accounts from Loreto

> I went on shore and waited on the Commandant Don José María Padrés to pay my respects and make arrangements.... He resides in the best house in the place, near the church, which was formerly celebrated for the richness of the Virgin's pearls; but in a visit paid by some Chilean or Colombian vessels in the year 1821 under pretense of making

the colony free, the crew thought it their duty, it is said, to relieve the Virgin from her superfluous weight of pearls and the church of the greater part of its gold and silver, so that in addition there is little in it worth seeing....

Don José is a short, dark phlegmatic-looking man of about 30 years of age...I now began to think that I had fallen into company with a scientific man whose talents I feared were thrown away in this retirement...He said he was not satisfied with his present situation and hoped soon to leave it. The government had readily sanctioned his proposal to remove the commandancy to La Paz....

Loreto stands in a valley of about two or three thousand feet wide, surrounded by wild and sterile mountains of which that called "La Giganta" is the highest and least picturesque. There are two gardens in the place in which the vine, peach, fig, quince, and date are cultivated. A considerable quantity of wine is annually made, notwithstanding the fruit is common property to all the inhabitants....

There is space only for the town and two gardens; and there being in consequence no possibility of raising either wheat or maize....I observed that the hills which surrounded the town are chiefly composed of primitive rock, granite, and hard sandstone, all intermingled with scarcely any appearance of soil upon them. They are thus capable of absorbing but little moisture; and during the heavy rains, which happily do not occur more frequently than once in five or six years, the rush of water through every part of the town as it comes down the ravine is so great that instances have been known of some of the houses having been actually carried away.

To prevent the recurrence of this danger, the former friars, many years ago, erected a stone wall to break the force of the water and give it a new direction towards the sea. In successive years the rains washed this barrier away, and another was built, which by the returning floods was washed down also, and at present there is but a slight trace of its ever having existed. No attempts have been made to restore it, and on some future day it may be expected that the inhabitants will be seen floating down the gulf! Although the natives are perfectly sensible of their perilous situation, the love of their dwellings is so great as to extinguish all fears for the future and all desire to change their residence...

The population of Loreto cannot exceed two hundred and fifty souls. The commandant is able to muster a force of about six soldiers, and there are two cannon with open breeches so that they might be expected to do equal execution among friends in the rear and the enemy in front. The exportations consist of soap, preserved fruits, wine, spirits, pearls, tortoise-shell, and salt, which latter article comes from a spring on the northeastern extremity of the Isla del Carmen in front of the mission.

In 1828 a severe hurricane brought heavy rains to the Loreto area. The arroyo flooded, many homes were swept away, and the church and public buildings were damaged. This served as an excuse to finally move the capital to the more populous south of the peninsula, first to San Antonio and then, in 1830, finally to La Paz, which was then a small town. Loreto became a little pueblo with only a local municipal government. *No Longer the Capital of Baja California*

A pattern of life in Loreto began at this period that lasted until the middle of the 20th century. Land grants had created ranches in the area, which provided cattle and goats for export. In the town itself, the population dwindled as many people went to Alta California where the lands were richer. The remaining inhabitants supported themselves with small kitchen gardens, fishing, and pearl diving; some families lived for most of the year on Carmen Island to work in the salt mine there.

The new government of Mexico was wary of the power of the Catholic Church and not interested in the church's problems in Baja California. Because of the lack of wealth to support the church and the decline in native population, priests who died or left the area were not replaced. In 1836 Padre Vicente Sotomayer was the priest in Loreto, and there were only six other priests on the peninsula. By 1855 there was one priest to serve Loreto, Comondú, La Purísima, Mulegé and San Ignacio. During that time and for almost the next hundred years, the women of Loreto increasingly took over the teaching of the catechism and continuation of the rituals of the church. *Decline of the Catholic Church in Loreto*

An attaché of the French legation to Mexico, M. Duflot de Mofras, visited Loreto in 1840 and found two hundred people living there. He reported: *Life in Loreto in 1840*

At one time this mission was the capital of Lower California, but it has fallen into decay. The presidio, mission and the church are now slowly crumbling away, although the buildings were designed by the Jesuit fathers to afford shelter in face of attack to the colonists. The presidio has a small esplanade defended by two bronze swivel guns; guns whose breeches are now wide open and whose gun carriages are missing.

He wrote that the church still had its paintings and silver cases and the doors were never closed. He also noted that "during the Spanish regime a messenger left Guaymas once a month, crossed the Gulf in a small boat and landed at Loreto. From there, letters were carried overland to Monterey. This service has been discontinued for some time, and frequently an entire year passes without news from California."

1846-1848 War With the United States

The invasion of Mexico by the United States in 1846 did not disturb the little pueblo. A few men from Comondú went to La Paz to fight the Americans there, but there is no record of any Loreto men joining them. The Treaty of Guadalupe between Mexico and the United States in 1848, which stipulated that Alta California would be ceded to the United States while Baja California would continue to be a territory of Mexico, did not bring any change to life in Loreto.

A Description of Loreto in 1850

In 1851, Rafael Espinosa, an author who also contributed studies of Baja California to the prestigious *Bulletin of the Sociedad Mexicana de Geografia y Estadistica*, published an article in *La Ilustración Mexicana* describing a trip he had made the year before on a sailing schooner from La Paz to Loreto. His account is vivid and worth quoting:

> About six leagues below Loreto, along the coast in front of Carmen Island, we discovered Puerto Escondido, the best in all the peninsula. In the port there is a stone house and a shed that served long ago as a storehouse for goods brought from Mexico for the missionaries; later it has served as a place for the governors to escape the heat of the summers.
>
> On the 24th (of June), between two and three in the afternoon, we dropped anchor in the port of Loreto, where we could see through our binoculars the church surrounded by a large olive orchard and beautiful date palms. After we landed, we went directly to the church accompanied by some people

156

who were waiting for us on the beach. We knew that the Virgin of Loreto that the venerable Jesuit padre Juan María Salvatierra had brought when he came in 1697, under the protection of the sovereign queen, to begin the spiritual and temporal conquest of the peninsula, was there, and we wanted very much to pay homage to her.

The temple that was completed in 1742, as one can read on the lintel over the door, doesn't deserve elegies for its architecture. We went about 80 varas from the entrance until we came to the great altar, keeping a religious silence; and my only concern was to give thanks to God that he had allowed me to pay homage and adoration to the image of the Sainted Mother who had been chosen, under her protection, to evangelize the heathen who had lived in ancient times on this ground. Kneeling at the foot of the altar, I gazed at the patron saint of this country and, after having spilled my heart into her divine hands, my attention was called by one of the group to observe on the face of the Virgin on her left eyebrow a nick which, according to tradition, was made by an arrow which she had received in an assault by the barbarians on Padre Salvatierra and his companions in front of their camp.

I doubted the truth of this, because in the history of Baja California written by Padre Miguel Venegas of the Company of Jesus, he wrote that the arrows shot by the Indians in this assault had not damaged anybody; and it does not appear probable that any damage to the Virgin, patron of the conquest, would have been hidden. At the exit of the church our attention was called to the full length painting of Saint John the Baptist; the drawing is excellent and the coloring beautiful.

The temple has two chapels attached, one to the right of the great altar which serves as the sacristy over whose door into the interior part is a portrait of Padre Salvatierra. One can see there on his Jesuit face, with a bell in his hand, the gift for calling to the neophytes to teach them the Christian doctrine. His aspect is that of a man consecrated to prayer and penitence. Possessing the most fervent charity toward the poor Indians of California, he entered voluntarily into the service of God to catechize them, scorning honors and esteem that were given to a provincial of his order. How sublime were the effects of the religion of the crucifixion on the souls who lived for the love of God and his fellow man! The gospel was propagated to the poor and ignorant by apostles all over the world, and God had chosen Padre Salvatierra as apostle to this barren corner of the earth where, forgetting his high position, he was a constant model of virtue to all who accompanied him in his glorious venture.

The ancient capital of ancient California had the look of one of those ruined villages of the orient, described by the poetic pen of Lamartine. Its half-ruined houses appear among orchards of olives, grapevines, figs and, towering over all, the colorful fans of the date palms; and, to carry the imaginary comparison further, there are, as in some places in the orient, some decorations of white marble and a house that has a marble floor taken from the island of San Marcos in front of the port of Mulegé. Its population is small, and those few inhabitants live well, especially under the protection of the Virgin of Loreto who watches over them. In spite of the absence of supplies, the excessive heat, and the abundance of mosquitoes that torment with their stings and buzzing, and the absolute lack of human resources in case of illness, one feels the attractions that keep a population there. Longevity is no exception in this place. An old man, his back bent with age and with a trembling voice, who was at least a century old, introduced me to an old lady who told me that she had seen the building of the church, and that its construction had been watched by most of the population. The house called the government house, the college of the Jesuits and the granaries that afterward served as storehouses for the belongings of the missions are all in ruins, and only indicate today the efforts that were made in that other time to develop this country.

The Jesuits knew that when it rained in the mountains the arroyo which runs through the town would flood and wipe out the town unless a wall was built to protect it. They constructed one, and today that has been destroyed by time and neglected by these inhabitants, and the prediction of the Jesuits has come to pass. The floods in the arroyo have carried away the earth and many of the houses that had formerly been part of the mission and damaged the church. The people who remained had never restored the wall. What a misfortune for Baja California! There is no river in all this vast area, the fountains are small and dry, and when it rains, the arroyos, which are dry all year, become torrents that carry desolation instead of comfort. The air is hot and dry, and two-thirds of the land is of frightening aridity.

The author visited San Javier on foot and was impressed by the beauty and peace of the mountain area and the simplicity and calm of the people he met there, in spite of their lack of material resources:

> One day was sufficient to visit the mission of San Javier, and we returned to Loreto, where Señora Larrinaga, who had provided us hospitality in her house, received us with the same attention she had given us when we first came. The name of this lady is gratefully remembered, since to her care we owe our good health in a land where everything is lacking.

Espinosa concluded by describing a night spent on board his ship waiting for a wind. He could hear, and was moved by, the music being played on the organ of the church in Loreto. He hoped that some day the potential of this beautiful place would be realized.

In 1857, a decree was issued by the president of the Mexican republic, Ignacio Comonfort, that required that the titles to all land purchased in Baja California since 1821 be nullified and that this land must now be repurchased for three hundred pesos by its present title holders.

This law was passed in reaction to the purchase by an American company of large tracts of land near the northern border, to the bitterness remaining from the 1846-1848 war with the United States, and to the abortive invasion of Baja California by the American soldier of fortune William Walker in 1852.

In 1859, Ulises Urbano Lassépas published a detailed account of conditions in Baja California, *Historia de la Colonización de la Baja California y Decreto del 10 de Marzo de 1857*, in an attempt to show the powers in Mexico City why this decree would cause undue hardship on this peninsular territory of Mexico and would not serve the purpose for which it was intended. About Loreto he wrote:

An Account of Loreto in 1859

> The town of Loreto lies on the shores of the gulf, in the center of the bay of San Dionisio, with the island of Coronados to the north and Carmen to the south. The flat terrain was con-

venient for building the town, although it didn't guarantee its survival. It is surrounded by mountains, between the peak of La Giganta and the small peak of Las Parras, from which a serpentine road goes to Comondú.

The buildings of the mission and the presidio are in ruins, and in 1829 a hurricane demolished a part of the government buildings. Many walls had disintegrated, and the floors were covered with debris.

Five or six paintings hanging on the interior walls of the church have defied time; the bats have taken up residence in the roof of the tower. Some poor families live in the blackened and deteriorated college and granary, an animal skin serving as a door. This is the sad appearance of the ancient and primary capital of the territory! The wrought silver of the chapel is estimated at 4000 pesos. The sacrilegious attack and foreign sacking, the greedy sexton, and necessity, mother of so much crime, have gradually reduced the Virgin to the most humble maid, she who had been literally covered with pearls of all shapes and sizes.

When the season for pearl diving opened, the padres in their vestments would go out in decorated boats to invoke a blessing on the divers and fishermen, a ceremony that the Indians repaid by consecrating to the Virgin the product of certain days of their work. This is the origin of the riches of the church.

The story is told that a pearl, shaped like a dove's egg, with a magnificent brilliance and irreproachable purity was given to the Virgin, but the missionaries gave it to the Queen of Spain. This pious and generous queen, appreciating this precious gift but not wanting to give offense to the Queen of Heaven, gave money from her private purse to pay for a candle to be burned perpetually before the Virgin of Loreto. After the revolution of independence, this custom was discontinued.

Seven leagues south of Loreto, Puerto Escondido offers the navigator a secure anchorage. It is almost a lagoon of five kilometers in circumference, deep, flat as a mirror, surrounded by rugged hills that give it more protection. To the east lies a small salt flat and a little spring of fresh water. The mouth or channel is encircled by a sandy point, hardly the width of a boat, and is entered or exited by the force of the wind or current but without power to tack in this narrow stretch. On the point of sand, the Spanish constructed a warehouse, once called the House of the King but now only a ruin. One leaves Puerto Escondido past the great beach of the island of Danzantes, passing between the land and the southern end of the strip of little islets that run out from Danzantes or to the east to Carmen Island.

He listed the buildings of Loreto: the school, the church, the storehouse, the granary, the house of the governor, the arsenal, and the town hall.

The census of 1857 showed a population in Loreto of 493. In 1829, a heavy flooding of the Loreto arroyo destroyed part of the public buildings, and in the following year, therefore, the center of government was transferred to La Paz, a more central point in relation to the population and better protected.

Urbano's report achieved its purpose, and the land owners of Baja California did not have to pay the three hundred pesos to repurchase their land.

Urbano also listed the soldiers of the missionaries and their descendants who owned land around Loreto. Juan de Vargas was listed as owner of Chuenque and Puerto Escondido as of 1781. Luis Romero was granted land at ranchos San Ignacio in 1786 and Santa Cruz in 1793, and Santos Ruíz received rancho Las Parras in 1793.

Urbano reported the results of a survey published in February 1858 of land devoted to agriculture, cattle or orchards. In the lands near Loreto, the families owning property were listed: Arce (whose English ancestor arrived in Loreto as a soldier in 1698), Castillo, Ceseña, de Cuevas, Davis, Gastélum, Higuera, Mesa, Meza, Molina, Murillo, Quijano, Real, Rodríguez, Veliz, and Verdugo. In the pueblo of San Javier were the Estrada, Ibañez, and Romero families. Most were descendants of missionary soldiers and artisans.

Loreto Settlers

He also listed some foreigners who had settled in the Loreto area since 1830:

Juan Bautista Tellechea: a native of Spain, sailor, owner of Rancho Notri as of July 4, 1834.

Juan Bautista Larrinaga: a native of Spain, sailor, owner of the property of San Matías, Santo Domingo, Rancho Viejo, San Ignacio, as well as various plots in Loreto.

Raymundo Mayoral: native of Manila, farmer, owner of the site of Corral de Dos Puertos and an orchard called San Ignacio.

Pedro Mayoral: born in Manila, brother of Raymundo, owner of the properties of San José and Ciujademí and a farm and orchard in the pueblo of La Purísima. He has held at various times important posts in municipal government.

Juan Dru: native of the United States, carpenter, owner of Rancho San Francisco, builder of coastal boats.

Tomás Taylor: native of England, owner of San Juan Londó through inheritance by his wife and children, property in Loreto and an orchard in Comondú, all in the name of the widow of Pedro Davis, English.

José Garayzar: Spanish, sailor, married in California with family; owner of land inherited by his wife, property in Loreto.

Most of the names listed in that census taken more than one hundred and fifty years ago still appear on the tax rolls, baptismal records, and school graduation programs of Loreto today.

New Families in Loreto in the Early 19th Century
Five men came to Loreto in the early part of the 19th century from different parts of the world and established families that have played a large part in the development of Loreto in the 20th century. From interviews with their descendants and from public documents, some fascinating stories of brave and adventurous men emerge.

PEDRO AND LUCAS DAVIS

In about 1820, the Davis brothers arrived on a ship from Alta California and never left. The family isn't sure if they were originally from England or were born in the United States. Lucas married and fathered several girls. Pedro married Susana Real of Comondú in 1823 and they had three sons, Pedro, Pablo and Lucas. José Jesús Davis Contrera, a grandson of the original Pedro, told us these sons of Pedro and Susana had large families, mostly boys, and these boys fathered more boys, sometimes ten or eleven to one family. Some left Loreto, but many of them stayed. Some have gone into business, some into politics, and some are fishermen, and there was one poet. Today, there are more than a thousand Davises in Loreto, and many of them live on Davis Street. Other people have told us that after the original Pedro Davis died, his widow, Susana, married the handsome Englishman Thomas Taylor, who squandered most of her inheritance on high living.

JOSÉ GARAYZAR

Rubén Romero Garayzar Verdugo and Ildefonso Green Garayzar told us that their great-grandfather José Garayzar Libaroni arrived in Loreto in a small sailboat with two other men in about 1830. Their long voyage had started in the Viscaya area of northern Spain, and the reason they came to the peninsula has been lost. But Rubén told us the family story that they had come ashore in Loreto because they needed water. Ildefonso Green thought they might have been looking for pearls. On the beach, the three men met Juan Bautista Larrinaga who, like them, was a Spanish Basque, and of course he invited them to his house. That was the end of the road for these adventurers. José Garayzar married Juan Larrinaga's daughter Dolores Larrinaga Gastelúm in 1835 and acquired two ranches, Bonó and Primer Agua, south of Loreto. Many of their descendants are prominent citizens of Loreto in the 20th century.

WILLIAM STUART CUNNINGHAM

William Cunningham arrived in Loreto in 1857. He came because his mother was in trouble. His grandson, Fernando Aguilar Cunningham, told us the story as he remembered hearing it:

After William's father, George Cunningham died in Brooklyn, New York, leaving his mother a prosperous widow, Caroline Cunningham met a charming British engineer who courted her and convinced her to invest her money with him in a copper mine just north of Loreto. She must have been an adventurous lady, because she left a comfortable life in Brooklyn to sail with him to the Baja California wilderness.

163

Unfortunately, neither the mine nor the relationship worked out, and the engineer abandoned her in Loreto. She wrote to her 18-year-old son William, who was attending college, and begged him to come to her rescue, and he did. William and Caroline worked the copper mine for a few more years, in the course of which William lost an arm in an accident. Then the mine filled with water, so William turned to ranching. He bought Rancho San Juan and three adjacent ranches, approximately fifty thousand acres, and raised cattle and horses and sold wood for the furnaces of the copper mines in Santa Rosalia and also the bark from the palo blanco tree which was used to dye leather. He had two wives and eleven children. So that his children could go to school in town, he built a house in Loreto on the foundations of the house built across from the church by Padre Jaime Bravo, which had been destroyed in the 1877 earthquake. He died in 1921. Many of his descendants are still living in the Loreto area.

CARLOS PERPULY

Leopoldo Perpuly told our friend Sandra Ryan, an author and playwright who spent some time in Loreto in 1973 and recorded conversations with interesting Loretanos, about his grandfather Carlos Perpuly.

My grandfather left Italy in 1832 when he was fourteen years old and made quite a bit of money in San Francisco, maybe in the gold rush. In about 1867, when he was in his forties, he lost the sight in one eye and was advised by a doctor to move to a warmer climate. He had a friend who was from Comondú, and he suggested my grandfather move there to regain his eyesight. He came here with money. He married a Comondú girl and moved to Loreto where he established a family and became a merchant, the biggest in these parts. His sons expanded the business, and my father used to bring merchandise from Mazatlán and Guaymas. He had to use sailboats, and there were many difficulties because of the weather. As a boy, I used to help unload the merchandise that came from Mazatlán. Often, the townspeople would be waiting desperately for the provisions to get here, and right here on the beach I would sell the major part of the provisions.

Pearl Fishing
1805-1855

Pearl diving, mostly carried out by concessionaires from the mainland, continued in the Loreto area. The boats worked

164

around the islands of Carmen, Coronado, Monserrat, and Danzantes, along the coast from Loreto to Puerto Escondido, and along the little islets of San Bruno and Arroyo Hondo. The diving was done during the time when the sea was warm, calm and clear from May until the end of October.

The best pearl-bearing oysters were called locally *chicharrones*. They were found on more or less sandy bottoms that were covered with a carpet of calcareous seaweed and old shells on which the oysters bred and developed. The pearls found in these shells were prettier and finer, and the famous pearls which were sent to the Spanish kings came from the beds of this class which were found in the bay of Loreto

In 1825 it was reported that from six to eight boats engaged in pearl fishing around Loreto. Each boat found four or five pounds of pearls worth from eight to ten thousand dollars in that year. Captain John Hall, an experienced navigator and trader in the Sea of Cortez, described the method of distributing the oysters in a published letter. He wrote:

> Every time the diver comes up, the largest oysters which he may bring with him are placed on one side for the Virgin. All the rest are then thrown into a large pile, and in the evening they are divided thus: eight shells are put on one side for the owners, eight on the other for the divers, and two in a third heap for the government.

In 1855, the Mexican government decreed that the divers should receive the equivalent of twenty-five percent of the value of the pearls they recovered. By that time though, because of the unrestricted and wasteful methods of pearl fishing the supply was diminishing.

In 1858, the War of the Reform between Liberals and Conservatives began, and fighting continued until 1861 when the Conservatives were defeated. The new president of Mexico, Benito Juarez, suspended payments of foreign debts for two years; and France, England, and Spain signed an agreement to compel Mexico to pay the debt. In 1862, the French army, which was supported by Mexican Conservatives, invaded Mexico, and the War of the French Intervention began. After two years of fighting, the second Mexican Empire was estab-

Years of Conflict and Change in Mexico 1858-1876

lished by the French army. Napoleon III hoped to capitalize on the American Civil War and the chaos in Mexico to return French rule to North America.

The Austrian archduke Maximilian von Habsburg was crowned emperor of Mexico in 1864. Three years later, in 1867, the Mexican Liberal Army defeated the Empire. Maximilian was executed, and Benito Juarez reestablished the Republic. In 1872, Juarez died, and Sebastián Lordo de Tenada became president of Mexico. In 1876, Porfirio Díaz overthrew Lordo de Tenada and became president for the first of seven times; his dictatorship lasted thirty-three years.

A Disastrous
Earthquake
in 1877
Empties
Loreto
During all this upheaval on the mainland, Loreto remained a quiet little village. Communication was so infrequent with the outside world that often the people didn't know what was happening in the rest of Mexico until several years later. Men and women worked each day to feed their families, while the children played in the gardens and on the beach when they could escape from their duties at home.

During an interview, Lupe Verdugo de Davis told us of a devastating time in the 1870s when an earthquake shook Loreto for all of April and two weeks of May.

In another interview, conducted in 1990 with ninety-five-year-old Ester Murillo, she described what her grandparents had experienced in the earthquake:

> My grandfather said the earthquake had occurred in 1877 and was so severe, lasting over a month, that all of the people left Loreto. Their family had gone to Rancho Viejo. Her grandmother told her the land was shaking so they couldn't make a fire, that the earth was separating and boiling water was shooting out, that they could roast corn on the ground. They said one child fell in a crack in the earth and was never found. When the quake occurred the sea went way out, and the people took the statue of the Virgin of Loreto to the beach to pray, and then the water came back up and stopped at the feet of the Virgin. The earthquake was felt in Comondú and San Javier but was not so severe there.

Loreto de los Santos, who was 101 years old when we talked with her in San Javier in 1999, told us that her mother was ten years old and living in Loreto at the time of the earthquake. Her mother remembered watching all the terrified people. There were repeated tremors, and the church tower fell little by little. She watched grown men crying and everyone on their knees around the church crying, "Miserericordia." Many people, including her family, left Loreto while the ground was still shaking. For many years after the earthquake, Loreto was almost deserted.

In 1973, Rebeka Davis interviewed her aunt Cruz Davis de Salorio on her 100th birthday. Sandra Ryan taped the interview. It is a first-hand account of the time the earth literally shook the people of Loreto away:

REBEKA: What year were you born?

CRUZ: In 1873.

REBEKA: How old were you at the time of the earthquake?

CRUZ: I was four.

REBEKA: Do you remember how it was then?

CRUZ: Some things I remember, others not.

REBEKA: What were you doing when the earthquake started?

CRUZ: We were in a little orchard cutting flowers. We heard women crying. We saw them. We were terribly frightened, and I looked for my mother. We started to run to the house. There were women in the patio in front, and others were kneeling on the floor in the house making the sign of the cross.

REBEKA: Who were you with?

CRUZ: My little brother Carlos.

REBEKA: And what were the people doing? Crying? Praying?

CRUZ: They were crying hard.

REBEKA: How long did the earthquake last? Do you remember?

CRUZ: No. It was terrible here in Loreto.

REBEKA: But did the earthquake last for many days?

CRUZ: Yes.

REBEKA: And what was destroyed?

CRUZ: Ranches.

REBEKA: What other things?

CRUZ: Many houses. The house of Jesús Arce. That one was completely destroyed; the whole house was totally ruined.

REBEKA: And what business did this señor have?

CRUZ: He was a trader.

REBEKA: And he had nothing after the earthquake?

CRUZ: Nothing. Absolutely nothing! He went away and never came back.

REBEKA: And the government house?

CRUZ: There was nothing left of that either. That house collapsed, and a little boy was hurt by the falling stones.

REBEKA: But didn't anything remain?

CRUZ: One room. The people called it a bolerita.

REBEKA: And the church? Did you see the ruins of the church?

CRUZ: Yes. I remember very well, because the ruins were not touched for many years, and there was a great deal of rubble.

REBEKA: When did they carry it away?

CRUZ: They saved it and used it to help build a new church. But that was later, much later.

REBEKA: Didn't the ocean rise up during the earthquake?

CRUZ: No. It didn't.

REBEKA: What was it that happened then? Did the earth open up?

CRUZ: That was only part of it. It was terrible. There was water all over the place. There was so much water.

REBEKA: What kind of water? Salt water?

CRUZ: Salty. Yes, it was.

REBEKA: And where did everyone gather to pray?

CRUZ: The place where the little park is today. That's where they took the Virgin. They built a little room there. It was made of twigs and branches, and they put the Virgin inside.

REBEKA: And was there a priest there?

CRUZ: Yes. One came from San Luis.

REBEKA: Did everyone go to this little house to pray?

CRUZ: At night many people went there. When they finished work they would go home to eat, and later they would go to the little house to pray.

REBEKA: And what did they finally decide to do?

CRUZ: Everyone wanted to leave for Rancho Las Parras. My mama told us that she felt that we ought to go, too. Our belongings were strapped down on the burros, and it was a difficult ride up to the top of San Masón. Oh, it pains me not to remember more details. I think it was on the 27th of April that we went away. Yes, that was when everyone left here for Las Parras.

REBEKA: And did you spend your saint's day there?

CRUZ: Yes. That's right.

REBEKA: And how old were you?

CRUZ: Four. Yes, and I made a little cross. They left the cross there. Don Santos and Guayacita de Los Santos set it up in the front parlor of the house, and they brought flowers from José Castillo's orchard. They arranged the little flowers all around the cross.

REBEKA: Who did they dedicate the cross to?

CRUZ: I don't know. I was very tired, and I went to sleep right after the cross was set up.

REBEKA: And the rest of the people, where did they go?

CRUZ: Everyone that was able to, left Loreto. Almost all of the people went away. Very few people remained in Loreto. Some went to San Javier, others walked to Las Parras.

REBEKA: And were there earthquakes in the mountains, too?

CRUZ: No, very little.

Many of the families never returned to Loreto, but slowly others drifted back and began to rebuild. Some newcomers came, including Chinese, who had been recruited from Canton by the Mexican government to help populate the peninsula. By the end of the 19th century a few wooden and adobe houses had been built. Most people, though, lived in houses built of palm logs, with walls of reed mats and roofs of palm leaves. There was no plan, and people built wherever they pleased.

The End of the 19th Century

169

Luis Arce Mesa, who was born in 1897, told us that the price of lots at that time was one cent per square meter; land and property taxes were twenty pesos. The church was in ruins, but an occasional priest visited, and the women of the town conducted the catechism classes and rosaries. Most of the men fished and sometimes dived for pearls, which were becoming scarce, or worked in the salt mine on Carmen Island. Hides, olives, and other products from the surrounding ranches were brought to Loreto where traders shipped them to markets. The school had reopened, although there were only four grades, and most of the Loreto children learned to read and write.

Chapter Five

CARMEN ISLAND

Carmen Island, which gazes back at Loreto from 7 miles out in the Sea of Cortez, has a parallel but separate history from Loreto.

The Sea of Cortez is dotted with islands. Most of these were low mountains which were not completely submerged when the ongoing activity of the San Andreas fault separated the peninsula from the mainland, and the waters of the Pacific Ocean moved in to fill the space between. There are various theories about the time of the islands' formation; some geologists believe they have existed as islands for about four million years.

Carmen Island is one of the larger islands, although not the largest. It is 18.5 miles long from north to south and about 12 miles at its widest near the northern end. A range of low peaks from 500 to 1,500 feet high runs the length of the island. The rocky precipitous shoreline is interrupted with small bays; some have sandy beaches with the lower slopes of the hills rising behind them. There are two large bays, Salinas on the east and Puerto Balandra on the west side of the island. Geologists describe it as "Upper Miocene with small deposits of sandstone (Paleocene)." In lay terms, this means the land was formed during the Tertiary geologic time period, from twenty-five to fifty-eight million years ago.

Carmen is not entirely a desert island. There are several sources of water on the eastern side. The vegetation and terrain are similar to that of the land around Loreto, rocky, with only desert vegetation. Early explorers found only rodents and snakes on the island.

There is a unique salt bed some 2 miles long and a half-mile wide on the northeastern side of Carmen, a mile inland from Salinas Bay, which has determined the course of the island's human history for many hundreds of years.

Early
European
Exploration
Padre Salvatierra noted that the native Monquí went to Carmen Island in dugouts or reed rafts on calm days to collect salt. But there were no people living on the island during the missionary period in Loreto or when it was first seen by early European navigators exploring the Sea of Cortez.

The first of these Spanish navigators was Francisco de Ulloa who had been sent by Hernando Cortés to survey this part of the world. In 1539, Ulloa sailed what he called the *Mar de Bermeja,* the Vermillion Sea, to its headwaters at the entrance to the Colorado River. In 1540, Ulloa sent a detailed report of his explorations to Cortés from Cedros Island off the Pacific Coast of the peninsula. He was never heard from again.

Ulloa was followed in 1540 by Hernándo de Alarcón who sailed up to the mouth of the Colorado and then in longboats possibly as far north as the Gila River. He also noted Carmen Island on his maps.

In 1633 Francisco de Ortega circumnavigated Carmen and wrote a description of it.

*The Jesuits
and Carmen
Island*
The Carmen Island salt bed was discovered by the Jesuits in 1697, when their ship, the *San José,* was taken into Salinas Bay for repairs. Several historians report that the Jesuits sold the salt in Sinaloa and with the proceeds bought the wood to build the mission in Loreto. Padre Salvatierra tried several times to get the Spanish government to give the missions a monopoly on the salt harvest to help support them, but he was unsuccessful. Shortly after Salvatierra's death, Padre Jaime Bravo again petitioned the Council of the Indies for the right to work the salt mines, but the council decided that permission to grant that right was a privilege of the viceroy, and the viceroy decided against it. The Jesuits were only able to supply their own needs for salt. In 1727 the Procurador of the Jesuits asked the Council of the Indies for the use of Carmen Island to run cattle, even though there was very little water there, and this may have been another attempt to gain control of the salt.

The Jesuit Padre Miguel del Barco, however, reported that

there was very little salt exported during the Jesuit administration by anyone because of the difficulties of transportation. In his *Natural History of California,* del Barco wrote a description of the island and the salt bed:

Among several salt pans that exist in California the foremost by far is the one located on the island called del Carmen, which is in front of Loreto and four leagues distant from it. This island is uninhabited not only by people, but also by animals, with the exception of rats and snakes, of which there is a great abundance. There is no doubt that this island is unpopulated on account of being afflicted by lack of water. This island has a circuit of at least 13 leagues. On the part which faces Loreto it has a rough mountain that runs in the same direction as the length of the island itself. On the opposite part, however, it is flat. And the salt pans are on this plain, about a half league from the sea.

This salt pan is large and it extends from north to south as far as the eye can see; the whiteness is still evident in the far distance, and no end of it is in sight. This salt is very white, beautiful and pure, without the slightest mixture of soil, sand or other things, and it is of a vigorous quality. It is made up and appears sort of kneaded out of little pieces that have a crystalline appearance. For this reason, and because of its whiteness, the reflections on the salt pans is so great that it dazzles and will not allow those who go collect the salt to work. In order to undertake this maneuver, it is therefore necessary to wait until the sun is nearing sunset or else in the morning at a corresponding time. They cut it with crowbars and they extract the pieces of any size they want, because the entire salt pan is a single piece. Though the salt is solid and hard, it is not as hard as stone, as it can be toasted and ground with no particular difficulty. They commonly cut the pieces in the shape of large bricks, so that a man can carry one of them to the beach comfortably on his shoulders. It is only when it has rained substantially that one cannot go fetch salt, as the salt pan fills with water and the salt softens and melts halfway. However, as it seldom rains there, this obstacle is not frequent, nor does it last very long. When they have loaded up a canoe or a launch with salt, the hole that resulted where they extracted the place appears as though nothing had been taken out of it. An explanation for this occurrence could be because of the subterranean communication that the salt pan has with water of the sea which, pushing against the salt walls, fills the empty space and recovers the level to correspond with that of the surface of the sea and of the same salt pan which, for this reason, is inexhaustible. Those who have seen and observed it well say that if a great fleet of thirty ships or many more arrived there, they could be promptly loaded up with nothing but salt. And, if after eight or ten days another similar fleet arrived with the same intention of loading up salt, they could do so without delay in the same place, because the second fleet would find the salt pan as full and whole as the first one had found it. When all the above-mentioned properties of this salt pan are regarded, one can say without temerity that it is one of the best on earth.

If it were located in another place where one could take advantage of all that salt, or at least where there was great consumption of it, one could derive great wealth from it, and its ownership would not be that of a private person but would be worthy of a monarch. However, where it is located it is totally useless, because what is consumed there is little – that is, the salt necessary for use in Loreto and a few missions. The miners of the south used to send a canoe to fetch salt, but this they did only rarely. There is no other consumption; all of the above is next to nothing with respect to the vast amount available in the salt pan.

The Franciscans and Carmen Island   One of the major disagreements between the Franciscans and the Spanish government, which led to the abandonment of the Baja California missions by the Franciscans, concerned the treatment of the natives working in the Carmen Island salt mine.

Inspector General Gálvez issued instructions to the new commissioner and acting governor Antonio López de Toledo, who arrived in Loreto in October of 1769, ordering that he "populate the salt works of Carmen Island with enough people, erect a warehouse there for the storing of salt, and take precaution that all the barks which had to return brought the salt to San Blas." He added that the Indians were not to be paid "because all subjects who are truly such have the obligation of serving the king."

Padre Palóu wrote:

> The commissary intimated these instructions to me and said
> that he would soon have to execute them, and that the Indians
> should, therefore, quickly make ready, and that, as there were
> few at Loreto, I should ask the missionaries of the neighboring
> missions to send laborerers for the royal service which must
> have a sufficient number.

Padre Palóu objected strongly to this order and refused to
obey it, since it meant that the families of all the men employed
on Carmen would have to be supported by the missions. Palóu
sent a circular to his fellow missionaries asking for their views
on the matter, and they replied unanimously that they should
give up trying to adminstrate the missions, since the economic
difficulties were impossible to solve.

Spain continued to be reluctant to give up an asset like
the Carmen Island salt bed, but it did not have the resources to
develop it. The salt bed lay quietly for many more years until
Mexico declared its independence from Spain and a new government took over in 1813.

Under the Mexican administration, the salt bed was
leased to concessionaires to develop. An official communication of May 23, 1851, from Colonel Rafael Espinosa, political
chief and military commander of Baja California, to the
Minister of Interior and Exterior Relations reports that the
Mexican government had taken charge of the salt production
on Carmen Island, leasing the right of exploitation to a contractor. Colonel Espinosa wanted to establish a presidio on the
island. Although this never happened, his report on the island
in the mid-nineteenth centery is thorough and worth quoting:

Carmen Island Under the New Mexican Government

> The island has an abundance of good salt of about ten kilo-
> meters in circumference, and in its environs a small and salty
> level surface, a place where some small huts can be put. There
> is no lumber for construction of buildings, only shrubs and
> thorny cactus. The closest point to the island on the peninsu-
> lar coast is a place named Agua Verde. It has four small fresh
> water sources: La Aguada, to the south a league and a half from
> the salt; El Carrizal, at three leagues in the same direction; La
> Higuera, two leagues to the east; and Lotó to the north. All are
> small, and the water is brackish.

It has no land capable of cultivation, because of lack of water and because the island is mountainous. There is only one place to the north that is capable of maintaining fifteen or twenty head of cattle. There are some wild goats there (placed there by the missionaries to breed many years ago), and along the shore can be found various seafood, pearls and sea lions. There are three ports, one to the southeast, the port of the salt works, and two others on the opposite coast called the bays of Marqués and Puerto Balandra.

The salt yield between 1852 and 1857, as reported by the maritime customs office in La Paz, which administered the salt enterprise, was between 432 and 1,204 tons annually. A ton of salt was sold in La Paz at the rate of six and one-half pesos, with four pesos going to the government and twenty reales to the salt extraction contractor.

Pearl Fishing A report made for the federal government by the Inspector General of Income Tax in 1857 reported that there were pearl fishing grounds around Carmen Island. He said pearls were found near all the beaches that surrounded the island, but the best site was on the southern point, Punta Baja. The pearls found there were white or blue and of good luster. They were from 1 to 14 *brazas** deep.

The inspector general noted that the exploitation of pearls was unregulated and that each year there were fewer and fewer. He predicted that without regulation they would soon be gone. There was never any successful regulation.

Russian As the salt bed on the island developed, Russian ships
Visitors to from Alaska began to visit Carmen Island every three years to
Carmen obtain the salt, which was excellent for curing furs because of its purity. On Christmas Day of 1841, a Russian ship, the *Naslednik,* commanded by a Lieutenant Bartram, arrived in Salinas Bay. On board was a young botanist, I. G. Voznesenskii from the Zoological Museum of the Imperial Academy of Sciences, Saint Petersburg. Voznesenskii collected plants and zoological specimens on the island and the peninsula during his visit and wrote a description of his observations there. A grisly footnote to that visit was that when the *Naslednik*

---

* A *braza* is a fathom.

returned to Sitka, Alaska, the captain was found dead in his cabin.

Another Russian visitor to the island was a writer named Alexander Markoff, who arrived in 1845 on the *Naslednik*. Markoff reported that when they arrived they found the salt bed covered by 2 feet of water. After a wait of a week, the water level had gone down only one foot. The captain decided they couldn't wait any longer and headed back for Sitka. Markoff noted in a description of Loreto that a little stream bordered with palms ran through the town.

Mexico was in desperate need of revenue after the disastrous reign of Santa Anna, the war between Mexico and the United States, and the war between the Mexican Conservatives and Liberals. President Benito Juarez sold Carmen Island to Fortunado de la Vega on May 28, 1862. Much of the salt was exported to San Francisco; in 1866 of forty-eight ships that arrived in that California port from Mexico, twenty carried salt from Carmen Island.

Carmen Island Changes Hands

De la Vega operated the salt bed until 1867 when he sold the island to the California, Oregon & Mexico Steamship Company. The American owners, who were associated with the Santa Fe Railroad, invested considerable money in machinery and other improvements, including a railroad, during the years they operated there. However, they eventually lost control because of a conflict of interests with the Santa Fe Railroad.

Captain John F. Janes visited Salinas Bay to pick up salt in February of 1875, and reported a narrow-gage railroad on the island that ran from the loading pier to the salt works, about one third of a mile. During most of the 19th century sails moved by the wind were used to pull the little platform cars along the tramway, although mules were also used.

Carmen Island was apparently not as devastated as Loreto by the 1877 earthquake, and the salt continued to be mined and shipped as usual.

By 1899 the salt works were under the control of the Viosca brothers of La Paz. A visitor at that time reported that the railroad had a steam locomotive, a tiny Baldwin *American* built in 1880, and forty cars.

In 1908, a severe storm carried away a part of the large pier in Salinas Bay, and a short time later, on July 22, 1908, the island was sold to the Pacific Salt Company Limited of London which improved the operation, including the purchase of new railroad equipment.

In 1920, Pacific Salt built a water storage facility with a windmill to bring water from underground to a level area about 1.5 miles east from Puerto Balandra on the opposite or western side of the island. The water ran out, and now only the concrete storage tank, watering troughs, and the toppled windmill remain.

The English company operated the salt bed until 1944 when it was sold to a Mexican company created for that purpose, Salinas del Pacífico, S.A. The Mexican company paid $366,767 American dollars for the complete salt operation and the island.

The Men Who Worked on the Island During those years, many of the men of Loreto worked the salt bed of Carmen Island and lived there with their families in the little town on Salinas Bay. Most of the current population of men born in Loreto who are over sixty years of age worked on the island in their youth. They remember that work on the island was very hard, but they all describe their time on the island as the happiest period of their lives.

ANDRES DAVIS

In 1920, Andres Davis Manriquez, age nine months, was brought to the island. He remembers wonderful years of playing on the beach with the other children, making fortresses out of seaweed, and diving for clams and conch. When he was fifteen years old in 1935, he started to work at the mine as a pumper and became a sacker when he was eighteen. Sacking the salt was very hard work, but in their free time the boys went fishing and played baseball and volleyball. He describes the island as a paradise:

The food was good – fish, *caguama* (turtle), caracoles. Vegetables were scarce. To prepare food, people needed firewood. As wood was scarce on the island, the people, usually on Sunday, took the boats and went around the island

The Carmen Island salt bed, early 20th century. Photo: Loreto Municipio Archives.

beaches to pick up driftwood. These excursions usually turned into a party.

In the 1920s, at the top of the mountain above the salt mine there was a cave. A man was always stationed there to watch for the boats that were coming to buy the salt and those that were bringing food and supplies and equipment. As soon as he saw a boat, he would light a wood fire to make smoke. When the people at the mine saw the smoke signal, they would get ready to ship the salt and receive the supplies.

Camen Island workers, early 20th century. Photo: Loreto Municipio Archives.

Mules were used to transport people and equipment from Puerta Balandra to the salt works. There were about eighty mules, as well as some cattle and goats. The mules were used for various kinds of work. Usually, only twenty were active. After one workweek, they were exchanged for another twenty, and the rest went back to Punta Baja to rest. To get the mules back to the mine took three or four days, and there were men employed by the mine who did nothing but tend the animals.

There are twenty or more people buried in a cemetery on the eastern side of the island. There are children, one American and some Chinese. Chinese were brought from Guaymas in the 1920s to work in the mine, but they were only there for four or five years. Chinese were not much liked in Loreto.

Foreign ships came to buy the salt. Andres recalls that in the period between 1950 and 1952 there were ships from Japan, North America, Russia, and one from Greece.

Andres lived on the island for forty-four years; his father lived and worked there for forty-one.

FERNANDO ROMERO

Fernando Romero, who was born in Loreto but moved to the island with his family as a child in 1940, lived and worked on Carmen for twenty-two years. He told us:

There were about eighty to one hundred families living on the island. Manuel Muñoz from Soñora had the supply concession. He had cattle, sheep, goats, deer, pigs, horses, chickens, turkeys, and peacocks; and he sold eggs, milk, meat, etc., to the families. In addition, the fishing was so good that the people ate very well. Señor Muñoz was related to the manager of the salt mine Gabriel Miller, and they were both very nice men. They taught the people and used to bring movies and organize dances on the island.

All of the buildings including a two-story house next to the school, were built of wood. There was a big oven at the mine, and the lime for its construction was made there.

The mine was very important to the area. Some of the families who lived on the island were Davis, Mesa, Romero, Rubio, Arce, Perpuly, Baeza, Murillo. The fishing was wonderful. The place was so beautiful. Work was very hard, but there was peace of mind there.

The docks on Carmen Island. Photo: Loreto Municipio Archives.

The dock was the meeting place in the evenings. After work, all the people used to meet there or on the sidewalk next to the store to talk, to see friends, to smoke cigarettes, to fish from the dock. After that, they went home. It was a healthy life, and the life style was so easy that the people had a lot of energy to do their work. When I first started working, I had to fill three hundred sacks with salt daily, each sack weighing 66 kilos. That was the minimum. But the houses, electricity and water were free.

The company didn't have a way to keep the houses cool or a way to avoid mosquitoes and gnats. During the stormy season it was very difficult to work and to get water. The tugboat used a hose to transfer the water to the *pangos*. It was difficult to get the water to the dock in a high sea. But, all in all, life was healthy and quiet on the island.

There weren't many safety measures at the mine. As most of the miners had been there since their childhoods, they knew their work. They wore glasses for protection from the glare and hats to protect them from the sun, and sometimes they wore boots. As the mine was so isolated, the company didn't comply with many safety laws, but liquor was not allowed on the island. Accidents didn't happen often. I remember only two or three. One time, some men had built a cave in one of the salt mounds which was as big as a house. They put a table and a candle inside for light and went into their cave to play cards. One day, the cave collapsed, burying two of the men. Only one was rescued. The mine had a lot of machines like tractors, power shovels, etc., and the people were trained to use them.

FRANCISCO BAEZA

Francisco Baeza, who was born in 1936, remembers boats from Japan coming to Carmen Island. He worked on the island as a young man when there were more than two hundred people working there.

Only spikes and shovels were being used to dig up the salt for the first five years he worked, but in about 1960 machinery was brought in. Francisco and many others who worked on the island believe that the machines lowered the quality of the salt.

Francisco was paid nine pesos daily and was given another three pesos daily for his three meals. The men worked from eight to twelve o'clock in the morning and from two to five o'clock in the afternoon. Most of the workers had their families with them, and they lived in wooden houses provided by the company. They left the island only if they were sick or there was a death in the family in Loreto. The Loreto priest visited the island chapel several times a year. There was no doctor, but a nurse took care of minor injuries and a doctor came from La Paz every six months to give a general checkup to all the workers. There was a primary school on the island with only one teacher.

Except during the hurricane season, July to October, salt ships arrived in Salinas Bay every month. About twenty-eight men called *estibadores* came out from Loreto to help with loading.

There was plenty of potable water on the island, although it wasn't of very good quality. There was a well about 50 meters from the salt works from which most of the water came, although it was not of good quality, and further away, about 800 meters, one which had very good water. This second well was 300 meters inland, and years ago engineers had installed a pipe to the shore where the water could be put on boats.

There was a relatively large company store and several small independent stores. Workers could not charge merchandise against their daily payments, but instead were trusted to take merchandise from the stores if they gave their word they would pay for it. Supply boats came from La Paz, and sometimes brought goods to Loreto, as well to Carmen Island.

HÉCTOR CASTRO ROMERO

Héctor Castro Romero was born in 1963 and lived on Carmen Island until he was seven years old. He remembers his childhood as an Eden, a paradise for children.

The beach on Salinas Bay extends for two or three miles, and the children went there in the evening to play and collect seashells. When the big boats came from Manzanillo and La Paz, they brought plenty of food and soft drinks. The teacher organized a lot of festivals and all the Mexican holidays were celebrated.

Electricity came to Carmen Island in 1954, ten years before it arrived in Loreto. Even though the houses on Carmen all had electricity, the women cooked on wood stoves. The wood came from the island, carried by burros or carts. Food tasted better when it was cooked on a wood fire.

In the afternoon, the families started to roast their own coffee, and when the bell signaled the end of the day's work, the whole camp smelled like coffee. They had coffee first, then ate. There were not many vegetables, but they had chile verde, garlic, pepper, zucchini, oranges, dates, apples, cheese, and fresh or dried meat, which came from Loreto. The bulls and cows came by boat and were pushed from the boat to the sea to swim ashore. Between May and July, watermelons arrived by boat from Rancho San Juan, and the fruit was thrown into the water, too. A lot of people swam out to get them or picked them up from the beach. In addition, the sea provided fish, turtles, and clams.

Sailboats were used by the local fishermen. Before 1950, there were canoes, which came from Jalisco, Manzanilla, Sinaloa, and Acapulco. They were carved from big trees and

A picnic on a Carmen Island beach, circa 1920. Photo: Loreto Municipio Archives.

were called *chalupas*.

The miners were paid by piece work, and the work in the mine was very hard. Work started very early in the morning, usually at four or five, and the miners worked until noon. Their families brought them breakfast of tortillas and beans every day between seven and eight o'clock. There were two shifts. The first shift finished at noon, and then they had lunch. If the miners didn't wear dark glasses, they ruined their eyes, and some became blind. The salt burned the miners' feet. (In Loreto, the miners were called *pata salada*, salty feet, but they didn't like that and preferred to be called *isleños*, islanders.) Their hands were callused, and the work was exhausting, but they were well paid, and the food was very good.

Some of the men worked digging in the salt bed. Some carried the salt. Others packed and refined the product. Some worked with specialized machinery. The heavy work was at the Estero. There they used rudimentary tools like picks and rakes. When the salt process was finished, the sacks went to the train. There was a lot of noise at the port. The salt sacks were carried to the conveyor belt, which carried it to the pongo, the small boat, then to the big boats. If the miners learned to do a better type of work, they could specialize and get better jobs. They could become drivers, machine operators, packers, etc. The miners needed strong muscles to do the heavy work. They used to compete with each other to show their strength. Extra people used to come from Loreto to help when the big boats arrived from Japan, mainland Mexico, or another country. It took almost fifteen days to load the salt from the warehouse to the big boats. Some times the salt went to the boat in sacks, and other times in bulk.

The people on the island were like one big family. Like any family, there were sometimes fights among them, usually over the children's behavior, but they enjoyed their life there. In the evening, people stayed inside their houses because of the mosquitoes and no-see-ums. Some houses had mosquito netting, but if they didn't the houses became very hot with windows and doors closed. Not many people had fans, but they were used to the heat. There were community bathrooms about100 meters from the houses, very primitive and not very hygienic. Toilet paper was scarce, but there was newspaper. They didn't have a drainage system, and all the used water went to a storage tank and was used again to water the streets. The children often didn't bother to use the toilets. They had common childhood sicknesses like chicken pox, measles, and mumps, but no epidemics.

SERGIO MORALES POLO

Sergio Morales Polo gave us a vivid and informative account of his experience on Carmen Island as a young man. Sergio went to work as an accountant at the salt works in 1961 when he was twenty-two years old, and he worked there for three years, becoming manager of the mine. During that time he fell in love with the island and Loreto, and after a successful career as an administrator in the Mexican government, he retired to Loreto in 1990.

Sergio was sent to Carmen Island by the company that owned the island, Salinas del Pacífico, from their office in the city of Salinas in the state of San Luis Potosi. After a harrowing flight from Guaymas in an old DC-3 plane left over from World War II, he landed in Loreto. At that time, there were only fifteen hundred people living in the town and three hundred living on Carmen Island. There were not many houses and only three buildings in Loreto with two stories: the government building and two houses which were owned by members of the Davis family.

With some misgivings, Sergio got into a small boat for his first trip to his new assignment. Of this boat ride and his first impressions of the island, he wrote:

The sea was stormy, the north wind was strong, and the waves were high. We started the trip after sunset, and it was a moonless night. The trip took four hours. I couldn't see the surroundings, so I rested for a while on some sacks. Finally, I could see the island lights in the distance, little points of light far away. I could see the lights of a big boat, the *San Luciano*. It was loading 2,200 tons of salt which it would take to Manzanillo, an important port on the mainland, and from there the salt would be distributed by railroad all over the country. I was really impressed when we came close to the ship because it was so big, as tall as a five-story building.

Because the bay is protected from the full force of the north wind by the mountains of the island, we landed safely at the dock. An assistant took me to the home of the general manager, Luis Martínez Gracida. As it was ten o'clock at night, we had awakened him and his attitude was not at all friendly. He received us in his slippers without enthusiasm or courtesy and, without a word, showed me to a small bedroom with a Baja bed, a canvas cot, that would be my home for a long time. I had never slept on a cot, but I was so tired that I didn't miss my bed at all. I had been so afraid of getting sick on the plane that I hadn't eaten since I left Salinas thirty-six hours before.

I woke up very early the next morning, and, as my bedroom window faced the sea, the view was really beautiful, a painter's dream. My first day, I thought, was starting well. If I could have had something to eat it would have been even better, but I had no time to reflect on that. I had to be at the office at 7 a.m. to report in and receive my instructions. The administration offices were on the first floor of an old building that was built around 1830. The rooms were dark and ugly, but the manager was planning some remodeling. Rudolfo Pérpuly Higuera was the head of the operation. He had been working at the mine for a long time. He was thirty-two years old when I met him.

Then I met Miguel Romero Lagos, the administrator with whom I was going to work for a long time. I also met Pedro Arce Talamantes, the storekeeper, and Jesús Meza, known as Pichuy, who was in charge of the electric power generators. I got involved in my work that morning and the time went very fast. All of a sudden it was twelve o'clock, and everybody disappeared. I was left alone in the office. It was lunchtime.

Outside I met a group of men who had been working on the island for some time. I told them I hadn't eaten since I left Salinas almost a day-and-a-half ago. They promptly invited me to the beach to find some clams and prepare them to eat country style. By then, I could have eaten a rock. Gratefully, I followed them. Between us we got some money and went to the store where we bought beer, flour tortillas, crackers, and Valvita tomato sauce. The sun was at its zenith, and the day was very bright, but, as it was November, the water of the sea was very cold. My new friends taught me how to feel for the clams with my toes and pick them up in my hands. It wasn't necessary to dive, because the clams were in shallow water. It was easy to gather them, because there were great quantities of them, and in less than a half-hour I had more than fifty, as did each of my companions. Enough, my friends said. They had provided me with a *costal,* a sack used for packing the salt which had a logo of a sea lion. After picking up the clams, we put them one by one on the sand close together. We made a bed of about two hundred clams. Close by, there were some *romerillo* and *chamizo* branches, shrubs which grew abundantly on the sand dunes, and we started a fire with them on top of the clams. After five minutes, all the branches were burned and all the clams were open. We put the tortillas on top of the clams to warm them. Then we put some clams and some tomato sauce on top of each tortilla, and we had the most unforgettable tacos. All this happened thirty-three years ago, and I remember every minute of it – the beauty of the place, the sea, the exotic food, and, so far away from home, the sensation of being among friends. It was a special moment in my life. Happy at last, I lay down in the sand, waiting to go back to the office at two o'clock.

The work hours were seven to twelve and two to five. Usually, I stayed later at the office. I left it about seven in the evening, just before dinner. The director, Rudolfo Purpuly, suggested I contact Héctor Castro who was in charge of the machine shop. His wife, Chata Romero, could give me breakfast, lunch and dinner – something I really needed. But, alas, that wasn't going to be easy. The island people were kind and hospitable, but they didn't like foreigners, especially people like me who came from the interior. Crime was unknown on the island, but some newspapers reached them once in a while. The people had read about the crimes and murders that happened on the mainland, and they didn't want to be exposed to people who came from there. I had to be quiet and prove that I wasn't a dangerous person.

The administration office was in very bad condition. Salt covered the walls, and they were rotting, so the company decided to cover the walls with wood planks painted an ivory color. Neon lights and new furniture were added. Also, an English water closet was installed. There were only three on the island, including ours. It was a novelty and made a big difference. In the town they used collective outhouses, one for the men and one for the women, consisting of little shacks made of laminated wood with board seats with holes. The smell was awful and the sanitary conditions worse.

We had to be in contact daily with the main office in Salinas by short wave radio and also with our office in La Paz, the capital of the territory, where all the administrative and legal work was done and which supplied most of the things for the island. Food, gas, medicine, clothes, electrical apparatus, timber, and many other necessities were sent by plane or by the motor boat *Arturo*. The 350-ton *Arturo,* owned by the Ruffo family of La Paz, was captained by Gumersindo Robinson, El Gume. El Gume was a wonderful sailor. His wooden ship was very old, unpainted, and looked as though it might never make it. Orders for the island were transmitted but took a long time to be sent, because many things were needed and the *Arturo* came only once a week. Its route was La Paz-Tembabichi-Agua Verde-Carmen-Loreto-Santa Rosalia-Guaymas and return. The *Arturo* broke down often and took a long time to be repaired. Sometimes, when the sea was stormy, the trip was canceled. If it was already on its way, the boat looked for shelter until the storm was over. These accidents affected our work, and we were often without fuel, without provisions. Then we tried to get in touch with our Manzanillo office and our Santa Rosalia office to get help. They sent us urgently needed supplies via the steamboat *San Luciano* and some other ships, but communication by radio was not always easy.

The general laborers in the mine received a little higher pay than the men who worked in Loreto, about two pesos more a day in the early 1960s. Special jobs, like engine and machinery drivers, paid up to twenty-nine pesos a day, and there were many opportunities for overtime. Most of the men didn't like to work overtime; life had always been hard in Loreto and the needs of the people very simple, so the men saw no need for making extra money.

One facet of life on the island that Sergio thoroughly enjoyed was the food. He wrote:

After a while, Chata Romero was kind enough to let me be a paid guest at her home. I had breakfast, lunch and dinner there. She charged me seven pesos a day, a reasonable price. The basic food was fish, and the Sea of Cortez had plenty of that. We had cabrilla, yellowtail, sierra, sardinas, shrimp and lobster. Sea turtle, caguama, was abundant on the island. In the summer the sea was full of sargasso. Fish laid their eggs on it, and that was the caguama's favorite food. In that time, people were allowed to catch the turtles, and I quickly learned how to catch, broil, and eat them. There is nothing so good. On the island they covered the shell with firewood and broiled it, or they made a stew with peas, carrots, green beans, tomatoes, garlic, onions and potatoes and added the broiled meat. It was a delicious but heavy meal, not easy to digest. The only time to eat it was in the middle of the day, and I didn't have breakfast or dinner on the caguama days. Coffee was good with this dish but not cold drinks, and I drank a lot of hot water all afternoon. After eating caguama for a few weeks, our bodies smelled like fish. Cabrilla was good broiled, breaded, and in fish patties. They used only the fish fillets to make soup, never the heads or tails. There were lots of sardines by the docks, and, as I liked them very much, Chata used to fry them for me. Children went to catch lobsters along the eastern shore of the island and sold them for fifty centavos each.

Sometimes there were no fish available because bad weather made it impossible to fish. Then we had recourse to canned sardines and tuna. There was also canned horsemeat from

Argentina that didn't cost much. It wasn't bad, but it was very red and had a sweet taste. In all the houses there was a store of shark and grouper, dried and salted, that was cooked like the turtle with tomato, onion, vegetables and turtle oil, and with corn tortillas it made delicious tacos. Chata served this garnished with French fried potatoes and black refried beans. Turtle meat was also salted and conserved for a long time. Turtle oil was collected when the turtle was roasted and kept in bottles to be used in cooking to give a taste to the fish machaca and for some household remedies.

The diet of the islanders, like that of the Loreto people today, abounded in carbohydrates like frijoles three times a day, tortillas of white flour or corn, a lot of potatoes, salt crackers, rice daily, soda pop and beer. Slim people were rare; in general the island people were robust and, in some cases, obese. When I arrived there I weighed 167 pounds, and after three years I left weighing 180 pounds.

On Sundays, we frequently organized fishing expeditions that helped to pass our day of rest. We left after our morning coffee, carrying with us all that was necessary to prepare our food, and on our way we threw out the bait and caught all the fish or turtle that we wanted. At mid-day we looked for a good place and drank our tequila and beer while we were preparing the tortillas, the fire, the salsas and roasting the entire fish, only taking out the intestines and washing it with salt water; leaving on the skin and scales while it was cooking. When it was ready, we gathered around in a circle and, taking turns, with our fingers we took the meat necessary for making tacos, added salsa and salt and they were ready. Few people in the world can boast about eating such fresh and natural fish in such a marvelous setting. Little by little, these experiences captivated me, and in less than a year I was profoundly in love with Carmen Island and Loreto.

Describing the process of salt production, Sergio wrote:

There is a theory that the depression where the salt mine is sited on Carmen Island was a volcanic crater which had been formed millions of years ago. In time, rain and erosion had covered it. At the same time, big pieces of crystallized salt sediment were formed. I could see, as the excavations of holes were made, that at less than 3 meters there was a layer of porcelain-white salt that contained some beautiful diamond-like polyhedrons about one inch in size. Underneath this layer we encountered salt water, due perhaps to the tides or the runoff from the nearby mountains. This water dissolved the salt above, producing a very high graduation salt solution, between 28 and 29 Baumé. It was the highest concentration that I knew about. For example, in Salinas, San Luis Potosí, the highest grade reached 14, and it was usually 7 grades. This high graduation made extraction very easy. The salt solution was pumped out by gasoline and diesel machines and was deposited in big ponds 250 meters square. When the solution reached a thickness of 10 cm., it was left to stand for about fifteen days, and, through the process of evaporation, it became a layer of white salt.

Then the graders started to work, and big mounds of salt were formed. These were gathered up by another machine with blades. A conveyor belt raised the salt to a dump truck, and, working together the truck was filled in a few minutes. The truck capacity was 4 cubic meters each. As soon as the trucks were filled, they were sent to the storage space where big pyramids of salt were formed with the help of mechanical shovels to a height of approximately 3 meters. At that time, we had a daily production of 300 tons, almost 40,000 tons a year.

Mine production was interrupted between July 15 and October 15 due to hurricanes, rain, and the hot weather of summer. Only maintenance work was done during that time. Most of the mine workers left for Loreto for a vacation. Only ten families and fifty workers remained on the island. Boats had to be hauled out and painted, motors overhauled, pumps cleaned, trucks painted. The pyramids of salt were left at the storage place to dry and then transported to the mill or to the screens or were sacked there.

During the time I was on Carmen Island, the salt was sold in two forms: "Sal Gruesa" which was collected from the pyramids of salt without milling and put into sacks made of agave fiber; and "Sal Fina Cribada," the product of separating the rough salt by grinding it in a mill with X-shaped metal bars inside, which rotated at great velocity and with deafening noise. This type of salt was put in cotton sacks, resembling flour sacks, imprinted with the logo of a sea lion. (The people called them *sacos de lobito* and used them to make sheets, shirts, pants, skirts and underwear. On Monday, the washing day, all the clothes danced on the lines like herds of lobitos.) The greatest amount of production was of the ground salt. The finely sifted salt was much in demand for use in cooking and various industries. The rough salt was used to cure animal pelts and by chemical plants and iron foundries.

Since production was reduced to 235 days per year, from October 16 to July 15, it was necessary to sack some 180 tons daily of salt, which was frequently difficult because the workmen were reluctant to work overtime. This made it necessary for us to bring personnel from the home office in Salinas, San Luis Potosí. This had an impact on the island.

The salt was transported from the mill by means of a small railroad and was slid from its platforms by way of a ramp into a boat that was called a "pango" which carried about 40 tons. At that time we had four pangos. The pangos were hauled by a small boat, a harbor pilot, to the side of the ship which was anchored a half-mile out, since the harbor was too shallow for large ships to come any closer to shore. On the side of the boat the sacks were put into a large net that was raised by hoists to the interior of the ship's hold where the nets were emptied and the sacks arranged until the hold was full. These maneuvers at the side of the ship and inside the hole were carried out by stevedores who came from Loreto each time a ship arrived and by a group of about thirty men who belonged to a union and stayed on the island during the nine months of production.

The principal destination of the ships was the port of Manzanillo, Colima, the second was to Mazatlán, Sinaloa, and sometimes to Acapulco, Guerrero. In those ports, the salt was loaded into railroad cars or stored in warehouses when there were not enough railroad cars available. The salt was then distributed along the route of the railroads throughout Mexico.

The many maneuvers – from the warehouse on the island to the platforms of the little railroad; to the smaller boat that took them to the ship; from the ship to the port; to the railroad car; from the railroad car to the warehouse of the client; plus the freight charges of the ship – significantly increased the cost of the salt and made it less competitive in the market. For a long time this could be sustained because the production of salt in

Abandoned town, Carmen Island. Photo: Sandy Harrison.

the country was insufficient, and the cost of Carmen Island salt was only a little higher than the cost of other producers.

Years later, production was increased in other salt production areas. Carmen Island salt was no longer able to compete and was unable to lower its costs. In 1978 it was seen necessary to close the plant, and this process took place over the next few years until 1983. This was after 278 years of exploitation, a few by the Jesuit missionaries who initiated the extraction of salt which they transported to Sinaloa to exchange for wood, mainly for the lumber that was used in the construction

The abandoned Carmen Island salt bed. Photo: Sandy Harrison

195

of the Mission of Loreto. Before the missionaries, the natives used the salt for thousands of years and considered the island a paradise where the spirits of good people went when they died.

The island is still owned by the company Salinas del Pacífico, S.A., the company that bought it in 1944. The owners have designated the island as a biological reserve. In 1995, a few animals were captured on the peninsula and transported to the island, the most important being twenty six *borregos cimarónes,* a protected species of longhorn sheep. A few Mexican and American biologists have been doing research on the island over the last few years, some living there for periods of three months to a year. Water is brought by boat every few days for their use from the island source that is piped to the shore, and a boat brings food and other essential supplies from Loreto twice a week. School children occasionally visit the salt mine to see the remains of the town and the rusting machinery

The abandoned docks of Carmen Island. Photo: Sandy Harrison.

of the salt works. There are plans to restore the chapel containing a beautiful Virgin donated by the company, and eventually they plan to build modest facilities for a few tourists to visit the island.

Chapter Six

LORETO IN THE 20TH CENTURY

Under a canopy of fluttering palms and spreading eighteenth century shade trees, her poor shoulders pressed close against the thorny thickets of a treacherous arroyo, the bereft Mother of the Missions sleeps the southern sleep of forgetfulness while the crooning voices of the Vermilion Sea whisper wistfully about her. They are telling of the days when the admirals of Cortez sought the Island of California; they are singing of the knightly Salvatierra, first of the Jesuits, of the earnest Franciscan, Junipero Serra, of cowled Dominicans, of haughty Dons, earliest Governors of the Californias, who here held court. They are murmuring of armadores de perlas who delved deep for brilliant pearls. With plaintive sadness they are whispering of storms that rocked the Mother Mission, of corsairs who bore away her wreaths of pearls, of the passing of the Padres, of glories lost, of oppression, of neglect and of dreams.

Arthur W. North, a California lawyer and adventurer, wrote this romantic impression of Loreto during his visit there in April of 1906. North began traveling down the Baja California Peninsula on a burro, camping and hunting along the way, in December of 1905. Before undertaking this adventure, he had read all the available literature he could find on the peninsula, and during his trip he developed a love and respect for the land and its people that were evident in his later writings.

He estimated that in 1906 Loreto had a population of about five hundred people, with a fringe of thatched houses and a plaza with 18th century buildings of adobe and stone. He

Visitors to Loreto in the Early 1900s

199

found the mission in a sad state of neglect.

A large church it was, built of stone, the rough and cut cemented together, flat roofed, with bells swung above the northeast corner. Off at the right were a cemetery and an ell forming a chapel; to the left extended a goodly patio. Entering, I noticed above me a projecting gallery, perhaps a choir loft, with a high carved railing...With walls five feet in thickness the windows and doors of the church are deeply indented; shutters and rounded wooden bars protect the windows. The flooring is part stone cubes, part earth – and the footprints in the dust are all of women. Though made of stone, the altar has been sadly dismantled. About it there are several one-piece onyx fonts, beautiful even in their fractured state. Above the altar hang three large oil paintings and five empty frames; above and back of the shrines – of which there are several – there are immense torn tapestries, sadly faded from the rain that has come through the leaky roof. At the left of the altar there is a closed room, used to store what has escaped the cupidity of vandals. From the patio a broken stairway leads through the choir loft and upwards to the roof and the bells, five in number. Dating back as they do to the close of the seventeenth century, it is not surprising that the rim surfaces of these bells have been worn smooth, the outer surfaces, too, for

Carmen Larrinaga, 1905, and the bells of the Loreto mission church
Photo: Arthur W. North, provided by Mary North Allen.

"Ancient Bells of Loreto", Sea of Cortez in the distance, 1905.
Photo: Arthur W. North, provided by Mary North Allen.

the usual method of sounding them seems to have been for a man to strike them in quick succession with an iron bar. The mission has suffered so severely from earthquakes and neglect that only a suggestion of its pristine beauty and majesty now remains – and unless repairs are promptly made, the main building will shortly fall asunder.

He noted that although a priest came to Loreto only once a year, the women of the town made regular daily visits to the church. He met and photographed young Carmen Larrinaga who, from the age of twelve, dedicated her life to caring for the church and teaching the Catholic catechism to the children. He saw fruits and vegetables growing in the gardens and was told

Loreto town square, early 20th century. Photo: Loreto Municipio Archives.

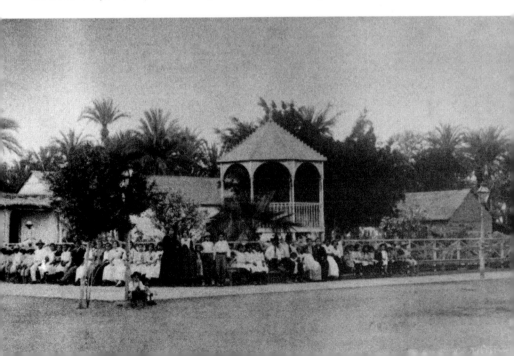

that there was considerable export trade, most of it fruit and vegetables produced in Comondú. With pleasure he recalled meeting young Amadeo Romero and his brother, whom he described as "the most thorough gentlemen and the most progressive men of their age whom I had met upon the Peninsula."

In the early part of the century visitors to Loreto were rare, but several north Americans wrote accounts of their experiences and impressions of this part of Mexico.

An unnamed person or persons came in 1919 to survey the trails around Loreto and the town itself on behalf of the Western Department of the U.S. Intelligence Service, which was preparing a handbook for the southern district of Baja California. It included a description of trails from Comondú "rough", and the anchorage off the town "good at a half-mile from the beach in ordinary weather, but not safe for a vessel not well found in ground tackle when the winds are strong". Nothing much to interest a spy.

In 1932, Griffing Bancroft, a wealthy American from San Diego, arrived in Loreto on his yacht, *The Least Petrel*. He wrote:

Life centered about the plaza; there the spirit of Loreto stood revealed. The bandstand was very old, as were its accompaniments, and over all its surroundings was thrown a pronounced atmosphere of decay and dejection. The long ago enthusiasts who had been fired with the courage to build have left descendants lacking both the ambition and the energy to maintain the inheritance. One cannot be long in Loreto and not feel the spirit of stagnation and depression.

Loreto has saved some things out of her past. The mission relics, for instance, include woodwork whose heavy relief is covered with gold leaf – the broken picture of bygone beauty. Old homes, several of which, in part at least, are still occupied by the families of the builders, a long street under a community veranda, and, strangest of all, a social prestige that permeates and dominates. In surroundings little less squalid than the simplest we have seen in other pueblos live people whose pride of ancestry is as strong as is such feeling in any other part of America. Moreover, the claims are admitted, and the influ-

Interior of the Loreto church, 1945. Photo courtesy of Nora Harlow.

ence of the impoverished aristocracy can hardly be exaggerated. Loreto is the Back Bay of Western Mexico.

We left Loreto with a feeling akin to that which comes from visiting a sick friend. We had found what we had expected, but we had not been fully prepared for the extent of the ravages of time. Of all the towns we visited in Lower California, this is the one that taught us the most: It is the place that connects yesterday with today, the spot that must have inspired the great Díaz to his famous phrase: "Pobre Baja California".

On March 17, 1940, the famous American writer John Steinbeck arrived in Loreto with his friend Ed Ricketts and the

The Loreto church, 1945. Photo courtesy of Nora Harlow.

crew of the *Western Flyer*. Steinbeck was accompanying his friend on a cruise of the Sea of Cortez to study its marine life. In his book *The Log From the Sea of Cortez*, he wrote:

A serious small boy attached himself to us...This small boy could have been an ambassador to almost any country in the world. His straight-seeing eyes were courteous, yet firm. He told us something of Loreto, of its poverty and how its church was tumbled down now; and he walked with us to the destroyed mission. The roof had fallen in and the main body of the church was a mass of rubble. From the walls hung the shreds of old paintings...We wormed our way up to look at the old bells and strike them softly with the palms of our hands so that they glowed a little with tone. From here we could look down on the low roofs and into the enclosed gardens of the town. The white sunlight could not get into the gardens and a sleepy shade lay in them.

One small chapel was intact in the church, but the door to it was barred by a wooden grille, and we had to peer through into the small, dark, cool room...The Virgin Herself, Our Lady of Loreto, was in a glass case and surrounded by the lilies of the recently past Easter. In the dim light of the chapel she seemed very lovely...We came back slowly through the deserted streets of Loreto, and we walked quietly laden with submergence in a dim chapel.

Before they came to Loreto, Steinbeck and Ricketts put in to Puerto Escondido. Leopoldo Perpuly was living there then, and he and some local ranchers escorted the visitors on a big horn sheep hunt in the mountains in back of the port. They went by mule and on foot to where "a tiny stream of water fell hundreds of feet from pool to pool. There were palm trees and wild grapevines and large ferns, and the water was cool and sweet." They fired a couple of shots but never hit anything, and they spent the evening around the fire telling stories. The stories were in Spanish and most seemed to be about a pretty young schoolteacher and a handsome student. The Americans never did get the punch lines because "the snappers were either so colloquial that we could not understand them or so filled with the laughter of the teller that we couldn't make out the words."

When Sandra Ryan interviewed Leopoldo in 1973, she

had the book with her and translated the part about their visit to Puerto Escondido into English for Leopoldo. Sandra wrote:

> When I read Steinbeck's account of their hunt, Leopoldo asked me to go over it again. When I finished the second time, he smiled and nodded with relief. It was all true. Everything that John Steinbeck wrote about the hunt was correct. It had happened that way, precisely that way. And most important of all was the fact that he had only written down some of the jokes they told that night, not all. It was better that way. When men are around a fire and wrapped in blankets, the stories they tell are not meant to be written down in books. And it was true that John Steinbeck must have been a great writer, because a great writer would know that.

LUIS ARCE MESA

To Luis Arce Mesa, born in La Purísima in 1897 and brought by his parents to Loreto when he was an infant, Loreto was not a romantic place of lost glories and dreams but simply the town where he grew up and lived for the next hundred years.

I first met Luis in 1995 through his niece Guadalupe (Lupe) Fernández Márques, who took us to the house where he lived with his great-niece Margarita. My lovely Chilean friend Juanita Swain went with me, as she did on all our subsequent visits to Luis, to clarify my Spanish and help interpret. We found him to be a small courtly man with a sharp mind and a keen sense of humor. His only handicap seemed to be deafness, but his nieces helped by shouting our questions in his good ear. We weren't surprised when his nieces confided that he had always had an eye for the ladies, and he obviously found Juanita enchanting and joked about taking her dancing. His nieces also told us his nickname was "El Huito", a slang term for frugal, because he had a reputation for not wanting to part with his hard-earned money. He was very generous to us with his time, however, and we spent wonderful hours talking with him over a period of two years.

When Refugio and Efren Arce Mesa brought baby Luis to Loreto in 1898, it was a very small town, and most of the houses were made of palms. A few people with some money had adobe or wooden houses. Luis told us his house was made of palms, but it was a good house.

Richer people had furniture made of wood that came from the mainland. Benches made from local wood were common in poor houses. Los pobres used to sleep on the floor on sacks, and there were a lot of fleas. Other people slept on beds made of wood frames with crossed strips of leather on top.

The food was good. We ate fish, turtle, and wild meat, especially venison. Some families kept a small garden where they planted tomatoes, chilies, cabbage, and onions. We also ate some of the native food. I liked chayote, similar to a sweet potato, and sweet and sour pitaya. Cardón was very good boiled in water with sugar, the heart of the mescal plant *tatimaro,* cooked in a hole in the ground, is delicious. Mescal is also a good medicine for colds and stomachache, and you can make tequila with it. I liked to have a glass sometimes on Sunday, and I liked sweet wine, too. The best wine came from Comondú, because it was very strong and was made without chemicals.

The gardens were watered from wells. There were wells for every three or four houses, but the water was somewhat salty and was only used for washing or gardening. There were only four wells in the town that provided sweet water, and the people went to those wells for their drinking water.

The church at that time was flat on top, because the tower fell down in the earthquake. Eventually, most of the roof fell down, too. There wasn't a priest in Loreto, but once in a while a priest came to baptize the children. The children learned their prayers from their mothers. There was a lady, Carmen Larrinaga, who celebrated the sacred holidays at Easter and Christmas and got the people together to pray at the church. Carmen had a beautiful voice, and she sang the old songs that were dedicated to the Loreto Virgin. Usually couples were married by law and had a big party. When the priest came they got married again in the church.

The school was very small, with first and second grades only. They didn't have writing paper. All the students' work was done on a small blackboard. I learned how to read and some arithmetic, but I didn't go to school often as, since I was six years old, I had to help my father fish. After the second grade most of the girls stayed at home, and only the boys and

Luis Arce Mesa,
age 100.
Photo:
Leland Foerster.

girls whose families could afford it and had family in La Paz or
other cities could continue their education.

Many years ago the fishing canoes were made in one piece
from a big tree trunk. They came from San Blas, Nayarit. There
were contractors in Loreto. They bought the boats and provided everything for the fishermen, their nets and food, and also
paid them some salary. The boatmen used oars and some simple sails. The sails were made of canvas, *manta* they call it here.
The poor people made sails from flour sacks sometimes. With
the sails the boats could go fast. They went to Isla Coronados,
Isla del Carmen, Catalana and far away. At times they went to
San Nicolás, Mulegé, to Los Barriles and Santa Rosalia.

When the sea was too rough for fishing, Luis' father took
him deer hunting. His father was also a skilled leather worker.
The animal hides were processed with a solution of lime and
water and the bark of the palo blanco tree, turning it every day,
and then hung out to dry. A stick or bone was used to scrape
off any leftover meat. Luis used to help by cutting the palo
blanco trees. The bark, called *cascalote*, was very high in tannic
acid, and boats came to Loreto to get it. Luis was paid one-and-
a-half centavos for each kilo of cascalote, and each bundle of

the bark weighed 50 kilos. The hides his father didn't use were sold in La Paz.

My father, who was called "Tata Cuco", used to make beautiful riding saddles. He made a special one for women, too. All the people had horses and bought saddles from Tata Cuco. Young and old people came from the ranches to Loreto for all the fiestas, and they promenaded on horseback in the streets, especially in December and the first part of January.

Luis started pearl diving with his father when he was ten years old. They dove off Coronados Island, along the coast near Loreto, and by the bay at Nopolo. When he went diving he didn't wear clothes, he said, just a *chapuza*, loincloth, like the Indians.

In order to dive for pearls you had to get a diving permit, which cost twenty pesos for the season. The seasons were between the growth of the *lama* (plankton), which begins to grow at the beginning of the warm weather in April, and the growth of the *sargazo*, a sea plant that grows in the winter. Sometimes during the sargazo we could dive if we could find a clear space. There is a lot of sargazo in the deep. There are some like fans, and they are strongly attached to the sand. There are some shells, too, that are strongly attached to the rocks. In the deep, there are places covered by small shells called *chicharon*. There are millions of them. Inside the shells some little crabs live that, being male and female, produce the eggs for reproduction. On the sandy spots there are no shells. One time Ramundo Romero found a big pearl, 40 karats, at Danzantes Island. They say it went to England.

The pearls were sold in Loreto, and there was a big demand. The Loreto buyers then took them to La Paz to sell. Divers were paid in silver or gold coins. Prices were set by the quality of the pearls. First class pearls paid very well. The pearl color was very important; they were white, green, black, blue, iridescent.

Luis told the story of one diver who found a 25-karat pearl:

The divers worked for Don Elias, but the diver who found the big pearl, instead of giving it to Don Elias, sold it to Don Romulo Davis. Don Elias then demanded it. The Loreto aduana (customs officer) demanded it, and then the aduana came from La Paz and took the pearl there. The diver didn't have a permit. Then Don Elias lost the pearl and Don Romolu lost the money, and the diver was sent to jail in Comondú. Everyone wonders what happened to the pearl.

We asked Luis about other kinds of work he had done. When he was ten years old he had helped make the adobe for the house that is on the property where we live. He and another boy made a mixture of mud and straw, called *zacate,* to make the adobe. A man brought some special soil in a cart. Luis remembered that it was very hard to do this work, because they mixed it with their bare feet in winter, and it was cold. The owner of the house at that time was Valentín Murillo.

Luis had also cut firewood to sell to the copper mine at Santa Rosalía. They cut mesquite, uño de gato, palo blanco, palo colorado, and mangalé. The woodcutters brought the wood to a storage place at the beach near the present-day marina, and the boats came once in a while to pick it up. The boats were able to carry up to five hundred logs. Luis, who is a small man, boasted he could carry three wood loads at a time from the storage area to the boat.

When my family first came to Loreto the streets were not laid out, and houses were built wherever the families pleased. The price of lots was one centavo a meter in 1897. Land and property taxes were twenty pesos. If the taxes were not paid on time, the people had to pay interest or the property could be

The adobe house of Luis Arce Mesa. Photo: Leland Foerster.

auctioned. There were houses around where the plaza is now. When I was eight years old, our teacher took the children to carry stones to help make the plaza.

The adobe house on the southwest corner of the plaza, which was torn down recently to build a hotel, has been there ever since I can remember. Later, Don Felipe Largo lived in that house. Felipe Largo came to Loreto as the aduana around 1912, and the aduana office was in that house. Other houses around the plaza belonged to Chavalo Romero, Romulo Davis, and Ricardo Larrinaga.

Luis remembered vividly the time of the 1910 revolution when Francisco Madero overthrew the Porfirio Díaz regime in Mexico:

There was a small group of Maderistas in Loreto. Nicolás Perpuly commanded it. Other Maderistas were Charnes Real, El Chep Villalobos, Adolfo Larrinaga, Pancho Verdugo, Arturo Romero, a small group. They called themselves revolutionaries, but they only went to the mountains to kill and eat fat cows. Soldiers arrived in Loreto to get them. Charnes Real escaped. The women of the town dressed him as an old woman, and he hid in the mountains. The soldiers went to Lupe Fernández' grandmother's house as she was sweeping the street and asked her if she was getting rid of evidence. A ship arrived at the port, full of soldiers, and they opened fire at Tierra Firma, a little hill. My brothers and I were still young, and we got so scared we hid in a well. Later on, we went to Divisadero, a high place where you can look around, and hid in a cave there. While we were there, a fox joined us in the cave. Divisidero and Cerro Colorado were full of very scared people.

He told us that in those days there were different names for money. Centavos were called *polas* or *politas*. One *real* was twelve centavos. one *peseta real*, twenty-five centavos. One of the coins had an eagle on one side and a scale on the other.

We asked him what they did for entertainment when he was a young man and he said that before electricity, people used to visit each other often:

They went from house to house after dinner to talk. For light, they used a plate filled with oil and a piece of rope, a *can-*

Loreto musicians, early 20th century. Photo: Loreto Municipio Archives.

tile. The families were close then; they knew all the cousins, aunts, uncles. People got together to tell stories and riddles.

We used to go dancing to a place called El Cajón. Cruz Murillo played the guitar there, and another man played the violin. The young men stayed until three or four o'clock in the morning, dancing, smoking, talking. Sometimes we offered our girlfriends a glass of sweet wine or beer. The young men and boys used to serenade the girls, but I didn't. I picked flowers for the girls to wear in their hair.

Luis liked to dance, and his nieces said he was a very good dancer and the girls liked him, but it was then that he became known as "El Huito". One of the traditional dances he enjoyed was called *"los juegos de la cruz"* (games of the cross). Like the other dances, this one was performed in people's houses or sometimes in the plaza:

It was a ritual, naming the five mysteries of the rosary. Five places were set up as altars, and each altar had two godparents, a man and a woman. They were supposed to be very respectful people. The cross was carried in front of the altar. Everybody knelt and prayed in front of the cross. Each time the cross was moved in front of the altars, there was a toast, and a dancing party followed. Small cookies, called "fruit of the oven", and a glass of tamarind tea were served.

211

The pastorilla was another celebration. The people prayed a novena in December, and everybody dressed up for church. There were celebrations on May 5 and September 15 and 16. Almost all the girls celebrated their birthday with dances. Everybody behaved. The first of May was celebrated in a big way on Carmen Island. In Loreto, the people, young and old, promenaded on their horses on December 25th. Then there was the Day of the Virgin of Loreto on September 8, the Rosary days, the San Javier festivities in December. It took my friends and me about seven hours to reach the San Javier fiesta on horseback. We took a blanket, some food, and one bottle of tequila for the trip.

Matachines (Indian dancers from the mainland) used to come to dance at the fiestas and the processions. They wore *cascabeles* (jingle bells) on their arms and ankles and played violins and drums.

On June 24, the day of San Juan, everybody would have a bath, at their homes or on the beach, and all the girls would cut their hair. The women used to wear their hair long. Some cut just a little piece, but some cut all their beautiful long tresses.

Sometimes a man would drink too much and fall down or make noise in the street. Then the neighbors used to take care

Loreto's main street, early 20th century. Photo: Loreto Municipio Archives.

of them. Now, if you do that, they take you very quickly to jail. People didn't worry about robberies. They went to sleep on the beach. Not anymore!

In the early days, the town had only one policeman. One of his duties was to light the kerosene lamps at the plaza. He was supposed to keep order. He didn't know how to read or write, but he was a good man.

Some men, after drinking got into fights, usually with knives. If one of them was cut badly, the other ran away to the mountains and came back a few months later when everything was forgotten. Not many people lived in Loreto then, and they all knew each other. The tequila and wine that usually caused the fights came from the mountains. As the wine was aged in leather bags, it tasted good. Around here, in Rancho Los Dolores, a man named Chavalo Murillo used to make very good tequila. His son drank it like water and died because of it. A liquor made of dates was made at Zacatal and was very good.

Luis never saw an automobile until he was a grown man. The first car to arrive in Loreto belonged to Santos Castro. The car came by boat from Santa Rosalía in 1920. Later on, Romulo Davis brought a small Model A Ford by boat. The top was made of canvas. (Several people have told us that the two cars met at a corner one day and collided.) Still later, an American somehow brought a car to Loreto over horse trails through the mountains.

Luis Arce Mesa, "El Huito," died peacefully in September of 1998. He had worked hard all his life at the kind of labor that most of the men in Loreto did to survive. He had been a fisherman, a pearl diver, a woodcutter, a builder of adobe houses, a vaquero. Juanita once asked him if he thought he had had a good life, and he replied, "Yes, why not? Besides I can't change anything now."

RÓMULO AND LUPE FERNÁNDEZ

Rómulo Fernández Real was born in Loreto and has written about its history. His wife Guadalupe Márques de Fernández is descended from a soldier who came to Loreto with Salvatierra in the 17th century. Together they described a

Rómulo and Lupe Fernández

typical household in the early part of the 20th century:

The walls were made of taco palms held by arches of *uña de gato* (ironwood). At one end of the main room was a turtle shell, framing a mirror on the wall, and the family's toothbrushes were kept in a horn hanging next to it. Nearby were several small basins. There was also a large jar made of stone or clay containing fresh water. If the container was made of clay, it was covered on the outside by cloth to keep the water fresher. If it was made of stone, it had a small pot placed underneath in order to collect any water that filtered through the stone. The wooden, brightly painted sink was nearby also. To the side of this was a large pot where the dirty water was deposited. There was also a shell to hold the soap and a large basin for washing, with a towel hanging to the side. The furniture was very rustic.

The kitchen was separate from the house and connected to it by an open corridor. In the kitchen there was a wood burning stove made of stone and a table holding a *metate,* a grinding stone, which was used to prepare meals. In the corridor there was a large wooden table surrounded by chairs, which were occupied by children with the exception of the head chair for the father and a chair at his side for the mother. The mother was the last to sit at the table. The father served himself first. Meals were silent and very formal. Once the father and the children were finished eating, then the mother sat down to eat. It was at this time that the formality gave way to informal conversation in which everyone participated. When this happened, chickens would enter and peck for whatever had been spilled on the packed dirt floor.

At the beginning of the century, Loreto was very poor, and a lot of people left. Fish was easy to catch, but other essential foods were expensive and not always available, because at that time there were no roads and everything had to come by boat. It was a little easier for people who had some cattle or a garden.

When an animal was killed, the meat was salted and dried. Both the meat and bones were used, the bones for soup. Dinner was eaten very early. Beds were pallets or cots and were folded up in the daytime and brought out at night. In hot weather, most families slept outside.

Water didn't come to our houses until 1960. Five faucets had been installed in various places around the town, and people went to the nearest one to get their water. We didn't get electricity until June 20, 1964, and that night all the people in the pueblo gathered at the square for a big celebration. Before then, people went to bed early and got up early. It was dark and quiet in those days. Women were always busy ironing, making tortillas, mashing frijoles, grinding coffee, washing, cooking on the wood stove, sweeping, sewing, watering the garden, taking care of the children.

ESTER MURILLO MESA

In 1990, we interviewed another of Lupe Fernández' elderly relatives, her aunt Ester Murillo Mesa, who was born in December of 1895 in Comondú and came to Loreto in 1900. Ester said there were about fifty families in the town then.

Everyone was poor, but every family had a garden where they grew vegetables and a few fruit trees. They had chickens, pig, cows, and burros and were pretty self-sufficient.

Boats came regularly from Guaymas via Santa Rosalía and Mulegé bringing petroleum, beans, rice, pasta, and other food supplies and clothing, The boats were named *Peninsular* and *Viosa I, II, III* and *IV*. Once in a while, a boat came directly from Guaymas to Puerto Escondido. From Loreto the boats took produce from Comondú, olives, dates, grapes, and dried fish, shark, goat skins, cheese and a lot of turtle back to the mainland. Fidencio Perpuly used to rent boats for trading. Some people called him the *cacique* (powerful man) of Loreto.

When I was a child, all the houses around the square were built of wood or adobe, but most houses in town were made of palm. The post office was located in various homes over the years, and the telegraph came to Loreto in 1917. In the early part of the century, people had to go to Comondú to marry or to go to jail.

There was no regular priest in Loreto until Padre Modesto Sánchez arrived in 1947. Priests came once in a while by ship from La Paz. There was Padre Cesar who visited the whole territory and on up to Ensenada. He died in 1946. He started coming here after the revolution in the 1920s. He was Italian. After the Dominicans left, priests occasionally came, but I don't know what order they were from. From 1925 on they traveled up and down the peninsula. During the presidency of Plutarco Elías Calles in 1924, he implemented the punitive articles applying to religion and deported all the foreign priests. The churches remained without clergy for three years, although the government kept them open and the people continued to worship in them.

My aunt Carmen Larrinaga was born around 1880, and when she was only twelve years old she took charge of the church. She knew all the old hymns and led the rosaries and

Salvatierra Street looking west from the sea, early 20th century.
Photo: Loreto Municipio Archives.

Ester Murillo Mesa, at age ninety.

taught the children their catechism. There were many years when there was no priest in Loreto, and Carmen was in charge. The church was in ruins from the earthquake. Everything was falling down. The main altar was a wreck. Then Padre Sánchez rebuilt it.

Santos Castro brought the first automobile to Loreto in 1920. Everyone was afraid of it; they thought it was a bull. The first airplane came to Loreto in about 1928. Everyone was terrified and ran and hid in their houses. I thought the pilots were very brave. There was no airport, only a five or six hundred meter runway. Teachers took their classes out to look at the first plane. In 1948 or 1949 Transmar de Cortés began to fly to Loreto. They flew Guaymas - Loreto - La Paz. Aero Lineas Contreras flew from Loreto to Tijuana. At about that time the boats stopped coming to Loreto.

Like Luis Arce, Ester remembered the federal soldiers coming to Loreto during the revolution:

The revolution of 1910 didn't affect Baja California very much, except that federal soldiers came to Loreto from time to time looking for Maderistas. Once, as they landed, a man named Real shouted, "Viva Madero!" and then ran. The soldiers couldn't catch him, because the women dressed him in a rebozo and hid him among themselves. That night they took him out and hid him in the mountains. The federales searched, but they never found him. In Comondú the federales shot and hung several Maderistas. They called it an execution. At every shot the people cried, "Viva Madero!" In the church in Comondú there are bullet holes from the revolution. One time when a coast guard ship came close to Loreto my grandfathers Don Romulo and Don Facundo went out with other men to visit, but the federales shot at them. They dove into the water to get away, Don Juanito Rubio also. The federales were looking for Maderistas and government employees. Many people tried to hide in Comondú and the mountains, but the soldiers followed them. The bravest people stayed in Loreto, and the soldiers didn't shoot them if they stayed in their houses. The soldiers ate the chickens and the pigs and whatever else they found. We hid whatever we could.

Ester told us there had been hurricanes in 1931 and 1946. But Hurricane Claudia in 1959 was the most severe and just about razed the town.

Romulo Salinas Benavides was the Delegado in Loreto when that hurricane occurred. People said when the storm started, Don Romulo went to the second floor of the municipal building and hid. The new school they were building and most of the houses went down. My grandfather's house also collapsed. By the arroyo there were many dead chickens, cows and burros, and then the bad odor started. The people who cleaned up after the hurricane were paid in food and clothing.

The Three Sisters of Las Parras   Rancho Las Parras (The Grapevines) is in the mountains west of Loreto on the road to San Javier. It is one of the oldest ranches in the Californias. Sandra Ryan, our friend who planned to write a novel set in Loreto, taped many conversations with Loretanos in 1973. When she recorded her visits with two of the three sisters living at Las Parras, Rosario and Lolita de los Santos, there were no men living at the ranch. The third sister, Loreto, was not well at the time and had gone to Loreto to recover. Their father had died, and their brothers had all left many years before. The orchard at Las Parras is in the arroyo, surrounded by high rocky cliffs. The ranch house is on one side of the road to San Javier and the family chapel on the other. The chapel was built in 1960 and consecrated by Padre Modesto Sánchez. Their mother, who died in 1967 at the age of 100, is buried there. The old ranch house was made of dark stone and its two rooms were connected by a ramada. Across the yard was a stone storage house and behind it was a clear, deep pool.

LOLITA DE LOS SANTOS

In January of 1973, Sandra interviewed Dolores "Lolita/Lola" de Los Santos, the youngest of the Las Parras sisters. Don and I had met her at the ranch many years ago and remembered her as a very heavy woman with a pretty face and a warm personality. Luis Arce had told us that she acted as the head of the family.

Lola started her interview with Sandra by saying:

I want to begin by telling you about the years when the orchards were planted. The men, the proprietors, were two Spaniards, Lalo Osorio and Enrique Juan García. They came to Las Parras to build the church of San Javier, and when they began construction on the church, they founded Rancho Las Parras. They planted the grove that is there to this day. They planted all kinds of trees in 1757. And today, 1973, there is the same grove. It hasn't dried up.

Las Parras first belonged to my father's great-grandparents, and from then it changed hands through sales until it came into our hands. The old house was built with the planting of the orchards in 1757.

All of the owners of the ranch have cultivated the grove successfully. There are all types of trees. The most important fruits of our harvest are the olives, oranges and mangoes. And the grapes! The ranch bears the name of Las Parras because there are many grapevines. They made wine, a magnificent wine. Now, no, but in those times. Now, grapes are cheap, and they don't bring in money. They only bring in three pesos a kilo, and it doesn't pay to use the land to grow them. Black figs pay well. We used to sell cowhides in Loreto, too.

There are many very old trees on the ranch, more than two hundred years old. Once we wanted to dig up one of the mesquite trees to reclaim the soil, because the tree was old and very big. Beneath the tree was a corpse, seated, and with a shell in the cheek and another in the head. He was an Indian, because he was buried in a sitting position. The long legs, the arms, and all of the bones were seated just as they had been when they buried him.

Sandra asked Lolita about rock paintings on the property, and she said:

I've learned how the Indians painted those with rocks. First, they put the rocks through hot fire, and then they threw them into water to soak them. A little old man whom they called Almadra told me that almadra was a yellow stone, which they smelted until it turned red.

How I used to enjoy the fiestas in the old days, especially when we girls went everywhere by horseback! We used to sell meat, fruit and vegetables at the fiestas. Then we put all the purchases aside and danced for four days. I used to dance a lot. I was young then.

ROSARIO DE LOS SANTOS

The first time Don and I stopped at Las Parras about twenty-five years ago, Rosario invited us into their house to see a mountain lion her brother Prisciliano had shot the week before. The sisters had stuffed the good-sized lion with paper and stood it proudly in the middle of the living room. We were introduced to the other two sisters who were attending to a little girl whose family had brought her to them because she was suffering from a persistent stomachache. Lolita was massaging the child's stomach while Loreto was explaining to the mother how to prepare the herbs she was giving her to take home. The low ceilinged, rather shadowy room was bustling with activity, and there was a rather overpowering smell of dead mountain lion, so Don and I were happy to accept Rosario's invitation to tour the orchard. She was a small, energetic, wiry woman, completely unlike her sisters. She dressed in pants and obviously spent most of her time outside supervising the workers and doing a lot of the work herself. She showed us their spring, which flowed from underground through rocks and told us it was very clean, very pure water, and she seemed to know every tree, plant, and animal on the ranch intimately.

This turned out to be true. When Sandra walked the ranch and recorded their conversation, Rosario demonstrated her knowledge. At one point they passed cowhide vats that had been slung between pieces of wood. Rosario went over to them:

These are to cure olives. The containers are made of cow skins. We take the skins and cure them. Then we cure the olives, first with lime and afterwards with a tincture. Then we put them in the skins. When they are cured, we take them out and put them in gallon glass containers or tin cans. We slit the olives while they're still green after they've been taken from the trees.

Those men over there are cutting wood into a plank so that they can make shredded beef. They dry the meat well, then they beat it, shredding it with a stick. Lola puts a chair there, and when the men come to work, she sits down and directs them.

Look at the white wing doves. There is a lot of water here, and they like to roost. They fly in flocks of about three hundred. We kill them with shotguns.

Those molds we use to make loaves of sugar candy. This is the macho, the male tree of all the olive trees in the grove. That's why we left this tree standing and have cut down some of the other old ones. It's a little broken around the trunk, but it will be cemented before the rains come. I think we will have a bumper crop of olives this year. One hopes there will be a lot of fruit so that there will be work for the men. As you know, we manage solely with strange men. We have brothers, but they all have their own homes now. This property has been transferred through our family for many years, and now only we remain. Lola wants to sell. I don't want to sell, I tell you. There are 1,500 hectares. When I can no longer work in the orchards, yes. But look! I go with the servants here and there. I climb the trees, and I pick the fruit. I carry it to the house. Olives, figs, mangoes. Everything. And Lola says we must sell because we are getting to be old ladies. I'm seventy-two years old, but they say a working woman lasts a long time.

Sandra noticed a young boy with the workers and asked who he was:

He's from over yonder, past that mountain range, from Parral. He's Rodolfo Calichi's son. He never saw an automobile before he came here. He and his family never saw people. No one other than themselves. Now, when he sees an automobile he runs to see what's going on. He chases after the moving car as far as the chapel until it's out of his line of vision. He doesn't seem to get his fill of strange and new sights. He's been with us for three months now. His father kept him secluded in the past, away from material temptation. His little sisters and brothers are raised the same way. His hair was never cut. Lola cut his hair, and when he went back to the ranch for a visit, they didn't recognize him.

Sandra and Rosario resumed their tour, and Sandra asked if the tangerines were in season:

Yes, they are sweet and good to make conserves with. We also make guayaba and orange marmalade. I make a lot of mango preserves, too. These are anise plants. They have a lovely odor; that's why I don't uproot them. They're fragrant and very good for a stomachache. See those grapevines. I propped them up. All of them. With the boy. And we removed the dead twigs and branches. Everything is dirty around here. But it must all be cleaned by the months of July and August. All of the tropical trees and vines, too. That's when the grapes will be drying to make raisins.

Sandra asked if Rosario was getting tired:

Truthfully, no. I keep going all day long. I never lie down during the day. Not even in the hot season. I always tell the girls, 'You go to sleep. Take a siesta. I'll watch over things.' Because everything here depends on me. I go around all day watching the boys as they work. Many of these orange trees are 150 years old, and more. Look at this olive tree. Look how old it is! My great uncles planted them. Over there are prickly pears. They're American ones. I brought them from the United States, from Hollister. I was visiting my brother.

Those olives that are lying on the ground are ripe. I gather them and make oil from them. I crush them in a metate with a little stone. Then I extract the oil by soaking them in pure hot, boiling water. The olives compress that way. Yesterday and the day before, I worked hard extracting oil. I keep working all the time. I never get sick. I'm always healthy. The other girls, Lola and Loreto, have high blood pressure. I always like to wear pants when I go through the orchards and to wear men's shoes, too. The shoes I have on are my aunt's. Right now, I don't have any of my own because I haven't gone to Loreto.

I was engaged once. I was going to be married, but then he fought with one of my brothers, and I broke off the engagement. If he fought before the wedding, think how it would be later. And so none of us married. Because, we said, if one of us gets married, the husband would be in charge of things. He would take over the business of running the ranch, and we would naturally have to turn things over to him.

Sandra and Rosario continued their walk, talking about the trees, the crops, the winter winds and the destruction they had brought. It was the middle of the afternoon before they got back to the ranch house. They found visitors there. A young couple had brought their daughter up to the ranch.

Sandra wrote:

The child had problems with the bones in her skull. There were, Lola explained, lesions. There were still parts that were soft and vulnerable. She had the skull of a newborn. They had been to doctors in La Paz and Guadalajara and Mexico City, and now they had come to the Chapel at Las Parras to pray in hopes of a miracle.

When we went to the chapel, Lola led the ceremony. She stood at the altar, close to the place where her mother was buried, and she read. She was a huge priestess, massive, wearing black, her deep voice echoing, reverberating against the walls of the shrine as she read from a Latin text. The child knelt between her parents with her head bent and, for a time, there was nothing in the world but Lola's voice and the early spring sun coming through the open door.

When the ceremony was over, we walked back to the house, as we went up the narrow path toward the ramada, the child shrieked with delight. She pulled off her red sweater and ran ahead, defenseless, fragile.

"Don't run," the mother shouted.

Lola took her arm. "You'll see," she said. "If it weren't for God, many things wouldn't be possible. You will see what will happen. For us, it's different because we've lost our youth. It isn't the same to be old and sick, but when one is young, one has hope in God and in the future. And then, of course, there will be a cure."

But Lola walked faster, almost trotted, her large swollen feet slapped the umber-colored earth until she caught up with the child. Then she put her arm around the girl's shoulders, and they walked into the house together.

LORETO DE LOS SANTOS

When I recorded conversations with the third sister, Loreto, in 1998 and 1999, she was living in San Javier, and Las Parras had been sold to Gilberto Amador of Loreto. The old ranch house has been torn down and replaced by a sturdy new modern house, but the orchard looks just the same.

Loreto de los Santos was born in Loreto on February 12, 1898, one of eleven children of Antonia Romero Higuera and Prisciliano de Los Santos. She is the oldest of the Las Parras sisters and had been considered the frailest of the three, but she celebrated her 102nd birthday in February of 2000 and is still enjoying life. She uses a walker to get around, but her mind is sharp, and she has a good sense of humor. She loves to talk and to recall her life and the people she knew. Loreto lives now in San Javier with her brother, Prisciliano de los Santos, the baby of the family, who is only ninety-two.

Just before she was born, she told me, a terrible fever was killing people in the area, and her mother promised her child to the Virgin of Loreto if their lives were spared. At that time, children were usually baptized with the name of the saint of the day they were born, but she was named Loreto to fulfill her mother's promise.

She lived in Loreto for the first ten years of her life and remembers it as a very happy time. She described those years:

After the earthquake in 1877, and for many years afterward, Loreto was almost deserted, and when I was born there were not many people living there. At the beginning of the century there was extreme poverty. Things were cheap, but as there were no jobs, people couldn't afford to buy them. Bread cost two centavos, one egg three centavos. One real was the equivalent of twelve centavos, one media was six centavos. Loreto people could manage pretty well, because they could get fish

Loreto de los Santos, at age 102. Photo courtesy of Marilynne Keyser.

and turtle and other seafood, but it was pretty hard for the mountain people. They often had only mescal and agave roots and other desert plants to eat. Loreto people had the opportunity to work diving for pearls and for shells that were sold for mother-of-pearl, but the pay was low. But even in Loreto, people often had to eat what they could get, including desert plants, to survive. If someone had a small lot, they could plant a small garden and get potatoes, cabbages, beans.

My family admired the first aduana to arrive in Loreto, Ricardo Vuelas. He was an intelligent, educated man. He taught children and adults as a private tutor and charged money for his classes. My father contracted with him to teach his children, especially the boys. We learned a lot from him.

She also has fond memories of Carmen Larrinaga who taught her the catechism and all the songs of the church. She remembers that once a priest came and questioned why they sang "Salve Regina" instead of "Salve Virgin of Loreto." The people explained that the song was sung as the Jesuits had taught the Indians. The priest agreed they should continue singing it that way. Loreto sang the song for me in a quivery but true voice. Even at her age she can carry a tune better than I can.

In 1907, Loreto's father and her brothers built an adobe house in Loreto, making their adobe bricks from mud and chopped palm leaves. The house is still standing on the corner of Francisco Madero and Baja California Streets. But a year later, when Loreto was ten years old, her father bought his brothers' and sisters' shares of Las Parras and decided to move the family there.

> When our father moved the family to Las Parras, we girls were very unhappy. We cried a lot. We were afraid of the solitude, the silence. Our father told us that the family would be safer living at the ranch. If anything should happen to him, we could survive there. Our mother brought books to teach the children at the ranch, but I wish I had a better education.

Las Parras originally came into the possession of the de los Santos family when a Portuguese sailor, Antonio de los Santos, jumped ship in Loreto along with nine other sailors, probably in about 1850, because they were being badly mistreated. Antonio wandered around for a while and then married Rosario Acevedo, whose family owned Las Parras. At that time it wasn't a very good business to have an orchard. Vegetables were grown, too, but the area of good soil for planting them was very small, only enough for the family. They had horses, cows and goats on the ranch.

Loreto and her brother Prisciliano told us a wonderful story about their Portuguese grandfather:

> One day, riding on a burro, Antonio left his pregnant wife and three children to search for a lost goat. The burro somehow took him all the way to Loreto, and there happened to be a boat there about to sail to Portugal. He went aboard and sailed away. Five years later, he sailed back to Baja California, this time landing in Santo Domingo on the Pacific side of the peninsula. He bought a burro and a goat and reappeared at Rancho Los Parras from the opposite side of the mountain. When Antonio left, his wife was pregnant, and when he returned the boy was five years old.

Antonio lived and worked on the ranch until he was quite old, but he was carried to Loreto when he got very sick. They said he had been hit on the chest by the boom of a sailboat when he was a sailor, and that caused his death. He is buried in the Loreto cemetery. His wife, Rosario, is buried in the graveyard next to the chapel at Las Parras with our little sister and older sister and our father. Only our mother, Antonia, is buried in the chapel. She lived to be 100. As the chapel was already built when she died, she is buried there.

Loreto described the meals at the ranch as very simple:

Breakfast usually was tortillas, meat, eggs, frijoles, olives and cheese. Lunch was soup and frijoles, and we didn't eat much at night. Food was abundant at Las Parras. People in San Javier were poorer; they had to eat roots, mostly mescal, and pitaya. They didn't eat meat often. There were not many houses in the San Javier area, and the houses were very primitive. Most of the walls were made of stone.

There were no doctors in the early part of the century. If you got really sick, you died. For medicine they used camomile, comino, oregano (very good for fever), cilantro, nopal, boraja. Other herbs my parents used were coriander seeds, yerba buena, and yerba de india. These herbs were boiled and used to cure colds, pains, stomach upsets, fever and earache. An old *curandera* (healer) named Pomoposa used salvia to cure throat infections. San Javier people lived a lot longer.

Loreto said that life was often very boring for young girls on the ranch, but she does remember some good times:

The whole family used to go to San Javier for the December festivities and to Loreto for Christmas and the New Year. When the girls reached fifteen, we were allowed to go to dances. Many of our family had birthdays in December, and they held dances at home. We grew grapes on the ranch, and our father made very good wine. People would stop at Las Parras on their way to San Javier for a glass of wine, so we had a lot of visitors. But it was hard work to produce the wine, and when our father died, the production stopped.

Our father became paralyzed when he was sixty-seven, and we older girls took care of him. After he died at age seventy-five, our mother, Lolita, Rosario and I remained. I lived on that ranch for sixty years.

Rosario died at Las Parras, and Prisciliano brought Loreto and Lolita to live with him in San Javier where Lolita passed away.

GUADALUPE VERDUGO DE DAVIS

When I taped conversations with Lupe Davis, she was living with her daughter Gloria Davis de Benzinger at the Hotel Oasis. Gloria and her husband Bill had opened this Loreto landmark in 1964, the first Loretanos to take advantage of the developing tourist fishing industry by building a hotel.

Lupe was born in Loreto in 1911 and says that when she was young it was very small, "maybe including the children, there were five hundred inhabitants." She talked about her life in Loreto when it was still a very small town:

In those early days of the century, there were three social classes. For example, in the first group were the merchants. They were the people who dressed better and lived better than most in the area. The families of Juan Antonio Romero, Fidencio Perpuly, and Romuló Romero Davis were in the first class. The women of those families all dressed well and in the latest style.

In the second class were the female cooks or maids who worked for their betters. The women cooks who worked in the kitchens and also looked after the children had very different lives. And they dressed differently because of their poverty. They lived with poverty, with misery, because we were all more or less poor then. Also in the second class were the fishermen and those who looked after the ranches and the animals. The third class were the laborers.

In this society there were different customs. For example, a servant couldn't enter a house without formal permission. Neither could a girl. I remember when I was a girl and I went to a house to perform an errand, I always had a written order from my mother. I would knock on the door, and if they opened it, you were questioned by the señor or señora, and you handed them the message. Then you left at once and returned to your own house.

When girls went to a dance or a party, their mother always went with them. And first they had to ask their father for permission to go.

Guadalupe Verdugo de Davis. Photo courtesy of Jack Foster.

We showed respect in those days. When my father came home from a trip, we would kiss his hand. Then we would hold hands and say, "Blessed be his safe return, his safe return and the Saintly Host of the Altar", and my father would respond, "God will make you a saint." That is how it was. It's different, now.

I remember Carmen Larrinaga who started taking care of the mission when she was twelve years old. She was noted for her piety. She taught the catechism to me and all the other children in town, and she rang the church bells and conducted rosaries every Sunday. There were many years when Loreto had no priest, and even though the Catholic Church was persecuted throughout the country, and in Loreto also, Carmen continued her religious activities.

In the early part of the 20th century there was no factory-made thread available. It had to be spun from locally grown cotton or wool. I made pillows for my children with this home-made thread and stuffed them with chicken feathers. I still have a comforter I made with pieces of silk cloth stuffed with local cotton.

Most produce in those days arrived from Guaymas. Unrefined sugar, called *piloncillo,* came from surrounding ranches and from San José de Comondú and Todos Santos. The sugar was shipped in wooden boxes called *huacales,* wrapped with sugar cane stems. The tasty sugar was made using a mule to power the wooden contraption that squeezed the juice out of the sugar cane.

Other people we talked with remembered there were Chinese people living in Loreto when they were young, that the men wore long pigtails, and some of them were merchants. I asked Lupe what she remembered about the Chinese:

> In the early part of the century, commerce was dominated by the Chinese. A Chinese had a large market on the land where the primary school is today by the town square which was owned by the Garayzar family. One of the prominent Chinese families in Loreto was the Yee family. They owned a large hardware and clothing store that was located, along with their house, on the same land as the market. These Chinese were mostly single men or men who had left their families behind in China. There was an anti-Chinese campaign during 1925-1926. Mexicans in Baja California and Soñora were upset that the Chinese owned the largest businesses in these areas. The anti-Chinese campaign was led by locals; the government had no part in it. A number of Chinese died because of it, though. The only Chinese in Loreto when the campaign was over were Felipe and Francisco Yee.

There was a literacy campaign in Baja California, and anyone could learn to read and write. The school went only to fourth grade, though, and when Lupe was twelve years old, her parents took her by boat to Guaymas to continue her education. Afterward, she taught school in Santa Rosalia for a year before returning to Loreto.

Lupe vividly recalled her first trip to Guaymas on a boat named *El Trieste* after the Italian town in which the owner was born:

> *El Trieste* entered a storm that tossed the boat around like a toy. Everyone had to be crammed into the boat's cabin and sit on the floor. We were all seasick from the violent wave action, and fumes from the engine exhaust filled the cabin, making everyone even sicker. My family and I thought we were going to die.

Only years after this trip in 1923 did larger, steam-powered ships arrive. These included the *Mavari,* the *Bonita,* and the more modern *Salvatierra.* Lupe made later trips to Guaymas

Chinese grocery store on the square, early 20th century. Photo: Loreto Municipio Archives.

on the *Peninsular* and the *Soñora*, and the *Arguan*. These boats made the Guaymas-Santa Rosalia-Mulegé-Loreto trip about every fifteen days, depending on the weather. When she was young, Lupe loved to ride out in the old wooden canoes, which were paddled out to see the large ships passing by.

When I turned off the tape recorder, Lupe smiled, held up her hands and spread her fingers wide. "That is how it was." she said. "It was that way, and it's all different now."

ALTAGRACIA AND MERCEDES PERPULY

Two sisters, Altagracia and Mercedes Perpuly were pioneers in the educational development of Loreto, which was one of the greatest factors for change in the town. Altagracias Perpuly Davis was born in 1905. Her early education was four years of primary school in Loreto, but she studied to be a primary school teacher in La Paz.

In 1945, the governor of the territory, General Francisco Rey Mujica, came to Loreto on an official visit. Altagracia had hoped for some time to start a kindergarten in Loreto, and, gathering her courage, she approached the general to tell him her idea.

The general asked me how many children would need it, and who was going to teach them. I told him there were a lot

231

of children, and I wouldn't mind being the teacher. The general's secretary took note of all this, and a few weeks later the kindergarten was approved and was supported by the territorial government. By then, I had collected eighty-two children. At first, the children had to sit on rugs on the floor because we had no furniture. Little by little, we got tables, chairs and school materials. I was the kindergarten teacher for ten years.

Mercedes Perpuly Davis was born in 1912. She also had four years of primary school in Loreto and later received teacher's training. Mercedes taught for forty-six years. She began teaching in her own house and then moved to the house of the de los Santos family. In 1944, the primary school was transferred to what is now the museum. She was called the "Teacher Mother" by everyone in Loreto, and is remembered as one of the pillars of the town. When we talked, she was eighty-two years old. She said that teaching had been the most important thing in her life, and she still regretted her retirement.

In the years between 1920 and 1940, about eighty Loreto children attended primary school. Only a few children from the ranches who had relatives with whom they could live in town were able to learn to read and write.

REBECA DAVIS DE MURILLO

One of the outstanding Loretanas in the 20th century was Rebeca Davis, teacher and poet.

Rebeca was born on October 4, 1900, one of nine children of the marriage of Símon Davis Monroy and Cruz Perpuly Márques. Rebeca worked in the post office from 1921 until 1923 during the government of General Álvaro Obregón. Her outstanding intelligence was recognized, and she was asked to be a primary school teacher. At age twenty-seven, she retired from teaching to marry Lorenzo Murillo Verdugo and went to live for a short time in Santa Rosalia. From there, they went to live in San Miguel Comondú. In that period, they adopted a child who died in a terrible accident when he was just thirteen years old. From that time on, she always had boys and girls living in their home "to give them love and education."

Rebeca became a widow when she was sixty years old. She came back to Loreto in 1970 to be with her mother, and here in Loreto the two volumes of her book of poetry, *Frente de la Vida*, were published, the first in 1974 when she was seventy-six and the second in 1978 when she was seventy-eight.

I first visited Doña Rebeca with my friend Sandra Ryan in 1973. She was a delicate woman with sparkling eyes and a sly sense of humor. She had a lively interest in literature, and we discussed books for a while. Rebeca told us that she had always written poetry from the time she was a child, and on her wedding day she had presented her husband with a love poem, perhaps this one:

Let me ask you for what you can give me.
A clean and pure love, sweet as honey.
For that you can give me, unless you stop loving me.
Let me tell you many things at the same time,
Those we only hear when love is deep in our hearts.
Let us enjoy the present.
The past is far away, and the future will come.
But today, let us enjoy.
This love I have for you will never die.

Her new husband read it, tore it up and threw it away, and forbade her to ever write poetry again. "Do you want the whole world to know our business?" he asked, "I can have nothing to do with you unless you promise me never to write like that again." So, for all the years they were married, Rebeca never wrote poetry, but when her husband died, she told us, "I sat down, toasted him with a glass of wine from the grapes of our vineyards, and I began to write. I wrote a poem to his memory and continued to write poetry from then on."

This remarkable woman died in 1990.

ELODIA VERDUGO PÉREZ DE CORTEZ

Elodia was born in 1913 and, like Lupe Davis, her life has spanned both the old and the new Loreto and she is related to many of the old families. Her father was Jesús Verdugo Osuna and her mother Blanca Pérez Larrinaga. "How can I explain it to you?" she asked. "In those days, it was a very small town, so we all got married to relatives." In 1998 when we talked, Elodia was still a pretty woman, warm and cheerful. She enjoyed talking about her life, which she considered to have been a very happy one:

Life was hard when I was young. My father died when I was five months old, and my mother was left with nine young children to support. My mother worked alone. She was only forty-four when my father died. Poor, poor we were, but we didn't need that much, and my mother worked a lot. She had a sewing machine, and she sewed men's clothing, women's clothing, and wedding dresses. She could sew anything. Sometimes she had to stay up until three in the morning sewing. When it was cold, she would put her feet in hot water to warm them up, and then she would put on her socks and go to bed. Loreto was a small town then, and there were no businesses. Almost all the people were poor. They lived on doing little jobs. My eldest sisters learned to knit so they could make their own clothes and also help my mother.

My elder sister Blanca, who married Juan Garayzar, was very strict with us, more than my mother. She would watch out for us and advise us. She had a guest boarding house, but not just anybody could be a guest in her house; she selected her clients. Many Americans liked to stay there. When Blanca started working, my mother's life also started to change. Blanca helped us with good meals, better dresses, everything. She helped us a lot. She was very smart and she liked to read. When she was young the school only went to fourth grade. There were some very smart people in Loreto. Romana Lagos, for example, was very intelligent. Like Blanca, if she had had access to education she would have been a very good student.

I was fifteen years old when I got married, and my husband was twenty-eight. Getting married at fifteen was a scandal because I was a girlfriend to him for so little time, only seven days when he asked me to marry, and after another fifteen days we got married. And you can't imagine what a happy marriage. Never did we have a disagreement, never a bad word. He was an educated man who had studied a lot, and he never used a bad word. We had been married sixty-two years when he died.

My husband was the school inspector, and he fought and fought to form a secondary school. He started one in a classroom upstairs in the government building. Ildefonso "Dunchi" Green as well as our son Mario gave English lessons. There was a physical education teacher, and they all taught for the pleasure of it. My husband struggled to form a real school where the teachers would be paid and was pushing and pushing the federal government to authorize a secondary school in Loreto. Then, our daughter Margarita went to see a person in the Department of Education in Mexico City with a document from her father asking that the Loreto secondary school become federated. When she gave it to him, the person said, "Look, miss, we are about to federate the Loreto school, so tell your father to give us a rest. Do you see that room, young lady? Well, the files in it are full of documents and letters from your father asking that the school be federated, and we are going to do it right away so he will leave us alone!" So my husband got the first secondary school authorized and supported by the federal government in Loreto.

We had five children, and they all got a good education. My son Carlos, when he was president of the Lions Club, fought

Wedding party,
early 20th century.
Photo: Loreto
Municipio Archives.

235

to introduce electric power to Loreto. In 1960, there was a generator for lighting at night. It used to start working at 6 p.m. and was turned off at 10 p.m. In order to provide electric power twenty-four hours a day, the electric company said the town had to raise sixty thousand pesos and have ninety clients. The Lions Club held a marathon and raised the money, and my son sent them the money and also told them there were ninety clients, even though there weren't that many. One day Carlos wasn't here, and the chief of the electric company came from La Paz to Loreto to see how they would introduce the electric energy. They held a meeting, and the chief was saying that they would install the electric power because there were ninety clients, when somebody yelled, "There are no ninety clients. There are not even fifty families!" Then Luis Arjona, my son-in-law, yelled, "No, no, there are ninety clients and maybe even one hundred." He said this, even though he knew it was a falsehood. The chief said, "Well, then, we are going to install the electric power." All this happened while Luis was making signs to the others to keep quiet. That's the way they worked for the people to have a better town.

Early Loreto architecture. Wooden house of Romana and Candelaria Lagos, which is still standing. Photo: Leland Foerster.

GUILLERMO ROMERO MAYORAL

Guillermo Romero was born in Loreto in 1919. His grandfather, Juan Antonio Romero Aguiar, was a leading merchant who owned boats and sold provisions to the people then living on Carmen Island. Guillermo attended the primary school which, by that time, went through the sixth grade.

Loreto was a small town, then, no more than two thousand people, and there weren't many children. Most of the adults were fishermen. There were a few cattle ranchers and some farmers. Many fishermen also dove for pearls and for mother-of-pearl. I remember that my grandfather bought and sold pearls, and I think it was around 1950 that there was a disease that wiped out the pearl oysters in the Sea of Cortez.

While Guillermo was still a young man, in the 1930s, he became justice of the peace of Loreto and was in charge of minor family matters that didn't involve much money. He described his position:

At that time you didn't have to be a lawyer to become a minor judge, or justice of the peace, in Loreto. There were no laws or lawyers involved in the decisions. The decisions were arbitrary, based on my own judgment.

In a little more than a hundred years after Loreto was the most important town in Baja California, it had become a remote pueblo at the end of the road. Until 1950, Comondú was the municipio, or county seat; and all marriages, births, and other civil matters had to be registered there.

Children born during those years were reported by their parents to an official in Loreto, and the papers were taken to Comondú to be registered. Many of the statements that were made in Loreto concerning these births never reached Comondú, and many of those that did reach Comondú were lost. A lot of people born in Loreto had trouble getting a passport later on, because they couldn't find a copy of their birth certificate. The only way a person could obtain a birth certificate was to be accompanied by two older witnesses to testify before the judge as to the person's identification. Besides this, he was fined for not being registered when he was born.

Part of Guillermo's job was to issue certificates to people whose papers had gotten lost somewhere between Loreto and

Comondú. At that same time, Mexican law required that all 18-year-old men had to have one year of military training. After that, the men would receive a work permit, although their status was that of a reserve in case of war. One of Guillermo's duties was to resolve conflicts with young men who didn't want to serve in the military.

Guillermo Romero was the Loreto justice of the peace until he retired in 1982.

FLORENCIO MURILLO NAVARRO

Florencio "Lencho" Murillo was born in Rancho Chuenque at Juncalito Bay, south of Loreto, in 1944 and was brought to Loreto to be registered. When they arrived in Loreto, his family decided to stay. Although he is younger than most of the people we interviewed, he has vivid memories of Loreto when he was young and before it began to change very much from the way it was during the early part of the century. Well known as a *curandero* (healer) he is visited by many elderly people who like to talk about their lives and the old days in Loreto. In addition, he is a great raconteur and a very intelligent man. He attended only first grade in school, but he taught himself and showed us his library of books, some of them medical, which he has absorbed. A few years ago, Lencho lost his sight, but he continues to help his friends who come to him with their aches and pains.

In the 1940s, Lencho's father repaired the town's pots and pans. People then were very poor. They couldn't afford new ones, so they brought their utensils to him to mend, which he did by using material from the lids. He also carved spoons, bean mashers, and meat pickers from the wood of the pimientilla shrub, which was very strong, and he made and sold leather rope.

Lencho's grandmother made soap using fat from the killer whale or the cow. She would extract the fats and oils from the rest, then mix it with a powder made from a plant which thickened it. The fat was then poured into a mold. When it solidified, she sold the bars of soap for five centavos each. This energetic woman also sold bread, cookies, produce, and pork. Her

Florencio Murillo Navarro. Photo: Jack Foster

pigs were fed on date seeds. She dug large ditches, filled them with the nutritious seeds, and watered them until they became soft and then drove the pigs into the ditch to eat.

Lencho remembers that when he was young, fishermen hunted killer whales in wooden canoes, They usually wore only two pieces of cloth, in front and back, and palm hats shaped like cones. They paddled close to the whales and threw an iron spear tipped with barbs into the whale's head. The spear was tied to a long rope, and when the whale was caught, they let it run until it got tired. Then they brought it toward the canoe and, using a spear with an oval tip, stabbed it in the head and floated it into shore. Often, several boats chased the whale and shared in the catch. In addition to making soap from the fat, the inner layer of skin was used to make chicharron similar to that made with pork. Whale meat was not eaten.

As a child, Lencho watched the Loreto men making mortar for building houses.

There used to be huge piles of shells on the beach, and these shells were boiled to clean them of meat. Then a big ditch was dug and covered with the thick part of date palm branches, called *penca*. The clean shells were put on top, and a fire lit. When the fire was out, all that was left was a thin dust from the burnt shells. This dust was then mixed with water and left sitting in large buckets overnight. The wet shell dust would rise, like a cake rising in the oven. Mortar was made by a similar process from a fine porous white rock called *risco*. To burn the rock, the penca date branches were put in the pit, then the rock, and, on top, cholla cactus skeletons were placed and ignited. The dust was left overnight and then mixed with chopped nopal and maguey. The sticky liquid from these leaves made this mortar harden like cement.

When questioned about the social life of Loreto, Lencho remembered:

In the past, there was not much drinking except on holidays. There were horseback promenades, and the girls would tie their braided hair with red ribbons, wear red lipstick, and color their cheeks with the dye from wet red paper. The boys and girls talked to each other and made dates while they rode. At Christmas and the New Year there were special horseback promenades, and races were held on the main street that now leads across the arroyo.

Lencho described the medicines and cures that were in common use in Loreto before there was a hospital:

The medicines were those used by the Indians. They used Indian wheat, pig weed, linseed, epozote, mesquite, mint, *yerba santa* (mountain balm), mustard, and chamomile. The bark (the white part) of the mesquite was cooked with mallow and chamomile and used for stomach pain.

For stomach problems, an enema was given of a solution of mallow, mesquite, chamomile, and lemon juice. This cleaned the intestine. A big glass of *ojasén* (cassia) mixed with milk was a good laxative and worked very fast to clean the stomach.

Headaches were treated with a paste made of camphor fried in lard and put on the head. Fig leaves tied on the head were really good for headaches, too.

For wounds or boils a coin was put on the affected part with a little piece of cotton on it. Then a match was put to the cotton so it would burn and heat the coin. They covered this with a glass, and when all the oxygen was gone the glass was removed. You had to be careful with this not to burn the skin.

A cast was made for a bone fracture from *romerillo amargo,* arabic gum, and tequila spread on a fabric called *manta trigeña,* a type of canvas, and small sticks were used to shape the cast. This was wrapped around the broken bone to prevent movement. To harden the cast and to clean it, it was washed with *aluma duro,* a white powder. This remedy was called *vilmas.*

The sap of lomboy is very good for blisters. A piece of cardon bark tied on a cut will cure it, and a piece of potato will do the same thing. Ashes mixed with lime placed on a hemorrhage will stop the bleeding. *Yerba del indio* is good for the liver, and mint helps the stomach. An herb called horsetail and the leaf of the avocado tree eliminate the toxins in the blood. For mouth blisters and coated tongue, boil alum crystals and put in your mouth without swallowing them.

We asked Lencho how he knew all this. He replied:

Other people showed me all these remedies. To cure anemia or weakness when someone was unable to eat, a mixture was made of one purple onion, chopped very fine with an egg. This was put on a very soft cloth, which was folded over and put on the stomach near the umbilicus. This was applied daily. White bread, cinnamon, and red wine were sometimes used in the compress.

For ear pain, you put garlic mixed with castor oil in the ear. For an infant with earache, an egg was boiled, the yolk removed and cooked in a flame, which produces an oil. The oil was put in the ear. If there is an ear infection, you liquefy *guatamote* (seep willow) with alcohol, put it in a bottle, and clean the ear with cotton soaked with this mixture. This also works for all kinds of skin infections.

To treat the pancreas, cumin fried in olive oil is applied to the pancreas area for nine days. Wearing a gold bracelet or ring with coral and a pearl is good for the heart. For removing cactus spines, the best treatment is to soak the puncture with one's own urine. This avoids pain and infection.

Doña Fidelia Verdugo was the midwife and for a time was in charge of all births in Loreto. When a child was to be born, she prepared boiled water, soap, and scissors for cutting the umbilical cord; and when the child was born, she put a bonnet on its head. A child was kept immobile for the first year of its life, because they believed it would grow stronger. Bags were made for the babies' hands, because they didn't cut the nails. People thought if they cut the nails during the first year, the babies would have problems with their eyes. At that time, children drank only mother's milk, no other. If the mother didn't have milk, another woman nursed her baby. For the newly born child, camomile, linseed, Castilian rose and other teas are very good. For children with eye infections, nursing mothers would put some milk in a thimble and bathe their eyes.

We asked if there was anyone to help when the children got too sick for the mother to treat, and Lencho told us there were some curanderas who helped them when they had stomach infections or diarrhea. They used various teas.

When the crown of a child's head was depressed, they made a compress of a gram of frijol, cooked with a little oil, and put on the head of the infant. This was covered with a cloth made from material similar to denim (but you can't get this any more). Then, they gently massaged the fontanel with the thumb. This was done for three days, and then the fontanel would return to normal. If the umbilical cord of a newborn didn't fall off within five or six days, they applied oil and alcohol to burn it, which left it clean. Almost all the curanderas were women, like Martína Talamantes, Doña Fidelia, the widow María, Delfina Davis de Baeza. The curanderas were paid with gifts of cheese, chicken, corn, hogs, and, rarely, money. This was because the people were poor.

In 1947, when Lencho was three years old, a priest came to Loreto who was to have a profound effect on his life and on the lives of all the people of Loreto for the next forty years.

PADRE MODESTO SÁNCHEZ MAYÓN

Modesto Sánchez Mayón was born in 1897 in the town of Atengo in the state of Jalisco. His mother, Leandra, decided when he was a child that he was destined for the priesthood. He was educated in seminaries in Jalisco and then in Guadalajara and, briefly, in La Paz. He graduated from a seminary in Culiacán and was ordained a priest in 1925. Shortly afterward, he returned to Baja California for a short time and then was transferred to a church in Quilá, Sonora.

In 1926, during the presidency of Plutarco Elías Calles,

the Mexican government initiated a campaign against the Catholic Church. Churches were closed, and priests were persecuted and killed by government soldiers. These soldiers were called "Brigades of Christ".

Padre Sánchez wrote of his experience with the anticlerical campaign when soldiers came to his church in Quilá:

> I was alone when soldiers of General Álvaro Obregón came with orders to apprehend me and take me to a nearby mountain. I thought I was going to be executed, but I got a big surprise. The soldiers conducted me into the presence of General Obregón and his family. The general asked me to perform a religious marriage ceremony with María Tapia and to baptize their two sons.

In payment for this service, General Obregón promised to help and protect the padre and told him he could go back, if he wished, to La Paz without trouble or interference from the Brigades of Christ.

Padre Sánchez traveled safely to La Paz, but the governor of the southern territory of the peninsula had orders from President Calles to apprehend and execute priests who were not properly registered according to the new laws. Friends felt it was not safe for Padre Sánchez in La Paz, and he was hidden for several months on a ranch near Todos Santos and then at the house of Fidel Valdivia in La Paz, where he celebrated Mass in secret. With the assassination of General Obregón in July 1928, the religious persecution accelerated, and his friends thought it safer to hide Padre Sánchez on the island of Espiritú Santo off the coast of La Paz. They brought him food and water every twenty days when the sea was calm, but there were times when he became very weak from hunger and thirst when his friends couldn't reach the island. Padre Sánchez remained on Espiritú Santo until June of 1929 when the government relaxed its opposition to organized religion and the churches were allowed to reopen their doors.

For the next few years Padre Sánchez worked in the diocese of La Paz, and in 1931 he was sent to the church in Santa Rosalía. His mother, Leandra, and two cousins, Hilaria and Petra Miranda Mayón, accompanied him there. In April 1931, he visited Loreto for the first time and was saddened by the ruined mission. During his eight years in Santa Rosalía, he made other visits to Loreto and San Javier, marrying couples and baptizing children in the area. In 1939, Padre Sánchez was transferred to Ensenada and then to Tecate.

In 1947, he requested and was granted permission to serve as priest in Loreto, the first permanent priest in over one hundred years. He celebrated his first official Mass in the chapel of the Loreto mission on November 29, 1947.

Padre Sánchez traveled from La Paz to Loreto with his family, which now included another relative Carmen Romo. The women, Leandra, Ilaria, Petra, and Carmen would devote their lives to serving the church in Loreto. They arrived in a Jeep. Padre Sánchez drove this Jeep for many years on the primitive roads and trails of the area to visit his parishioners in the remote villages and ranches. Lencho Murillo described Padre Sánchez' first days in Loreto:

> Padre Sánchez arrived in Loreto in 1947 with a Jeep and no shoes. He asked for a glass of wine to warm up. He was always a very humble and polite man. There was no priest like him ever in Loreto, no one as humble. He slept on the floor or on pieces of wood; he never had a bed. The nuns slept on benches. When he first arrived, he stayed in the house of Inocencio Verdugo Higuera, the father of Lupe Verdugo Davis. It was a large house with an orchard and was located across the street from the present Pescador supermarket.
>
> When he first saw the church, it was in ruins. Local people had looted the ruins for the cedar ceiling supports and for a scarce white rock called cantera. Only the east and west wings of the church remained standing. Local people had stolen many pictures of saints and Virgins because they had silver and gold frames. The few pictures that were left in the church include Saint John, the Virgin Mary (La Virgin Pegrina), and the Virgin of Guadalupe, a painting brought by the Spaniards in the 1600s.

In January 1948, after meeting with all the people to ask for their economic help in rebuilding the church and appointing a committee of women to raise funds, Padre Sánchez began the restoration of the mission. He enlisted the help of the bish-

Modesto Sánchez Mayón in his famous Jeep, circa 1948.
Photo courtesy of Rómulo Fernández.

op and the governor of the territory as well.

His female relatives visited all the families in town during the first month to ask for help in the reconstruction project. Carmen taught the catechism classes and helped to clean and decorate the church for special occasions. Hilaria attended to the clothes and food of the padre and the preparation of the Host for communion. Petra was in charge of the housework and cooking for the family. A house was built for Padre Sánchez and his relatives on land donated by Ricardo Larrinaga Davis.

The first working party gathered to clean out the debris in the nave of the church and the annex, which is now the Museum of the Missions. They used the few remaining cedar beams to hold up the ceiling, which was in bad condition, and also exhumed the bodies which had been buried in the inner court and reburied them in the cemetery.

During the early months of 1948, Padre Sánchez also initiated the construction of an automobile road to the San Javier mission. Local men started the road building, and the padre went out in his Jeep every day to check on their progress. He convinced the governor of the territory to help, and in 1949 the governor ordered an infantry battalion to assist on the project. The road was finally completed on November 26, 1952. Padre

Sánchez drove the first automobile, his famous Jeep, up the new road. The governor and the mayors of Loreto and San Javier were his passengers.

In addition to the road building, the reconstruction of the church, and his religious duties in Loreto, Padre Sánchez attended to his parishioners in Comondú, La Purísima, San Isidro, Valle de Santo Domingo, San Nicolás, Carmen Island, Ligüí, Agua Verde, Juncalito, San Javier, and all the ranches in the area.

Padre Sánchez wanted to restore the church to its original state, and he wrote many times to Mexico City asking for drawings or plans of the Loreto mission as it had been before the earthquake. But he never received an answer. He even made the trip to the distant capital to try to find someone who could help him. But the little pueblo of Loreto in the remote territory of Baja California was of little interest to anyone in Mexico City, and he was unable to find any help. Padre Sánchez had to continue reconstructing the church using his own judgment about the architecture.

Over the next seven years, many men of Loreto and a few artisans from other parts of Mexico continued working on the building. The lack of money slowed the process, but the padre persisted. And then, on September 15, 1955, a miracle happened! Padre Sánchez won the Mexican National Lottery! Except for a few charitable donations, he devoted the money to completing the reconstruction of the Loreto Mission.

When it came to finishing the bell tower, the local story goes, he had some money left and thought maybe he would buy watches for everyone in the pueblo so they could get to Mass on time. But then he decided to do something more permanent. He put clocks in the tower, facing in four directions, so people would always be able to see the time. In later years, the Mexican government recognized that the missions of Baja California were important and allocated money to restore them, where it was possible, to their original state. When they arrived in Loreto, intending to remove the unauthentic clocks, Padre Sánchez and his parishioners lined up in front of the church and refused them admittance. They said, "This is our

246

Monsignor Modesto Sánchez near the end of his life. Photo: Rómulo Fernández

miracle, and don't you touch it." And they didn't.

Education was another area the padre thought very important, and he used his considerable energy to acquire better schools for the children of Loreto. The primary school classes had been held in the rooms of the former Royal Treasury next to the church since 1944. Padre Sánchez was instrumental in getting the first primary school built next to the municipal building, which opened in 1959. The secondary school (grades 7-9) then moved into the Royal Treasury until 1967 when the secondary school building on Calle Salvatierra was completed.

1960 was a momentous year for Modesto Sánchez. He visited Rome and was named a Monsignor by Pope John XVIII. While he was in Italy, he visited the Basilica of the Virgin of Loreto, where he saw the house of the Virgin Mary enclosed in the gigantic cathedral. He decided, then, that one day he would build a replica of the Italian church in his Loreto in Mexico.

In 1974, he initiated the construction of the church he called the Basilica of the Virgin in Loreto and which the people call the Santa Casa. He had begun fund raising on his return from Italy, and he started his project by building a replica of the house of Mary in Nazareth, which stood alone for some years until he had enough funds to start the construction of the surrounding church. Until the church was finished, he held masses in a little shed outside it. We attended a fifteenth birthday Mass there for a young girl we knew well. The service in the shed was unforgettable. Padre Sánchez was eighty-nine, and he nodded off at intervals during the Mass, but the women in the congregation carried on, singing the service until he awoke with so much love and devotion that it was a poignant experience. The Santa Casa was not completely finished before his death in 1987, but it is now a busy church out by the highway near the entrance to Loreto.

On June 26, 1987, eleven days after his 90th birthday, Modesto Sánchez Mayón died and was buried in the Loreto cemetery beside his mother. On the tenth anniversary of his death, his body was interred beneath the altar of his replica of the Italian Basilica of the Virgin of Loreto, and his famous Jeep was installed along the highway at the entrance to the road to San Javier.

ILDEFOSO GREEN GARAYZAR

Ildefonso Green Garayzar, who was called "Al" by his English-speaking friends and "Dunchi" by his fellow Loretanos, very generously spent many hours allowing me to tape his memories. He was born in 1929, and had known Padre Sánchez all his life and loved to talk about him:

Padre Sánchez had been coming to Loreto for many years before 1947. He married my mother and father. He baptized me. He married me. He baptized my children. Everyone who met him recognized him as a pioneer, a man with a strong will, hard working, and always for the benefit of the people. He had the same spirit as Salvatierra. He worked real hard to open the road to San Javier. He did many, many things. I was very lucky to know him. He helped raise the whole town. We saw him as a real father to everybody. He had won the right to scold us and spank us and tell us whatever he had to say.

I mentioned that when Don and I first came to Loreto in 1973 women and girls went swimming in dresses. Few women wore slacks, and there were no shorts or bathing suits. We were told Padre Sánchez was strict about womanly modesty, and I asked if this was true:

> Oh, yes. A friend of mine from Tijuana wore pants to church, and he sent her out. But she argued with him, and he accepted her reasoning. But he never accepted people in shorts.

Ildefonso Green grew up in Loreto and spent his school vacations on Primer Agua and Zacatál ranches, which were owned by his grandfather Juan Garayzar. Other people we talked to remembered that early in the century his grandfather raised opium poppies at Rancho Primer Agua and brought men and women out from town in horse-drawn wagons to process them. The federal government heard about it, and he discontinued that operation. Al's grandfather also grew grapes on his ranches:

> I remember the winery at Primer Agua where the workers crushed the grapes with their feet. They danced over the grapes. And then they put the juice of the grapes in these cowhides, and that's where they fermented. It was a long process, but was an excellent, real excellent wine.

> Later on, when my grandfather was dead, somebody gave my Uncle Juanito Garayzar the idea to make brandy, and he started making brandy. This was not really legal. But it was with the knowledge of many authorities, because it was just a small operation, and he didn't make a lot. It really was very fine, very exquisite brandy. Then somebody informed the government, and they said, "Okay, Juanito, we know you're doing this. All you have to do is pay the taxes and make it legal." But the taxes and other costs made it not a profitable operation. He only made ten barrels at the most, and it didn't amount to a lot of income, so he stopped making his fine brandy.

Even as a youngster, Ildefonso was aware of political movements in Baja California Sur. In an interview in 1992, he talked about politics:

> When I was a just a young kid, I remember my grandfather went to jail, unjustly, for about thirty-five minutes. The government sent him to jail because he didn't want to back their candidate. The whole town, about 750 people, sent telegrams, and the federal judge in La Paz, who was a family friend, sent a writ of habeas corpus, and they freed my grandfather.

As time went by, the territory of Baja California Sur continued to be the poor relative of the politicians in Mexico City. Every time they wanted to punish or get rid of a politician they sent him to Baja California Sur as a governor or some kind of official. It was so difficult to travel between the peninsula and Mexico. There were no planes, and the boats were very small. Then, back in 1956, they sent a general as governor, General Salinas Bonifacios. He was a hard-handed general and he wanted to be president, but they didn't want him. Then, of course, he brought his own people in, and the government of Baja California Sur was in the hands of strangers. The people in Mexico City didn't give us the opportunity to rule our lives. They thought we were not politically mature.

Then some courageous and patriotic politicians in La Paz formed El Frente Unificación Sudcaliforniano to fight against General Salinas. In the past, the governors had been more or less paternal and some had tried to do good things, but with Salinas the people had had enough of military governors. Mexico City sent another governor, this time a young lawyer, but by then the people believed that the time had come to achieve statehood.

So a movement was started from Guerrero Negro to Cabo San Lucas by a political group, headed by a newspaperman, Felix Ortega. Many people, including me, started working in this movement. We wanted to be equal. We wanted roads. Finally, on October 11, 1970, more than two thousand people from all over Baja California Sur gathered in Loreto. I made one of the main speeches in that meeting. What we wanted was a beautiful movement, in peace and quiet, with no disturbance of any kind, with real class. We wanted to show the government of Mexico that the inhabitants of Baja California Sur were politically ready to handle our destiny. This meeting was called "Loreto 70".

Our representatives took the minutes of the meeting to Mexico City and presented them to the government. Echeverría was about to finish his term. The government sent us a native of Baja California as governor. But we were still a territory. The new governor was Felix Agramon Cota, born in Todos Santos, and he persuaded the federal government to establish municipios, which are similar to counties in the United States. Baja California Sur was divided into three counties – Mulegé, Comondú, La Paz. From Concepción Bay to Santa Rita is the county of Comondú, with the seat in Constitución, and from Santa Rita south is the county of La Paz, with the seat in the city of La Paz.

In 1976, Governor Agramon Cota called for a vote, and we voted for a young lawyer Cesar Mendoza Aramburo as constitutional governor of the free State of Baja California Sur. Since then, we have had three governors and nine municipal presidents. The county of La Paz was divided into two counties, and now Loreto is fighting to get the fifth county for Loreto. And that is the political movement in which we are engaged right now in 1992.

Ildelfonso also spoke to us about the weather in Baja. There were five hurricanes reported in the 20th century in Loreto, in 1912, 1918, 1921, and 1931, but the most destructive and the one everybody still talks about is Hurricane Claudia on September 9, 1959. Ildefonso described it vividly:

It destroyed the whole town, killed Don Francisco Higuera, an old policeman and his grandson. It destroyed whatever we had for roads. The town was flooded. More than five thousand palm trees were on the ground. After the hurricane, the town looked naked. Where before you couldn't see through a curtain of palm trees, you could now see from one place to another. Loreto was just a whole bunch of little islands. One of those islands was my mother's house, the old house on the southwest corner of the plaza in front of the church. That night, I was out

Ildefonso Green speaking at the "Loreto 70" meeting.

in the street bringing people into the house. About 150 people were in the house and in the church. The house of Doña Blanca across from the church had three feet of water inside. The water was up to the sidewalk of the church. That's one of the highest points in town. That was a terrible experience. A lot of people in their homes had to jump on top of their furniture, and they could see the water flowing through their houses. Ernesto and Lupe Davis were on top of a standing clothes closet all night long. We saw St. Elmo's Fire, caused by the friction of the air, in the church and houses. It was the worst hurricane in my lifetime. It isn't often that hurricanes come here. The hurricanes form in the Isthmus of Tehuantepec and they go up north. They hit the tip of Baja California and deviate to the Pacific or inside toward Mexico City, but they very seldom come up the peninsula. But I was told that Hurricane Claudia made a 350-degree turn and came right into the Gulf and came all the way. It killed people in Mulegé, Santa Rosalía, San Felipe. But that was quite unusual.

ANNETTA CARTER

Annetta Carter, a botanist from the University of California at Berkeley, made her first trip to Loreto in 1947. She was invited by Annie Alexander, heiress of an Hawaiian sugar fortune who had a strong interest in natural history, on a three-month expedition to Baja California. Annetta was 40 at the time, and Annie Alexander would celebrate her 80th birthday on the trip. Annetta drove Annie and her friend Louise Kellogg down the peninsula in a truck, after first learning to repair it in case it broke down on the primitive road from the border.

When the women arrived in Loreto, they decided to explore the plants of the La Giganta mountain range, and Annetta organized an expedition with the help of local ranchers. Annetta earned their respect and affection when she was able to make the difficult climb to the top of La Giganta, the highest mountain in the range. She was the first (and, so far, the only) woman to accomplish that difficult feat.

Ildefonso Green remembered her with admiration:

Annetta Carter is the only woman who has climbed La Giganta. She discovered three or four unknown species of plants. She used to hire men from Loreto on her expeditions. She used to lead them, and they got tired long before she did.

Lupe Fernández remembers that when Annetta first came to Loreto, she and the two women with her stayed at Doña Blanca's guesthouse.

It used to be full of people. I met Annetta when I was six or seven years old. At that time Loreto was very small, and everyone knew everyone. Many of us learned our catechism from Lucha, the daughter of Doña Blanca. We used to go to her house, and we all knew and loved Annetta.

Many people in Loreto still remember her with love and admiration. Several women told me they have a picture of her in their house, and the men she rode with speak of her endurance with awe.

In a letter to us written in 1990, Annetta recalled her first memories of Loreto in 1947 as "a lovely little village with neat tiny houses having petate-sided walls and thatched roofs, especially on the side streets like Independencia, and a few little corner stores." At that time, light was provided by kerosene lamps (with chimneys to wash every day).

The 1959 chubasco destroyed a lot of the palms. And there was a beautiful estero between the Lupe and Ernesto Davis home and where the Hotel Mision is now. I tried to promote the idea of making this estero a historical park, because it was the "agua dulce" area that brought Salvatierra to Loreto. Doña Lupe told me that following the chubasco you could again hear the burbling of water coming in to the estero. Unfortunately, the mayor at the time considered the estero nothing but a pest hole, and he had the whole area filled in with debris from the chubasco.

Annetta returned frequently to Loreto, often bringing groups of students from Berkeley to study the botany of the peninsula. The botany of the Sierra de la Giganta became her major interest. After she retired, Annetta and her brother Robert dug a well and built a small one-room brick house with a thatched roof on a hectare of land leased on the outskirts of Loreto. She used it as a base for her continued exploration of the Sierra de la Giganta. At the time we met her in the early

1970s, she had started a botanical garden on the property. She intended it as a place where people interested in the unique plants of the Baja peninsula could come to study them, and she hoped it would attract people from all over the world to Loreto.

Upon returning to Loreto from a trip to Berkeley, Annetta was horrified to find her garden being bulldozed by the government as part of a proposed tourism development. Ironically, the plans called for a botanic park, which has never happened.

However, Annetta had introduced Loreto to many botanists who continue to visit the area. She was also a pioneer advocate of the importance of preserving the valuable plant, animal, and sea life of the area.

ED TABOR

Ed Tabor was another American who introduced many people to Loreto and helped to establish a growing economy through tourism in the small pueblo. Born in 1917, Tabor got an engineering degree in electronic communications. He learned to fly and, at age twenty-three, acquired planes for non-stop commercial flights from San Francisco to New York. His interest in radio led him to a second career as a prominent radio disc jockey and talk show host in San Francisco. When World War II broke out, he became a Marine pilot, flying transport planes and bombers. After the war, he continued his careers in radio and aviation.

He first came to Loreto in 1954 to study the possibilities of tourist fishing in the Sea of Cortez. He decided that the idea had great potential, and in 1959, the year of the hurricane, he finished building a hotel on the south side of the Las Parras arroyo, which he called the Flying Sportsman's Lodge. There was no highway to Loreto then, so he flew his guests down in two war surplus B-25s.

Ildefonso Green worked for Ed Tabor and was his friend. He said:

> Ed Tabor came with a big machete, opening the brush for the tourism in Baja California, and he should be recognized for what he did. He was the worst hotel man that I have ever seen in my life, but he was the biggest tourist promoter I have ever seen. Ed Tabor could convince anybody. He had talent. And he

was a very active man, a very good-looking man, with a tremendous personality and facility of speech. When he was a young man he was an actor in Hollywood. But when it came to administrating his hotel, well...I worked for him three times.

Tabor continued to operate the Flying Sportman's Lodge until about 1980 when he became ill, and the hotel closed.

ENRIQUE ORTEGA

Enrique Ortega was born in Mexico City but moved to Los Angeles as a young man. He started a travel agency with his wife Doris, specializing in trips to Baja California. In 1954, he traveled to La Paz and Loreto to study the possibilities of bringing tourists there for fishing. Ortega also stayed at Doña Blanca's guesthouse, the only one in town, and there he and Ed Tabor met. The two men decided to work together on the Flying Sportsman's Lodge venture, with Tabor running the hotel and Ortega supplying customers from his travel agency. After a few years, the two men bought a DC-3 to fly the customers to Loreto. Then other airlines started service, and, as other hotels were built, Enrique and Doris sent many fishermen to Loreto.

RAY CANNON

A book called *The Sea of Cortez,* published in 1966, also helped promote the developing tourist industry. Ray Cannon, the author, had worked in the movie industry and was another charismatic character. Cannon put together an outstanding book about this unique and relatively unknown body of water. His chapter on the Loreto area, describing and illustrating its beauty and incredible fishing, attracted many tourists to the town.

During the thirty years between 1943 and 1973, there were other changes in the pueblo. In 1948, the first airline began regular flights from Tijuana. In 1952, the automobile road to San Javier was completed and the first hospital was built. In 1955, the first high school opened, and a boarding facility, called the Internado, for children from the ranches and fishing villages, was established so they could attend primary

Growth and Change

255

school. In 1957, a dirt road was completed to Constitución. In 1964, electricity replaced the gas lamps. In 1965, a secondary school was built. In 1974, Baja California Sur became a state with its own elected officials. As job opportunities increased, people started to trickle in from other parts of Mexico. From the north, a few Americans and Canadians who came for the fishing decided to retire in this quiet beautiful place. The building constructed on the orders of Visitor General José de Gálvez as the King's Treasury in 1769 was restored by the federal government and opened as the Museum of the Missions on December 10, 1973.

The Transpeninsular Highway

One of the principle factors in the growth of Loreto was the construction of the transpeninsular highway, which was completed in 1973. Before the highway was finished, the only access to Loreto from the United States was by plane or boat or by a primitive dirt and rocky road from the Alta California border. Only adventurous foreigners and a few equally adventurous traveling salesmen came down the old road. It took a month to drive from Tijuana to the Cape.

Don and I drove the new highway in the spring of 1974 before it had bridges, and it only took two days to reach Loreto on the smooth new road. Since then, we have driven it many times and have watched the development of agriculture and more prosperous towns along the route. Thousands of tourists now travel on it every year. Many of them come to Loreto, and more and more come back to stay.

FONATUR

As tourism gradually grew in Loreto, the federal government turned its attention to the small pueblo. The government agency FONATUR, an acronym for the National Fund for the Promotion of Tourism, began to plan the development of Loreto and Cabo San Lucas in 1976. The government had already developed the resorts of Cancún and Ixtapa and was looking for new areas to expand the tourist market. Loreto was chosen because the government was able to trade land in Cancún and Ixtapa for land in Nopolo and Puerto Escondido to the ICA company in partial payment for the construction of the transpenninsular highway.

Over the centuries, Loreto had been settled in a haphazard way, and one of the government's first efforts was to straighten out the ownership of land. This caused some disruption and anger in the community but was eventually accepted.

The initial planning included the urbanization of 860 acres in Loreto and the remodeling of the old town. The second step was planned to be the development of 8,777 acres of land at Nopolo as a tourist zone, with hotels, a golf club, tennis club, villas, houses, and condominiums. The third step was to be the development of 16,815 acres at Puerto Escondido as a harbor with zoning for hotels, restaurants, residences, and recreation.

In 1976, with a credit of $225 million from the World Bank, the improvement of Loreto was begun. Streets were dug up to install a water distribution system, and two water treatment plants were built. Electrical energy was brought up the peninsula from La Paz to replace the local generator, which was located south of the arroyo in Colonia Zaragosa, and a substation was installed between Loreto and Nopolo. The airport, which had been moved from the north to the south side of town, was enlarged, and a telephone network designed.

In the period from 1977 to 1982, the infrastructure of Loreto was completed and development of the tourist zones of Loreto and Nopolo initiated. The church and museum in Loreto were improved, the opening into the harbor at Puerto Escondido enlarged, and the construction of the Hotel Presidente at Nopolo began.

During that time, the runway of the airport was extended to 7,920 feet to permit jet planes to land, and a contractor began to sort and store gravel for the runway in the arroyo west of the highway. Someone warned him that if there was a heavy rain, his gravel could be washed away. "I've been here for ten years," the contractor said, "and I could drink all the water that has come down this arroyo." And he was right.

But in 1979, the thunder roared and the lightening flashed and the rains came, and in two days the arroyo flooded to within a few inches of the tops of the dikes. Everything loose in the arroyo from as far up the mountain as Rancho Las Parras came tumbling and floating down in the turbulent waters, including the gravel stored for the runway. Before the rain stopped, Don went with a neighbor, Jesús, to see what was happening, and while they were standing there, a man hurried by and shouted a question at them. Don asked Jesús what the man said. "He wanted to know if we had seen a palm tree go by with his burro tied to it," Jesús told him. When the skies had cleared, a peninsula had formed in front of the Hotel Oasis where before the sea had come up to the walls of the hotel. Each year, the peninsula grows a little more, and a lagoon has formed at the end of the arroyo.

Loreto Citizens Protest

In March of 1989, the generally peaceful citizens of Loreto staged an angry demonstration by blocking off the transpeninsular highway. There were two serious problems facing them: Aeromexico, which had been flying in the tourists to fish, discontinued service, which severely damaged the local economy; and the town water supply had become salty as the water table sank and mixed with sea water after a long period of drought. The Loretanos had other complaints, too. There were few paved streets, and those had huge potholes. The malecón, the sea wall, was falling down and had become dangerous to walk on. Appeals had been sent to the governor, who came and made promises and went away and forgot them.

Finally, the town had had enough. Impromptu parades and speeches were held, and then someone had the idea of blocking the highway. This got the attention of the politicians and the press, and the governor responded by sending his aide to make more promises. The citizens politely gave the aide a glass of water, and, when he claimed they had put salt in it, ran water from the tap into a new glass and insisted he drink it. The governor came back and was met at the airport by a thousand quietly determined Loreto citizens demanding action. Newspapers reported the events.

The Visits of President Carlos Salinas de Gortari

Three months later, airline service resumed, and a year and a half later the president of Mexico, Carlos Salinas de Gortari, visited Loreto to initiate a new water system which would bring clear water by pipeline from Rancho San Juan 25 miles to the north.

Ildefonso Green described another important result of

this first visit by the president:

> We have the new malecón thanks to a young kid who accosted the president of Mexico. That is one of the most beautiful stories. During the first visit to Loreto of President Salinas de Gortari, he had his driver stop the car in the middle of town. The president got out and started walking to the malecón. By chance, there was a class of third grade youngsters there. Their teacher had brought them to see the ocean. When the president jumped up on the malecón, which was all broken up, the teacher recognized the president and told the kids. "There is the president of Mexico. Go and say hello to him."
>
> And one of these mischievous kids says, "Hey, are you really the president of Mexico?" Very properly, Salinas says to the kid, "Yes, young man, I am president of Mexico."
>
> "That means that you are the boss of everything?" And the president, continuing with the game, says, "Yes, I am the boss in this country." "If you are the boss," the kid says, "why don't you order to make us a new malecón, because this one is all broken up, and it's dangerous to walk and play on." The president was absolutely surprised at what the kid had said. The secretary of tourism was there, and he turned to the president and said, "You have listened to the petition of the children of Loreto. When I come to Loreto to inaugurate the new water viaduct, I want to inaugurate the new malecón of Loreto." And that's how we got our new malecón.

President Salinas returned in August of 1992 to dedicate the new water system and the malecón project, which included a two-lane paved boulevard along a mile of the waterfront and a marina with a launching ramp. A platform was set up in the parking lot of the new marina, and on a beautiful moonlit night, the whole population assembled to hear the president dedicate the new water project and the new malecón. Salinas said: "As the children asked, here is the place where they can walk safely with their parents in the evening to enjoy the fresh air and the extraordinary moon like the one tonight that lights and enhances these proceedings." José Narcizo, the boy who had asked for a new malecón, was invited to be on the platform, and he made a very good speech, thanking the president on behalf of the children of Loreto.

Ildefonso Green contributed to another of our favorite Loreto stories, the story of the bell from the Loreto mission that was lost and the bell that was found.

We had first heard the bell story from Manuel Fernández, a good friend with whom we shared many fishing adventures. Manuel and his wife Choly were very kind to us when we first came to Loreto and helped us to adapt to life in our new home. Manuel had been born in Loreto in 1913 and started fishing for shark in sailing canoes when he was eight years old. As Manuel told it, the story went something like this:

A hundred years ago, the people in Loreto were very, very poor. One night, very late, when the moon showed only occasionally through the swiftly moving clouds, two men silently left their small palm huts and made their way to a rendezvous at the ruined Church of Our Lady of Loreto. Nodding to each other, they crept up the stairs to the roof and, working quickly, cut down one of the great bells that had been brought by the Jesuit fathers on a sailing ship to the Loreto mission. The men thought if they took only one bell and had it melted down in the new smelter at Santa Rosalia, about one 100 miles north by sea, the gold and silver it contained would feed their families for a long time.

The bell was very heavy, and they had a difficult time getting it down the steps and through the town without arousing anyone. They crossed the last few feet of sandy beach and, with grunts of relief, put the bell in their sailing canoe and prepared to cast off.

The scudding clouds should have warned them that a *turbonada,* a short but violent storm that comes up suddenly in the Sea of Cortez, was approaching. But they were so frightened of getting caught that they disregarded the danger signs. They had only sailed a short way north up the coast when the storm caught up with them. They were quickly overturned in the turbulent sea and never seen again.

About a hundred years later, in 1976, a shrimp boat was trawling in the waters near Coronados Island and picked up a large metal object in its net. The captain was from Loreto, and he remembered the story of the stolen bell. He took his ship to the pier and hurried to the church to tell Padre Modesto Sánchez of his find, which, even covered with barnacles and shells, appeared to him to fit the description of the lost Loreto bell. At this time, Padre Sánchez was an elderly man. He was about to leave on the plane to Tijuana and told the captain he didn't have time to deal with the bell right now. The padre thanked the captain, but he had a plane to catch, and he asked the man to come back when he returned from Tijuana.

The captain had a boat full of shrimp that he had to get to La Paz, so he shrugged and took off, taking the bell with him. Meanwhile, word had gone out around the pueblo of the finding of the bell. People got upset that their bell had come and gone. They alerted the coast guard. When the shrimp boat arrived in La Paz, police and military officers were waiting at the dock and demanded that the captain turn over the bell to them. The captain, of course, complied, and the bell was whisked off to a warehouse and there it stayed.

When the federal government heard about the find, they wanted the bell for the Institute of Natural History in Mexico City. La Paz, the capital of Baja California Sur, thought the bell should be in their museum. Even some museums in Alta California offered to take care of it. The Loretanos, however, were most determined to have the bell where it belonged: in Loreto. For two years Padre Sánchez led the campaign to get it back. They petitioned the governor, who came to Loreto and promised he would deliver it in person to Choly Fernández' aunt, who was 103 years old and alleged to be the great-granddaughter of one of the thieves. But time passed, and Choly's aunt couldn't wait any longer. She died.

On September 5, 1978, the Feast of the Virgin of Loreto, Padre Sánchez led the congregation out to the highway, because he had received word that the bell would be delivered that day. They planned to meet it and escort it back to the church. We were a part of the crowd that stood around for a long time at the entrance to town to welcome it. But the bell didn't come, and it started to rain, so everyone went home.

Ildefonso Green told us that finally César Mendoza Aramburo, the governor of Baja California Sur, decided to take matters into his own hands. He sent a pickup truck to the warehouse. His men somehow got the bell out of the building and into the truck, covered it with an old quilt, and drove furiously to Loreto. The governor alerted Padre Sánchez it was on its way. The truck arrived just before midnight. The driver was met on the church steps by Padre Sánchez and three leading citizens, including Ildefonso. They locked the bell away in the church, and the next day it was placed in the Museum of the Missions next door where it still rests.

Some people think that the bell delivered from La Paz in a pickup was not the bell that was found, because the stolen bell had been so big and so loud that it could be heard all the way to Nopolo. It is true that it is not the same bell the town thought it was. The markings on the bell showed it was a bell that had been lost when the ship that was delivering it from the mainland sank in a storm not far from the town. The placard on the bell in the museum reads:

Church Bell (Spanish). Saint Augustine. Typical 18th century.

Cast in bronze.

It was one of the bells given to the ship San José in June of 1769.

It was lost during the crossing of the San José between June and

September of the same year. It was found February 17, 1976

by a fisherman 23 fathoms deep in front of Rancho Juncalito,

18 km. South of Loreto.

The bell that was stolen on that dark and stormy night so many years ago still rests on the bottom of the sea.

Congress Decrees Loreto as a Municipio For many years Loreto was in the municipio (county) of Comondú. Constitución, a farming community about 90 miles south of Loreto, was the county seat, and taxes paid in Loreto went to Constitución and were doled back from there for local needs. As Loreto grew, it became increasingly difficult to make needed improvements in local services, since the town had no control over the necessary tax money to make them. For several years a large group of Loreto citizens petitioned the federal government to form a new county with Loreto as the county seat. Meetings were held, speeches were made, and delegations sent to Mexico City.

Finally, in October of 1992, the Mexican Congress decreed the new municipio of Loreto. On October 29, the governor of Baja California Sur came and installed a provisional government until legal elections could be held the following February. A joint council of seven, headed by the mayor of Loreto Dr. Santislaus Collins, administered the new county in the meantime.

April 3, 1993, Alfredo García Green took office as the first President of the Municipio of Loreto. He held the office for a three-year term, and gave the new municipio a good start by administering it well and leaving it with a balanced budget.

Museum of the Missions

Twenty years after its foundation by the government agency INAH, the Loreto Museum of the Missions took on a new life with the appointment in 1973 of Estela Gutiérrez as the director. She had studied art history at the university in Mexico City and done graduate study at the Sorbonne in Paris. She brought to the museum a unique knowledge, taste and dedication. She redesigned the interior and the courtyard, brought in new and interesting exhibits, inaugurated a series of concerts in the courtyard, and encouraged the school children and local people to participate in programs in the museum for the first time. Tourists from many countries visit the museum.

Ecological Concerns

When we first came to Loreto in 1973, the fish were so plentiful that no one imagined that this could ever change. Yellowtail swarmed and boiled so close to the shore we could sometimes catch them from the beach in front of our house. There were enormous grouper and marlin and swordfish and a countless variety of other fish out there for the taking. Whales spouted in all seasons, from giant blues to pilot whales. Dolphins and porpoise accompanied us on most of our fishing trips, and sea lions sometimes stole the fish from our lines.

But all night long we could hear the chugging motors of shrimp boats passing back and forth between our beach and

Carmen Island. Occasionally, the lights of a Japanese factory ship would light up the sky beyond the peaks of Carmen Island. Tuna boats came in with helicopters and nets to spot and round up huge schools of tuna and other fish. Gradually, the fish were no longer as plentiful.

Men who had become dependent on taking tourists fishing began to lose customers. Concerned local citizens appealed to the federal government, but nothing was done.

In 1995, Grupo Ecologista Antares (GEA) was founded by a dedicated group of local people. The goals of the organization were to study, conserve, and develop the environment and its ecological equilibrium. Headed by Fernando Arcos, GEA has established a marine museum and study center with a library and audiovisual materials. A successful program of education in the schools was initiated to make the children aware of the fragility of their environment and the necessity of preserving and protecting it. Ecological groups on both sides of the Sea of Cortez have been formed and are working together to save the sea before it is too late. Education and publicity have made more and more people aware of the danger to this unique body of water.

In 1996, the Mexican government established a national marine park, the Parque Marino Nacional Bahía de Loreto. The marine park includes all of the islands from north of Coronados to Catalana to the south. Shrimp boats, tuna boats, and other large commercial fishing boats are prohibited in the park. After four years of protection, there are signs that the fish population is becoming more stable.

Tricentennials We could find no record of celebrations held on the past two centennials of the founding of Loreto. The circumstances of those times didn't lend themselves to big celebrations. But the celebration of the 300th anniversary of the founding of Loreto began in January of 1997 with concerts and expositions and commemorative ceremonies held monthly. In October, three days of programs were sponsored by the Instituto Nacional de Antropología e Historia in coordination with the government of Loreto, the government of Baja California Sur, and the Fondo Nacional para Turismo. Eminent historians,

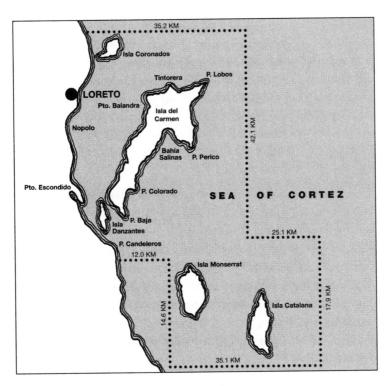

Area of the Parque Marino Nacional Bahía de Loreto.

including Miguel León-Portilla from Mexico of the Universidad Nacional Autónoma de Mexico and Harry Crosby, author of *Antigua California*, paid tribute to the founding fathers and discussed the history and future of Loreto and Baja California Sur. On October 25, five bishops and eighty priests from Mexico and twenty-five clerical delegates from other parts of the world came to Loreto to hold a solemn Mass in front of the mission. School children put artifacts of the present day and notes describing life in Loreto in 1997 in a chest to be opened in fifty years by the children of that time. Costumed citizens reenacted the landing of Salvatierra on the shore, followed by folklorico dancing and speeches by the governor of Baja California and other dignataries. The oldest city in California celebrated its survival for three hundred years with gusto.

On December 2, 1999, San Javier celebrated its three hundredth year with a three-day festival. The governor of Baja California Sur, historian Miguel León-Portilla, and many officials from Mexico City and La Paz made speeches. The bishop conducted a Mass attended by a huge crowd of local people and visitors in the magnificent old mission church. The paintings, sculptures and altar in the church had been beautifully restored by a group of artisans from the leading school of art restoration in Mexico City with money donated by local citizens in cooperation with the nonprofit Adopt A Work of Art Council, Inc. in time for the celebration.

In May of 2000, Lupe Verdugo de Davis, now ninety years old, went to the bank. She had not been downtown for some time, and was overwhelmed and saddened by the changes. "In that crowded bank I only saw three people I knew. I used to know everyone. Now, people have come here from the other side and from other parts of Baja California to live. Everything is changing."

Great changes have taken place in Loreto in the last twenty years. Nearly everyone watches television. There are computers and Internet access. There are four primary schools, one Catholic colegio, two junior high schools, two high schools, and a teacher's college. New suburbs have been built to the north, south, and west. Most of the streets are paved and a sewer system added. More stores and restaurants and hotels have opened for business. All this growth means more opportunities for the children of Loreto.

In spite of all the changes though, Loreto has preserved its sense of history and culture. The growth has been slow and has not destroyed the beauty and character of the area. The mountains, the sea, and the desert surrounding the town remain the same: timeless and aloof from the concerns of the humans who inhabit their domain.

Donald Clarke O'Neil
(May 1912 – December 1998)

Don died before the last chapter of our book was finished, but he was an active participant in our project until he left. Researching, writing, and publishing this book was just one of the many activities we enjoyed together during our wonderful and fascinating years in Loreto.

Don was affectionately called "Tio" by his many friends in Loreto and we have named our publishing company "Tio Press" in his memory.

Ann Caldwell O'Neil

Acknowledgments

Over the past twelve years, many people have helped and encouraged us. We are very grateful to all of them. There were special friends and acquaintances, though, who gave us invaluable help.

Esther Lev and Thalia Zapatos read and edited the various versions at least six times. Author and photographer Bill Evarts donated his editing skills to get the book started in the right direction. Sandra Ryan Hayward generously made available to us her 1973 interviews with Loretanos. The eminent California photographer Leland Foerster contributed his beautiful photographs of the people and buildings of the Loreto area.

Historian Harry Crosby, my daughter Jody Reed and Don's daughter Catherine O'Neil, Joyce and Art Bertoldi, John and Marilynne Keyser, and Graham Mackintosh all contributed valuable editorial suggestions.

People who heard about the project and came to us with material and resources we never would have found on our own included: Trudi Angell, José María Agruel, Glen Dawson, Rómulo Fernández, Estela Gutíerrez, William Hendricks, Tony Kinninger, Miguel Léon-Portilla, Sergio Morales Polo, Barbara Olsen, Rafael Padilla, and Edward Vernon.

Because my Spanish was learned late in life, I relied on friends to listen to the interview tapes and interpret them correctly into English. These patient translators were Victoria Benavent, Adrian Fernández, Oscar Fischer, Yolanda Furio, Estela Gutíerrez, Hugo Quintero, and Juanita Swain.

And *mil* gracias to the Loretanos who shared their stories and their time with us to narrate this history of Loreto, which would otherwise have been lost.

Bibliography

The books and articles we have consulted are listed below, but there are several that deserve special mention because we have relied most heavily on the information they provided.

Norman Roberts' *Baja California Plant Field Guide,* 1989, also has good information about the geology and climate of the peninsula. In addition to being useful for our book, we always carry it along in our camper when we are exploring the deserts and mountains and shores of Baja California.

Of the research we did about the indigenous people of the Loreto area, we found the Jesuit Padre **Miguel del Barco** (1706-1790) to be the best source. Padre del Barco spent almost thirty years in Baja California, most of that time in San Javier and Loreto. He was a keen observer, and after the expulsion of the Jesuits in 1768, he wrote what he called "additions" to the work of the Jesuit chronicler Miguel Venegas who had never been to California. Del Barco's "additions" were actually corrections and amplification based on his own experience and observations. His writings remained in manuscript for almost two hundred years and were first published in Mexico by Miguel Léon-Portilla in 1963. Del Barco's manuscript was published in two parts in English by Dawson's Book Store, Los Angeles, California. The first part, *The Natural History of California*, was published in 1980 and the second part, *Ethnology and Linguistics of Baja California,* in 1981.

Harry Crosby's *Antigua California* is the most complete, thoroughly researched, and brilliantly written account of the Jesuit period in California. We were grateful to have this excellent resource and for its author's encouragement in our project.

We also depended on **Herbert E. Bolton's** *Rim of Christendom: A Biography of Eusebio Francisco Kino,* 1936, as well as the published letters of Padres **Juan María Salvatierra** and **Jacob Baegert** for information about the indigenous people and the seventy years of the pioneer Jesuit presence in Loreto.

The Franciscan **Father Zephryin Engelardt** contributed an extensive, somewhat biased account of the experiences of the Jesuit, Franciscan and

Dominican missionaries in Loreto in *The Missions and Missionaries of California,* published in 1929.

The letters of the Franciscan **Francisco Palóu** and the Dominican **Vicente de Mora** also illustrate graphically the many problems of the era after the Jesuits left and the missionaries and Spanish government were trying, and failing, to manage the peninsula.

Amao Manríquez, Jorge Luis. *Mineros, Misioneros y Rancheros de la Antigua California.* Mexico: Instituto Nacional de Antropología e Historia, Editorial, 1997.

Baegert, Jacob. *The Letters of Jacob Baegert, 1749-1761: Jesuit Missionary in Baja California.* Translated by Elsbeth Schulz-Bischof, introduced and edited by Doyce B. Nunis, Jr. Los Angeles: Dawson's Book Shop, 1982.

Baegert, Jacob. *Observations in Lower California.* Translated and with an introduction and notes by M.M. Brandenburg and Carl L. Baumann. Berkeley: University of California Press, 1952.

Bancroft, Griffing. *The Flight of the Least Petrel.* New York: G.P. Putnam's Sons, 1932.

Bancroft, Hubert Howe. *History of the North American States and Texas, Vol. 1, 1531-1800.* San Francisco: The History Co., 1886.

Bancroft, Hubert Howe. *History of the North American States and Texas, Vol, II, 1801-1889.* San Francisco: The History Co., 1889.

Bolton, Herbert Eugene. *Rim of Christendom; a Biography of Eusebio Francisco Kino, Pacific Coast Pioneer.* New York, The Macmillan Co., 1936.

Bolton, Herbert Eugene. *Outpost of Empire.* New York: Alfred A. Knopf, 1939.

Breschini, Gary S. *The Portolá Expedition of 1769.* CSU Monterey Bay Social and Behavioral Sciences Center. 1969.

Burrus, Ernest J. *Juan María de Salvatierra, S.J., Selected Letters About Lower California.* Los Angeles: Dawson's Book Shop, 1971.

Cannon, Ray. *The Sea of Cortez.* Menlo Park, CA: Lane Magazine & Book Co., 1966.

Carter, Annetta M. *Log of a Journey from Tijuana to Cabo San Lucas, 1947-1948.*

Carter, Annetta M. *I. G. Voznesenskii, Early Naturalist in Baja California.* Mexico, Taxon 28:27-33, 1979.

Castillo Negrete, Francisco. *Geografía y Estadística de la Baja California, 1853.* Boletín de la Sociedad Mexicana de Geografía y Estadística, Tomo VII, Mexico: Imprenta de A. Boix, 1859.

Castro Agúndez, Jesús. *Resumen Historico de Baja California Sur.* Mexico: Federation Editorial Mexicana, 1981.

Cochran, Harrington W., Capt., M.I.D. *Data for a Handbook on the Southern District of Baja California.* San Francisco: US Intelligence Office, Western Dept., 1919.

Corle, Edwin. *The Royal Highway (El Camino Real).* New York: The Bobbs-Merrill Co., Inc, 1949.

Crosby, Harry W. *The Cave Paintings of Baja California: The Great Murals of An Unknown People.* San Diego: Sunbelt Publications, 1997.

Crosby, Harry W. *Antigua California: Mission and Colony on the Peninsular Frontier.* University of New Mexico Press, Albuquerque, 1994.

Crosby, Harry W. *The King's Highway in Baja California*. San Diego: Copley Books, 1974.

De la Guerra Ord, Angustías. *Occurrences in Hispanic California*. Translated and edited by Francis Price and William H. Ellison. Washington, DC: Academy of American Franciscan History, 1956.

del Barco, Miguel. *The Natural History of Baja California*. Translated by Froylan Tiscarena. Dawson's Book Shop, Los Angeles, 1980.

del Barco, Miguel. *Ethnology and Linguistics of Baja California*. Translated by Froylán Tiscareno. Los Angeles: Dawson's Book Shop, 1981.

Ducrue, Benno. *Ducrue's Account of the Expulsion of the Jesuits from Lower California*. Translated and edited by Ernest J. Burrus, S.J. Rome. Jesuit Historical Institute, St. Louis, MO, 1967.

Dunne, Peter Masten. *Black Robes in Lower California*. University of California Press, Berkeley and Los Angeles, 1968.

Engelhardt, Zephyrin. *The Missions and Missionaries of California: Vol. I. Lower California*. Santa Barbara: Mission Santa Barbara, 1929.

Engelhardt, Zephyrin. *The Franciscans in California*. Holy Childhood Indian School, Harbor Springs, MI, 1897.

Espinosa, Rafael. *Viage a Loreto y a San Javier en la Baja California*. La Ilustración Mexicana. Publicada por I. Cumplido, 1831.

Espinosa, Rafael. *Reseña Estadistic sobre La Antingua ó Baja California*. Boletín de la Sociedad Mexicana de Geografía y Estadistica, Tomo IV, Imprenta de I. Cumplido, Mexico, 1854.

Esteva, José María. *Memoria Sobre La Pesca de La Perla en La Baja California: Informe hecho para el Gobierno por el Visitator General de Rentas en 1857*. Boletín de La Sociedad Mexicana de Geografía y Estadistica, Tomo X. Mexico: 1863.

Fernández Real, Romulo. *Modesto Sánchez Mayón, Evangelizador y Pionero en la Reconquista Espsiritual de la Península de California (1897-1987)*. Imprenta López, Loreto, BCS, 1997.

Fierro Blanco, Antonio (Walter Nordhoff). *The Journey of the Flame*. Boston: Houghton Mifflin Co., 1933.

Fondo Nacional de Fomento al Turismo. *Ciudades Turisticos, Una Estratega Mexican de Desarollo*. Mexico: FONATUR, 1998.

Forbes, Alexander. *California: a History of Upper and Lower California*. San Francisco: J.H. Nash, 1937.

Geiger, Maynard. *Franciscan Missionaries in Hispanic California 1769-1848, A Biographical Dictionary*, The Huntington Library, San Marino, CA, 1969.

Gerhard, Peter. *Pirates in Baja California*. Editorial Tlilan, Tlapalan, Mexico, 1963.

González Rodríguez, Luis. *La Fundación de la California Jesuítica, Siete cartas de Juan María de Salvatierra, S.J. (1697-1699)*. Autonoma de Baja California Sur, Mexico, 1997.

Gutiérrez, Alfonso René. *Edición Crítica de la Vida del V.P. Juan María de Salvatierra, Escrita por el V.P. César Felipe Doria*. Prologue by Miguel León-Portilla. Mexico: Consejo Nacional Para La Cultura y Las Artes, 1997.

Historia del Ferrocarril en el Estado de Baja California. Instituto de Investigaciones Historicas de Baja California. Mexicali, BC: El Instituto, 1988.

Ibarra Rivera, Gilberto. *Vocablos Indigenas de Baja California Sur*. Gobierno de Baja California Sur, La Paz. 1997.

Island Biogeography in the Sea of Cortez. Edited by Ted J. Case, Martin L. Cody. Berkeley: University of California Press, 1983.

Jordán, Fernando. *El Otro Mexico: Biografía de Baja California.* Secretaria de Educación Publica, México, 1987.

Kirchner, John A. *Los Ferrocarrilés de Baja California Sur,* 1982.

Krauze, Enrique. *Mexico: Biography of Power: A History of Modern Mexico, 1810-1996.* Translated by Hank Heiftez. New York: Harper Collins, 1997.

Lassépas, Ulises Urbano. *Historia de la colonización de la Baja California y decreto del 10 de marzo de 1857.* Colección Baja California: Nuestra Historia UABC, Mexicali, 1995.

Leigh, Randolph. *Forgotten Waters: Adventures in the Gulf of California.* New York: J. B. Lippincott Co., 1941.

Léon-Portilla, Miguel. *Loreto's Key Role in the Early History of the Californias (1697-1773).* California Mission Studies Assn., 1997.

Léon-Portilla, Miguel. *Cartografía y cronicas de la antigua California.* Coyoacan, D.F.: Universidad Autonome de Mexico, Fundación de Investigaciones Sociales, 1989.

Léon-Portilla, Miguel. *Loreto, Capital de las Californias: Las Cartas Fundacionales de Juan María de Salvatierra.* Mexico: FONATUR, Universidad Autónoma de Baja California, Consejo Nacional para la Cultura y las Artes, 1997.

Lindsay, George E. *History of Scientific Exploration in the Sea of Cortez.* Berkeley: University of California Press, 1983.

Martínez, Pablo L. *A History of Lower California.* Translated by Ethel Duffy Turner. Mexico: Editorial Baja California, 1960.

Martínez, Pablo L. *Guía Familiar de Baja California, 1700-1900.* Mexico: Editorial Baja California, 1965.

Martínez, Pablo L. *First Government in Baja California: Transcription of the Act.* La Paz: Contacto #18, a trimestral publication of the Historical Archive 1995.

Massey, Lee Gooding. *Baja California Climates.* Pacific Coast Archaeological Society Quarterly, Vol. II, No. l. 1975.

Massey, Lee Gooding. *Chacuaco: The Tubular Stone Pipe in Baja California.* Pacific Coast Archeological Society Quarterly, Vol. 12, No.1, January 1976.

Massey, Lee Gooding. *Jesuits and Indians: A Brief Evaluation of Three Early Descriptions of Baja California.* Pacific Coast Archeological Society Quarterly, Vol. 10, No. l, January, 1974.

Mathes, W. Michael. *The Conquistador in California, 1535: The Voyage of Fernando Cortés to Baja California in Chronicles and Documents.* Los Angeles, Dawson's Book Shop, 1973.

Mathes, W. Michael. *The Missions of Baja California, 1683-1849: An Historical-Photographic Survey.* La Paz: Gobierno Autonoma de Mexico, Instituto de Investigaciones Historicas, 1973.

Mathes, W. Michael. *Historical-Biografical Introduction to Obras Californianas del Padre Miguel Venegas, S.J.* Universidad Autónoma de Baja California Sur. La Paz, 1983.

Mathes, W. Michael. *San Bruno, First Mission and Fort in The Californias, 1683.* XXI Simposio de la Asociación Cultural de las Californias. La Paz, 1983.

Mathes, W. Michael. *Medicine in The Jesuit Missions of Baja California.* Baja California Symposium XXX, Santa Rosalia, 1992.

Mathes, W. Michael. *Conchó, Dionisius, Loreto: Historical Vignettes of the Capital, 1684-1829.*

Meigs, Peveril. *The Dominican Mission Frontier of Lower California.* Berkeley: University of California Press, 1939.

Morales Polo, Sergio. *Loreto: Some Relevant Facts About the History of the Keystone of California Culture.* Editorial Londó, S.C. Loreto, BCS,1993.

Morales Polo, Sergio. *Carmen: An Island With Much History*. Gaceta Lauretana, Aug. 28, 1993.

Nelson, Edward W. *Lower California and Its Natural Resources*. Riverside: Manessier, 1966.

North, Arthur Walbridge. *The Mother of California*. San Francisco: Paul Elder and Company, 1908.

North, Arthur Walbridge. *Camp and Camino in Lower California, Explorations and Adventures on the Baja, 1908-1910*. Glorieta, NM: The Río Grande Press, Inc., 1977.

Piccolo, Francisco María. *Informe On the New Province of California, 1702*. Translated & edited by George P. Hammond. Los Angeles: Dawson's Book Shop, 1967.

Pourade, Richard F. *The History of San Diego, Vol. II: Time of the Bells*. San Diego: Union Tribune Publishing Co., 1960

Priestly, Herbert Ingram. *José de Gálvez: Visitor-General of New Spain (1765-1771)*. Berkeley: University of California Press. 1916.

Roberts, Norman C. *Baja California Plant Field Guide*. La Jolla, CA: Natural History Publishing Company, 1989.

Robertson, Tomás. *Baja California and Its Missions*. Glendale, California: La Siesta Press, 1978.

Ryan, Sandra. *Before the Road*. Bancroft Library Collection, University of California, Berkeley, 1973.

Salvatierra, Juan María. *Selected Letters About Lower California*. Translated and annotated by Ernest J. Burrus, S.J. Los Angeles: Dawson's Book Shop, 1971.

Serra, Junípero. *Diario (1769)*. San Diego: Don Diego's Libraria, 1964

Steinbeck, John. *The Log from the Sea of Cortez*. New York: Viking Press, 1941.

Sudcaliforniano. *The Stone House of the Republic*. La Paz, Aug. 16, 1993.

Trasviña Taylor, Armando. *Que Desea Saber de Baja California Sur?* Mexico: 1989.

Valadés, Adrian. *Historia de la Baja California, 1850-1880*. Prologue by Miguél León-Portilla. Mexico: Universidad Nacional Autonoma de México, 1974.

Venegas, Miguel. *A Natural and Civil History of California, Vols. I and II*. Madrid, 1757. Readex Microprint Corporation, 1966.

Wiggins, Ira L. *Investigations in the Natural History of Baja California*. Proceedings of the California Academy of Sciences, Fourth Series, Vol. XXX, No. l, San Francisco, 1960.

Wiggins, Ira L. *Flora of Baja California*. Stanford: Stanford University Press, 1980.

Zepatos Thalia. *The Pueblo That Roared*. Portland, OR, 1993.

Index